TABLE OF CONTENTS

Top 20 Test Taking Tips

1. Carefully follow all the test registration procedures
2. Know the test directions, duration, topics, question types, how many questions
3. Setup a flexible study schedule at least 3-4 weeks before test day
4. Study during the time of day you are most alert, relaxed, and stress free
5. Maximize your learning style; visual learner use visual study aids, auditory learner use auditory study aids
6. Focus on your weakest knowledge base
7. Find a study partner to review with and help clarify questions
8. Practice, practice, practice
9. Get a good night's sleep; don't try to cram the night before the test
10. Eat a well balanced meal
11. Know the exact physical location of the testing site; drive the route to the site prior to test day
12. Bring a set of ear plugs; the testing center could be noisy
13. Wear comfortable, loose fitting, layered clothing to the testing center; prepare for it to be either cold or hot during the test
14. Bring at least 2 current forms of ID to the testing center
15. Arrive to the test early; be prepared to wait and be patient
16. Eliminate the obviously wrong answer choices, then guess the first remaining choice
17. Pace yourself; don't rush, but keep working and move on if you get stuck
18. Maintain a positive attitude even if the test is going poorly
19. Keep your first answer unless you are positive it is wrong
20. Check your work, don't make a careless mistake

Introduction to the CEOE Series

Why am I required to take this CEOE Assessment?

Your state requires you to take this CEOE Assessment in order to test the breadth and depth of your knowledge in a specified subject matter. Oklahoma has adopted the CEOE series in order to ensure that you have mastered the subject matter you are planning to teach before they issue your teaching license.
Because the issuance of your license ensures competence in the subject area it is important that you take studying seriously and make sure you study thoroughly and completely.

Two Kinds of CEOE Assessments

The CEOE Series consist of two different kinds of assessments multiple choice questions and constructed response test.
The multiple choice test consists of questions followed by several answer choices. From these answer choices you select the answer that you think best corresponds with the given question. These questions can survey a wider range because they can ask more questions in a limited time period.
Constructed response questions consist of a given question for which you write an original response. These tests have fewer questions, but the questions require you to demonstrate the depth of you own personal knowledge in the subject area.

Business Management

Basic Organizational Structure

Any business organization of a decent size will have a division of labor, a structure for making decisions, and some formal rules and policies. A typical vertical division of labor has three levels: top executives, middle managers, and low managers and laborers. The horizontal division of labor is the division of each level into groups with a specific and unique purpose. Decision-making structures vary depending whether the top executives make all-important calls, or whether authority is delegated. The delegation of authority is the process through which managers give the authority to make decisions or take action to individuals or groups under their control. Rules and regulations may be either formal or informal, depending on whether they are written and known to all, and are crucial in maintaining efficiency in a business.

Functional structure, territorial structure, product structure, and matrix structure
Successful businesses always select the organizational business model that best fits their needs. A functional structure divides the parts of the business up by what they do. Possible divisions in such an organization might be production, accounting, marketing, and so on. A territorial structure is typical of businesses whose operations are spread out among a series of locations; it just makes sense to have each location operate somewhat independently. Some large companies have what is known as a product structure, in which divisions are made among the parts of the business that sell different products. An auto manufacturer, for instance, might have different divisions for trucks and cars. A matrix structure simply combines functional and product structures, such that there are both financial and production managers overseeing a given project.

The line and staff organization structures
The chains of command in a business organization can be considered to follow either the line or staff organization structure. In a line organization, the chain of command runs from a top executive to his subordinate executives, to their subordinates, and so on. All employees consult only with their immediate superior. In a line and staff structure, however, that line of command remains, but individuals are also advised by other departments depending on the project. Most large businesses use a line and staff structure, so that responsibility to one's immediate boss is emphasized without removing the potentially beneficial advice provided by other superiors. Executives will often give functional authority over their subordinates to department heads who are knowledgeable on the current project.

Management Problems

There are a number of ways that the organization of a business may hinder its operation. Some businesses have what are known as span of management problems, in which managers have too many immediate subordinates to be effective. On the other hand, if every manager has only a few subordinates, it is possible that the organization will have too many levels, which will require more managers than are necessary and will therefore be needlessly expensive. Generally, managers can afford to have more direct subordinates if job assignments are clear, if the manager is a good communicator, and if the business is relatively stable. If subordinates are well trained and independent, it is possible to broaden the manager's span of control.

Authority

A business organization is centralized when there is little delegation of authority, and decisions are mostly made by the top executives. Obviously, the most extreme version of centralization is when one owner makes all the decisions in a business. Decentralization, conversely, is exhibited in a business where authority is dispersed widely throughout. Most businesses operate in degrees of centralization and decentralization. Important decisions, particularly those regarding large amounts of capital, will probably be reserved for top executives; more trifling decisions are likely to be left to lower managers. Business analysts have noted that most businesses tend to be too centralized in their early years, but can become too decentralized once they have had some success and established a company policy.

Organizational Planning

It is extremely important for business managers to continually be adjusting the business organization structure and anticipating what adjustments will need to be made in the future. Organization is essentially a setting in which employees can perform; as the needs of the business and the demands of the market change over time, the setting appropriate to maximizing employee performance will also change. It is important that roles in a business be clearly defined, and that the leaders of the business envision what roles will be needed in the future. It is impossible to recruit or train the appropriate workers without having a vision of what the business' needs will be. Most businesses will discover that as they grow over time, their organizational structure will become more and more complex.

Business Budgeting System

A budget is a formal document that describes the financial history of a business and projects the expenses, income, credits, and debits for an upcoming period, typically a year. A complete budgeting process entails planning long-term goals, assigning the budgeting process to a specific group of trained individuals, organizing information from every area of the business, directing authority so that managers at every level assist with the process, and controlling future activity to make sure that it is in line with the approved budget. Successful budgeting enhances the ability of managers to see long-term goals, alerts the business to potential problems, coordinates the various activities of the business, evaluates the ongoing performance of the various divisions, and shapes the accounting department's overall view of company history.

Management Styles

Exploitative-authoritative -- There are a number of different approaches that managers can take to overseeing the operations under their jurisdiction. The styles of management that can be described as exploitative-authoritative is one in which managerial decisions are imposed on subordinates, and high levels of management typically have much greater responsibility than lower level workers. In this environment, workers are motivated by threats to their future employment or pay, and there is very little communication overall between the various levels of the organizational hierarchy. This sort of structure is often found in the worst sort of factories, where the employees' dependence on their jobs to sustain them is so strong that it can be exploited by management. This has not been shown to be one of the more effective ways of increasing employee productivity.

Benevolent-authoritative -- The benevolent-authoritative style of management is one in which there is a clear distinction between management and labor, though unlike in the exploitative-authoritative model, there is the assumption that management acts in the best interest of the workers. In this model, managers have a great deal of responsibility and workers have very little, and there is almost no communication between the various levels of the company hierarchy. In the same line, there is very little cooperation between the different levels of the business. Managers tend to adopt a patronizing attitude to their employees, and may frequently fail to understand and take into account their employee's feelings. The benevolent-authoritative model is much more common and unremarkable than the exploitative-authoritative model of management, but it too is considered to be ineffective.

Consultative style -- In the consultative style of management, leaders place a small degree of trust in their employees, but still do not allow them an equal voice in the operations of the company. In this model of management, employees are motivated by potential rewards for productivity, and there is some quality interaction between the various levels of the business hierarchy. More so than in the authoritative models, all employees may feel some responsibility for the success of the business, and there may be a degree of teamwork between the various groups. In this model, managers somewhat trust their subordinates, and therefore give them freedom to act on a host of minor issues. Still, ultimate responsibility is seen to be in the hands of management, and so lower-level employees are not trusted with very important matters.

Participative-group style -- The participative-group style of management is considered by most analysts to be the most effective means of leading a business. In this model, managers have absolute trust in their subordinates, because they have ensured that every employee is properly trained and competent. Employees in this kind of business will be motivated by rewards rather than punishment, and they will have a clear idea of the company's objectives. There will be a large degree of cooperation and communication among the various levels of the business, and all employees will feel that their work directly impacts the success of the company. According to business analysts, this model results in the most profitable businesses with the most satisfied and productive employees.

Sole Proprietorships

A sole proprietorship is any business that is completely owned and operated by one person. Sole proprietorships are relatively easy to open: the individual only needs to obtain the relevant licenses. This is the most common form of business. Sole proprietorships are attractive to many entrepreneurs because they offer the opportunity for total control, as well as the flexibility in decision-making afforded a one-person management team. Such businesses need much less government supervision and licensing, and are therefore less expensive to start. On the other hand, sole proprietorships frequently suffer from limited source of capital, and the risk for the owner is often great. The success of the business also is dependent on the health of one person, so any illness or infirmity is devastating.

Advantages -- The owner of a sole proprietorship has the most concentrated control of any businessman. He or she is not required to share plans, policies, or methods of operation with anyone else. Since the owner has the sole right to all profits, he or she is likely to be more motivated to succeed than the employee of a corporation or partnership. It is also extremely easy to start up or dissolve a sole proprietorship. There is no need for a contract, as in partnerships, or incorporation papers. The owner is subject only to the relevant government regulations. Last but not least, the proprietorship (unlike the corporation) does not have to pay income taxes on its profits; the owner must simply pay the taxes on his personal income.

Disadvantages -- There are some disadvantages to running a sole proprietorship. For one thing, it is often difficult for a single individual to assemble the capital necessary to start the business. Whatever startup investment is going to be made is limited to the resources of the proprietor. There is also a great deal of personal risk, as the proprietor is responsible for all the losses incurred by the business. It is quite common, as well, for the personal assets of the proprietor to be combined with the assets of the business, so getting in trouble with creditors can result in the loss of personal property. It can also be difficult to attract top managers to a proprietorship, because they will desire some financial ownership. Lastly, the ease with which sole proprietorships can be formed and dissolved means that they will often start without adequate planning, and are therefore more likely to fail.

Corporations

A corporation is a company or group that has been granted by the government the rights pertaining to a distinct and viable entity. Ownership of a corporation is held by individuals who own shares of the corporation's stock. One of the main advantages of the corporation is that individual shareholders are not responsible for the actions of the corporation; they can only lose their initial investment. Indeed, employees of the corporation cannot be prosecuted for the acts of the corporation at large; many critics say that this system of corporate rights has led to much immoral business. In any case, large corporations have enormous influence today in the global economy: they can attract the best managers, manipulate government policy to suit their ends, and in many ways become national economies in their own rights.

Corporate governance -- In a corporation, stockholders elect the members of a board of directors, who oversee the operations of the corporation. Typically, one share of stock amounts to one vote in a corporation election. In this system, a few major stockholders may hold sway over much larger groups of small shareholders. Usually, though, real power is held not by the stockholders but by the management group in power, who often cooperate with a few major stockholders to ensure that they remain in power. This arrangement is frequently aided by proxies, the permission given by stockholders to someone else to manage the stockholder's interest in the corporation. Oftentimes, corporate officers cultivate these proxies to maintain their position.

Advantages -- The owners of a corporation, the stockholders, have only a limited liability over the fortunes of the business, and so they do not stand to incur devastating losses. Since the corporation is considered a legal person, is responsible for its own debts. This limited risk makes it easier for corporations to attract investment. The vastness of most corporate structures makes it possible for them to place authority in the hands of the most qualified individuals, and to specialize job roles so that everyone does the task for which they are best suited. Ownership of corporations is easily transferable, and the transfer of ownership rarely has any effect on the daily operations of the business. For these reasons, corporations tend to have longer and more stable histories than other forms of business.

Disadvantages -- One disadvantage of the corporate form is that it results in double taxation; that is, the corporation is taxed as a legal entity, and shareholders must pay income taxes on their dividends. Furthermore, these individual stockholders are unlikely to have any real control over the business, and so they may feel powerless to make needed changes. Corporations, because of their size, can face difficulties in organization and management that smaller proprietorships and partnerships avoid. Also, corporations are required to make regular reports to their shareholders, and so they cannot preserve too many secrets of their operation. Lastly, there is always the danger of low motivation among corporate employees, as managers may not have much direct interest in the long-term success of the business.

Partnerships

A partnership is a business that is operated by two or more principals for the purpose of making a profit. It can also be a legal contract agreed to by two or more parties, in which they agree to jointly provide capital and labor for some enterprise, in exchange for a determined proportion of profits or losses. A limited partnership is any business partnership in which the responsibilities and liabilities of one party is restricted to a certain amount. A joint venture is any business enterprise in which the parties share responsibility and benefits to a predetermined degree, and in which the parties are bound together until the conditions listed in the original agreement have been met to the satisfaction of all.

Advantages -- Partnerships have many of the same advantages as sole proprietorships. There is a great amount of control concentrated in the partners, and their motivation to succeed is likely to be very high. Partnerships are a good chance for individuals with different sets of skills to team up. No government permission is required for a partnership, and business affairs do not need to be shared outside the partnership. Partnerships are easy to form and dissolve, and it may be easier for two people to raise sufficient startup capital than it would be for a single individual. Also, the partnership as a business form is not required to pay income taxes, as the corporation is. Most partnerships are less heavily taxed than individuals in a corporation.

Disadvantages -- The most serious disadvantage of the partnership is the high liability for losses assumed by the members. Moreover, any general partner in a partnership has the ability to bind the business to contracts and other obligations, so it can be a very risky form of business in which to participate. Partnerships are notoriously unstable. Any injury or illness to one partner may seriously hinder the business, or force it to seek a new ownership arrangement. Even worse, if one partner is discovered to be incompetent, it is extremely difficult to force that person out of the partnership. Deciding on appropriate compensation for an unwanted partner can amount to long court battles and crippling legal fees. Many members of a partnership wishing to exit the agreement have a very hard time finding people to take their place.

Cooperatives

A cooperative is a group of individuals or smaller groups that join together to achieve some common goals. Cooperatives are often formed by minority interests who want to improve their power in the market. An example of this kind of cooperative is a farm collective, in which small farmers band together in an effort to get better prices and a bigger market for their crops. The cooperative model has also been extended into credit unions, retail consumer groups, residential organizations, and marketing associations. Many retail cooperatives offer their members the chance to receive a significant discount in exchange for working in the store. The cooperative model has been praised for giving the worker a clear stake in his or her labor, as well as returning some market power to smaller interests.

Board of Directors

The board of directors is the group that is elected by the shareholders of a corporation to manage it. The board of directors selects the upper-level management, including the chief executive officer, and supervises strategy and financial objectives; all this, theoretically, is mean to be done in the best interests of the shareholders. A typical model has the board of directors subdivided into committees dealing with nominating future members of the board, determining executive compensation, overseeing internal audits, and supervising financial operations. Many members of a board of directors will be senior executives at other companies. In recent years, some have criticized corporate boards for mindlessly following the whims of a popular CEO.

Managers

Purpose -- Some businesses that have only one employee may be able to do without managers, but any business larger than one or two people will eventually require some leadership. Managers, simply, are people who are responsible for the performance of one or more people below them in a hierarchy. As businesses grow and become more complex, it becomes necessary to create more layers of management to oversee all the aspects of the business. In some very large companies, there can be up to ten or twelve layers of management. If they are functioning effectively, business managers are catalysts: that is, they are agents that make a business work more effectively. However, in order to do this a manager must know his or her job, must be excellent communicators, and must have excellent judgment.

The ways that managers attempt to create a situation in which employees feel obliged to do their best -- One of the most important jobs for managers is to create an environment in which employees can operate at their maximum potential. This is perhaps a rebuttal to the stereotypical view of a manager as one who sits behind a desk all day doing paperwork. Managers try to ensure that all the members of their team are pulling in the same direction, and that, moreover, the goals of the company are clear and known. Managers are charged by their superiors with using their authority to create a situation in which employees will feel obliged to do their best. Of course, no manager has unlimited power; organizations typically rein in their managers by creating a set of company rules that govern how managerial authority may be expressed.

Some important elements in the business environment that will help to take advantage of the natural strengths of the employees -- Managers need to keep a few key things in mind when developing a proper business environment. First, it is essential that every position have a defined set of goals; business plans and objective must be fully understood by every member of the team. In order for this to be achieved, the manager must ensure that all of the roles in the company are clearly defined. Furthermore, managers should try to remove any obstacles that may be preventing the business form reaching these goals. These could be money obstacles, which can be altered, or legal restrictions, which cannot. The manager must also keep in mind the motivations of his or her employees: what is it that will entice them to do their best work? Finally, managers should consider how best to tailor the workplace to take best advantage of the natural strengths of the employees.

The ultimate goal of all managers -- Every manager has surplus in mind as his or her ultimate goal. Businesses that create surpluses create profits (the amount by which sales dollars exceed expense dollars). In order to achieve a surplus, of course, managers have to have a good idea of what their goals are, regardless of their position in the organization. They must treat management as both a science and an art. Management is a science insofar as it has certain reliable rules and can be studied in an organized fashion. Management is an art, too, insofar as it requires a degree of flexibility and intuition. Simply knowing the "rules of management" will not make someone an effective manager: that person must also have intelligence, compassion, and an innate understanding of how to make teams work effectively.

Successful managers -- Successful managers tend to have a bias towards action. That is to say, their immediate response to a problem is to act, rather than to sit and ponder the problem's cause. Well-managed companies quickly assess troubling situations and determine a proper course of action. If this course is unsuccessful, they have no qualms about changing course and trying something else. An effective manager will strive to avoid what is known as "paralysis by analysis." Good managers will also try to keep their teams small, so that they can effectively oversee everyone, and so that everyone on the team feels integral. Even large corporations try to keep their divisions small, so that every individual's job seems more important, and no one feels as if they are buried by the bureaucracy.

Managerial goals concerning continued contact with customers and productivity improvement -- Successful businesses almost always are driven by their customers; that is, they make decisions based on the desires of the people to whom they sell their products. This means that companies do not make decisions based on technology, or on production, or on their overall strategy. All of these things are important, but they should be determined by the demands of the consumer. Moreover, well-managed companies tend to emphasize improving productivity by means of helping people to be more effective, rather than improving machinery. Good companies find that they can improve every aspect of their operation if they can motivate and satisfy their employees. Employee satisfaction tends to positively influence many aspects of a business besides just basic productivity.

Some managerial goals concerning freedom to encourage entrepreneurship and stressing a constant set of goals -- Successful businesses will strive to create the opportunity for employees to conceive, develop, and implement profitable new ideas. In order to do so, of course, managers cannot keep employees too tightly under their control. Entrepreneurship within a company will be encouraged if the management makes a point of rewarding successful innovations, and employees feel they have the freedom to experiment in their work. Successful businesses will also try to emphasize a particular business value with almost religious zeal. If management transmits a consistent message to staff, there is less chance of confusion and chaos. Maintaining a constant set of goals ensures that all employees will know how best to perform their jobs.

Some managerial goals concerning emphasis on specialization and "loose-tight" controls -- Although diversification seems to be a popular trend among large corporations, the businesses that are consistently successful are those that stick to the area of production with which they are most familiar. Some businesses may be more effective at new-product innovation, or manufacturing, or marketing: they should work to accentuate these strengths. Another consistent feature of successful businesses is simultaneously loose and tight controls. This vague-sounding description simply means that businesses should have fairly tight control on some things, while still allowing operating managers a great degree of freedom in others. While top executives should always have a firm grasp on the overall workings of the business, it is best if they give their various divisional managers the freedom to operate in their areas of specialization.

Business Planning

The managers of a business are engaging in business planning when they envision a desired future for the business and define strategies for reaching that future. Productive planning will honestly assess the business' current status, anticipate trends in the market, and consider the financial implications of proposed plans. It should follow the scientific methods of observation and experiment, and include every aspect of the business. Planning is impossible without good records from the accounting department, as well as cooperation from every division of the business. Out of the planning process, a management team should arrive at a set of long-term goals that will be the aims of short-term budgeting decisions. Ideally, coherent business plans allow every member of the company to understand the long-term goals of the business, and thereby most efficiently contribute to their realization.

The first step of the business planning process -- The first step in planning is to become aware of an opportunity, or of a problem that needs a solution. Once a problem or opportunity is discovered, business managers should undertake an analysis of it to determine the best way to proceed. This analysis should move in several directions, as managers must consider the potential market, the actions of competitors, and the strengths and weaknesses of their business. The company should also consider practical matters like how long the proposed process will take, and how much it is likely to cost. All of these questions are essential if a business is to set goals that are appropriate and attainable; every company has limits to its resources and capital, and they will do well to appreciate their limitations before setting their goals.

The second step of the business planning process -- In order to be a plan, a business' proposed course of action must have a clear and verifiable objective. Once the business has determined and considered an opportunity in the market, the next step is to set their goals. Of course, profit is the general goal in almost all business, but there must be more concrete production and distribution goals if a business is to proceed knowledgably. A business may establish tapping a new market as a goal, even if that new market does not immediately provide financial benefits. Large objectives may be supported by smaller objectives, like making a certain amount of money in one division or increasing productivity in another. These objectives are the end points for all the plans that the business will soon be constructing.

The third step of the business planning process -- After noting an opportunity and setting objectives, a business must begin to envision the necessary environment for the objectives to be met. In other words, they must develop the premises of their future plans. This might entail forecasting changes in the market, assessing population growth, or anticipating changes in the price level. Envisioning the planning premises also means considering which resources the company will be required to use in order to bring a plan to fruition. Sometimes, the larger plans can become the premises for smaller plans, as for instance if the construction of a new factory creates a need to hire temporary employees. It is essential that planning premises be consistent and widely understood, so that managers can establish their own plans without contradicting the general plans of the company.

The fourth step of the business planning process -- Once the managers of a business have decided on their objectives and established planning premises, they must consider the various means of getting the job done. Managers cannot afford to look at an unlimited number of options, so they must determine the critical (or limiting) factor in every situation. The critical factor is the one aspect of an operation that will make the most difference. Some highly intelligent business managers flail during the planning process because they take too much time weighing the various alternatives. It is more effective to choose the alternative that offers the best results for the critical factor, and accept whatever problems may arise as necessary evils. This problem illustrates the constant struggle in management between doing something right and doing it quickly.

The fifth step of the business planning process -- If all of the steps in the planning process have been performed properly, selecting a course of action should be fairly simple. Unfortunately, it is often the case that real-world choices are not easy. Managers may be concerned about the way the market will change, or about the actions of their competitors. Occasionally, it may make sense to delay planning certain future events until external factors can clear up a bit. Some managers will construct a partial plan, and leave some later choices to be made once the market develops. Of course, unless this decision to postpone planning is made known to the organization, and is sound strategy rather than procrastination, it can result in a rudderless company. One thing is certain: the market will not give time extensions to companies that fail to act.

The sixth step of the planning process -- Once a major business plan has been constructed, managers set to work developing all of the supporting plans that will enable the greater plan to be followed. The major plan sets the objectives and premises for all of the smaller or derivative plans. At this point, managers will also need to develop specific budgets for their plans. In order for a plan to be meaningful to the people with money invested in the business, it must be expressed in its financial form. A proper budget will include the costs of the plan, as well as the number of labor hours it will require. Budgets are important because they set a specific numerical target for a plan, and give managers something to measure their actual expenses against. Budgets are a way of making business plans concrete.

Business Objectives and Policies

Business objectives, or goals, are the end points to which the business is aiming. In order for a business to be successful, objectives must be clear and attainable. It also must be something that can be verified; it is much less motivating to ask an employee to do his or her best than it is to set a specific production goal. Business policies, on the other hand, are statements of purpose that will define the way a business goes about achieving its goals. The managers of a business must have certain rules to guide them in making decisions; company policy is there to help guide them. A successful set of policies, however, will not only set limits to business activity: it will also encourage initiative. Setting policy is a way for a business' founders to stay in control without directly overseeing every aspect of the business. Policies must be regularly revised if they are to remain relevant.

Business Strategies and Procedures

Business strategies are the overall plans that take into consideration such external factors as trends in the marketplace or the actions of competitors. A business strategy implies a certain course of action, and as such implies a commitment of human resources and capital. Strategy is determined by what kind of company the managers want to create; it does not bother with small-scale plans, but instead is a loose framework of objectives for the company. Business procedures, however, must be very clear. Procedures specify exactly how future actions should be performed. Business managers often publish extensive lists of business procedure, in the hopes of ensuring that employees will perform properly even when the managers are not around. There is always the danger that procedures will become too various and extensive, and that they will ultimately undermine their intention to aid productivity.

Business Rules and Programs

Business rules are things that employees are either required to do or forbidden from doing. Rules are in a sense similar to procedures and plans, in that they control future action. Procedures might even be considered as sequences of rules. Rules are often very necessary, but too often they are conceived simply to prevent anyone making a mistake. Some rules may discourage innovation. Managers should often consider whether making something a "guideline," rather than a rule, might be a more humane means of suggestion. Business programs are the combinations of goals, policies, procedures, rules, job assignments, and resources that are necessary to carry out a certain plan of action. Business programs must be clearly supported by a budget that covers operating expenses and capital expenditures.

Career Clusters

In this extremely specialized modern economy, it is useful to consider various "clusters" of careers that have similar attributes. The United States government has established sixteen career clusters: agriculture and natural resources, arts/audio/video technology and communications, architecture and construction, business and administration, education and training, finance, government and public administration, health science, hospitality and tourism, human services, information technology services, law and public safety, manufacturing, retail/wholesale sales and services, scientific research and engineering, and transportation distribution and logistics. These clusters have been created in part to aid vocational educators, who may be overwhelmed by the variety of potential careers and can benefit from a system of summary.

Career clusters utilized to determine job aptitude -- One of the main uses of the system of career clusters as devised by the United States government is to provide vocational educators with a simplified way to look at the skills and standards for various types of jobs. The government has developed extensive paperwork regarding each of the sixteen skill sets, complete with specific training required and skills that must be acquired. Oftentimes, vocational teachers will administer a questionnaire to students that determines which career clusters best suit their interests and aptitudes. Then, with the help of the available literature, the teacher can work with the student to develop a plan for attaining the skills necessary for employment in their chosen field.

Work Standards for Employees

It is very important that an employer enforce clear standards for employees. In order to do this successfully, the employer needs to make sure that standards are posted visibly and that employees are introduced to them during orientation. Employers should also lead by example by following all the rules themselves. Employers should strive to present the image to their employees that their business prizes accuracy and honesty. Finally, a good way to ensure that employee work standards will be attained is to set certain performance goals and reward employees for reaching them. Work standards may have to do with customer service, accuracy in bookkeeping, cleanliness, punctuality, productivity, or safety.

Office Managers

Office managers have a wide variety of responsibilities, but their main goal is to ensure that the office runs smoothly and is an environment in which all employees can work productively. Office managers are typically involved in bookkeeping and may work closely with an accounting department. They are responsible for acquiring and maintaining all office equipment, from facilities to furniture to technology. Office managers may oversee the mailroom and workflow software used by a company, as well as ensuring that all of the company's communication systems are working properly. Office managers are required to set strict budgets for office expenditures, and monitor use of company property closely. They may also be responsible for office security.

Treasurer

The treasurer of an organization is charged with various responsibilities concerning the company's finances. First, the treasurer is responsible for paying the bills of the business, especially those pertaining to office supplies. The treasurer will receive all of the checks and securities given to the business, and will deposit them in an account authorized by the management. Treasurers are also required to maintain the check register, to keep a record of deposits and withdrawals, and to make and keep receipts for all the money that flows throughout the business. The treasurer also may be required to prepare an annual budget for the business, and to have this budget approved by management. The treasurer will also likely have to prepare an annual financial report summarizing the financial activities of the business.

Comptroller

A comptroller is the head accounting officer in a company. In a corporation, the comptroller (also known as the controller) is responsible for managing cash flow. The comptroller will oversee the company's accounting, meaning he or she will establish the accounting principles to be used, and will make recommendations regarding accounting to the company's management. Most comptrollers are certified accountants. The comptroller will also help management develop an annual business plan, monthly sales and profit forecasts, expense budgets, daily operating reports, and will provide advice to management as to how the company can best reach its financial goals.

Chief Executive Officer

The chief executive officer, or CEO, of a company is typically the individual with the most responsibility for the business' success or failure. The CEO is responsible for basically everything: human resources, operations, marketing, strategy, financing, sales, and public relations. Obviously, no one person can perform all of these functions in a large business, so the CEO exercises his or her authority through the people that he or she hires. The main duty of a CEO in a large business, then, is to set the overall strategy and vision of the company. The CEO is also responsible for making sure that all of the various departments in the company are working together well, and that strong channels of communication exist throughout the business.

Chief Financial Officer

The chief financial officer of a business is responsible for figuring out what the company's financial needs are, and then determining how to satisfy those needs. The CFO is also responsible for communicating the financial activity of the business to the shareholders, employees, and management of the business. In order to do his or her job effectively, the CFO will have to establish the best capital structure for the company. Capital structure is the particular blend of cash, debt financing, and equity financing that the company uses to continue operations. The CFO will also have to maintain good working relationships with commercial and investment banks. The CFO assists in the creation of sales and expense forecasts and budgets.

Receptionist

A receptionist is charged with providing the company's face to the outside world, whether by greeting visitors or answering phone calls. Obviously, this job is quite important, as every business wants to make a good impression on the outside community. Therefore, a receptionist must always maintain a professional and courteous demeanor. Receptionists will also be required to sort and direct mail that arrives for the people they represent. More generally, a receptionist is a source of general information for visitors as well as for fellow employees; if a receptionist can provide basic information, it will save time and money for more senior employees that have other, more important tasks at hand.

Promotion From Within

One of the most important tasks of a business manager is the selection and training of new employees. Promotion from within is a straightforward concept, but besides indicating that a company tries to advance its own employees, it has come to mean more generally the philosophy of establishing loyalty among employees. Many businesses claim to have a promotion-from-within policy because it is attractive to employees, though the company may do a considerable amount of hiring externally. Sometimes the current employees of a company simply aren't appropriate candidates for management. Furthermore, if a new area of business opens up for a company, it will always make more sense to hire an external candidate who specializes in that area.

Open Competition

In the matter of hiring, most companies these days have what is known as an open competition policy. That is, they fill vacancies or make promotions based on who is the best candidate, not on any predetermined criteria. Obviously, this policy results in the best employees being hired, and therefore seemingly in the best interests of the company. However, repeatedly hiring external candidates can have a demoralizing effect on a company, especially if current employees feel they are not being given a fair chance at promotion. If a company cuts staff development programs and then hires a series of external candidates, the workforce may have serious grievances. Most companies, though, find it to be in their best interests to encourage the development of their present staff.

Improving Employee Attitudes

There are some business analysts who note a mismatch between the passion for personal liberty in the United States and the authoritarian hierarchies of American business. Over the course of the twentieth century, statistics have shown a gradual decrease in the trust of the American worker in his or her employer. At the same time, the average age of American workers and management has decreased, so there is reason to suspect that communication between employer and employee may improve. One means of increasing employee satisfaction is through the formation of quality circles, groups of people that meet together to discuss work-related issues. Many statistics show that workers are now more concerned with being challenged and feeling important than with earning money to survive; the modern manager will have to do more than pay his employees to make them feel their work is worthwhile.

Peer Relationships

It is essential to maintain solid relationships among employees if productivity is to be maximized. Oftentimes, individuals who focus intensely on their work can actually undermine an organization by alienating their coworkers and inhibiting the flow of knowledge throughout the company. As a manager, it is crucial to monitor the relationships among staff and ensure that positive communication is taking place. Many businesses devote time to building the relationships among staff, as they feel that taking a bit of time away from work to develop trust and friendship in the company will ultimately lead to greater productivity in the long run.

<u>Building strong relationships among staff</u>
There are a few easy ways for managers to develop positive working relationships among the members of their staff. One way is to set aside some time for company lunches or outings, so that fellow employees can get to know one another personally. Passing on compliments and bestowing praise on positive behavior is another way to nurture a good work environment. If a manager wants to encourage communication among his or her employees, then he or she should set a good example by keeping the staff informed and involved in the managerial operations. Most importantly, a manager should always be a good listener, so that employees will get the impression that their ideas are valued and appreciated.

Personnel Needs

The first thing a personnel manager in business has to do is determine what employees the business needs. This is best done by arranging an organizational chart and making sure that there will be enough employees to advance the business' agenda. Personnel managers often make organizational charts and then hypothetically "remove" certain positions, to try and determine whether the business could function without it. After establishing what positions are needed, the manager should determine what skills are needed for each position. Then, it can be determined what precise qualifications candidates must have to be considered for the various positions. Personnel manager must also consider when employees will be needed, and for how long.

Recruiting Personnel

Good business human resources managers do a great deal of preliminary work before they select employees. They must have a good description of organizational needs and necessary qualifications. It is also important for a business to have a standardized method of selection. If there is no standard procedure for hiring, a manager is likely to make one of three mistakes. The first mistake is to ignore the necessity of envisioning and planning for potential future problems. Another common mistake is to assume that the right employees will be available when they are needed. The last common mistake is to trust personal judgment to an inordinate degree. Companies may administer psychological exams and demand resumes, and then ignore them to follow some personal intuition. Rather than doing this, managers should have a clear idea of their selection needs and process.

Sexual Harassment

Sexual harassment is any inappropriate verbal or physical conduct of a sexual nature, specifically when it is directed at an individual because of his or her gender. The Supreme Court has determined that sexual harassment violates the protections for employees that were set forth in the Civil Rights Act of 1964. There are also state laws against sexual harassment. In order to prove that sexual harassment has occurred, a plaintiff must be able to demonstrate that the alleged harassment was either severe or consistent enough to affect their work, and that the employer is liable because of their knowledge of the harassment. In many cases, the courts have leveled extremely harsh punishments against businesses that neglect to stop or punish sexual harassment.

<u>Quid pro quo and hostile work environment</u> -- Most sexual harassment cases are either built on the idea of quid pro quo (literally, "this for that") harassment or the existence of a hostile work environment. In order for a plaintiff to prove that quid pro quo harassment has occurred, he or she must be able to demonstrate that harassment was considered a necessary part of having the job, that tolerating harassment affected the employee's progress in the company, or that the harassment clearly affected the plaintiff's ability to work. In order to make the case that harassment created a hostile work environment, the plaintiff must prove that he or she was discriminated against on the basis of gender, that this discrimination was pervasive and regular, that he or she was negatively affected by this discrimination, that any reasonable person would have been similarly affected, and that management either knew or should have known about the harassment, and did nothing to stop it.

Job-Hunting

As part of preparing students for entry into the job market, teachers need to show them the various places to look for jobs. One of the best places to find a job is still the classified ad section of the local newspaper. However, there are now many on-line listings for jobs as well. These are constantly changing, so business teachers will want to keep abreast of the most popular sites. Many part-time and odd jobs will be advertised on bulletin boards and message boards at local supermarkets and libraries. Magazines and trade journals often have job listings, too. One of the most obvious yet often overlooked ways to get a job is simply to ask for one. If students are interested in working for a particular company, they should have the skills and wherewithal to call and inquire about openings.

Human Resource Accounting

Many business analysts believe human resources are even more valuable than physical assets; some even go so far as to say that human resources should be listed as assets on the company's balance sheet. Most businesses spend a substantial amount of time recruiting and training their employees. Some analysts even say that, in the event of a recession, companies would do better to get rid of machinery or downsize inventory rather than fire trained employees. Oddly, though, human resources is one of the more neglected and undervalued areas of business. There is speculation that this is because effective human resource accounting requires a feel for employees that goes beyond objective charts and graphs.

Writing Job Descriptions

In order to attract the right kind of candidates for an available position in his or her business, a manager has to be able to write a clear and precise job description. A good job description is similar to a job contract: it outlines what the employer wants, and indicates what the employee is likely to get in return. It should include a description of the physical tasks of the job, the training that will be provided, the authority and responsibility of the job, the goals and objectives of the job, and a brief account of the payment offered. In a medium to large business, it is always good idea for managers to run a completed job description by the employees who deal most closely with the person performing that job, to make sure that they concur with the summary.

Application Forms

Large businesses can be overwhelmed by the volume of resumes that they receive, whether they are advertising vacancies or not. For this reason, it often makes sense for them to compose a standard application form that every prospective employee will have to fill out. This allows the business to inquire directly about the things that are important to them, rather than allowing candidates to mention anything they believe to be significant. By law, application forms cannot inquire about age, marital status, arrest records, gender, religion, citizenship, or nationality. All of these things are considered to be possible sources of discrimination in hiring. Application forms should be concise and clear, so that managers can look through a large number of them quickly.

Internal Candidates

If at all possible, managers should try to promote individuals from within the company to fill upper-level vacancies. There are a number of reasons for doing so. First, it is good for company morale to see an employee rewarded for his or her good work; internal promotion gives the impression that hard work will be rewarded. Moreover, internal candidates already know the basic structure and workings of the organization and will therefore require less orientation and training. In order to give current employees the best possible chance to fill a vacancy, managers should advertise job descriptions in the company newsletter and mention vacancies at any company gatherings.

External Candidates

In some cases, especially for newly-created positions, it will be appropriate to search exclusively outside the company for new employees. There are a number of ways to do this. The most common way to attract external candidates is to advertise in the print media. This approach often results in an overabundance of unqualified applicants, however, so many businesses have taken to using headhunters, people who have made a career out of matching individuals with companies. Employment and staffing agencies are also good ways for a business to fill their vacancies with minimal stress. Perhaps the best way for a manager to discover great job candidates is simply by asking around in his or her business network.

Conducting Job Interviews

Learning how to conduct a proper job interview takes experience. However, there a few fundamental tips that a manager should know before meeting with prospective employees. First, be prepared. Unless interview questions are planned, an inexperienced manager will not be able to use the interview to get to know the candidate. Instead, he or she will be occupied trying to remember what questions to ask. Besides the specific information that should be acquired about the candidate, the job interview should give the manager a general sense of the candidate's character, confidence, and intelligence. A well-structured interview allows a manager to focus on developing an overall impression of the candidate, and gives him or her to pursue any interesting subjects at his or her discretion.

Interview Questions

The questions that are appropriate to a job interview will depend on what job is being offered; a manager will need to ensure that the candidate has whatever skills or training is requisite to the job. Still, there are some general questions that are appropriate for just about any interview. For instance, most managers like to ask a candidate why they are interested in a job, or where they first learned about the vacancy; these questions give the candidate a chance to speak at length about his or her interests and goals. It is important for a manager to ask questions that require more than a simple "yes or "no," so that he or she can gat an idea of how the candidate's mind works. Asking for opinions, or for a description of some past experience, is a good way to draw the applicant's personality out.

References and Tests

Although checking references is not always a fun experience, it is an invaluable tool for learning more about job applicants. Most managers are astonished by the honest information they can find out about potential employees just by calling up their previous employers. Even if the company finds its applicants through a headhunter or employment agency, it is a good idea to check with the applicant's references. Companies may also find it helpful to administer psychological, medical, IQ, or dexterity tests to their applicants. It is a good idea to limit testing to those areas that are directly relevant to the position offered; IQ testing for a receptionist position, for example, might be unnecessary. Drug testing is also frequently employed by businesses, although it is illegal in some cases.

Offer Sheets

Once a manager has decided to offer employment to a particular candidate, the next step in the hiring process is to design an offer sheet. An offer sheet should include the job description and title, the starting date, the starting salary, a summary of the compensation package, a copy of the business' organizational chart, and a deadline for acceptance or refusal of the offer. It is not at all rare for a first job offer to be refused. Still, managers should always make sure that their payment offers are consistent with the company's pay scale, to avoid jealousy within the company. Also, it is a good idea to hire new employees on a three-month probationary basis. Finally, managers should avoid drawing up employment contracts, unless it is a good idea to prevent any employees from working for a competitor for any length of time.

Salary Agreeement

Managers, after appraising all the objective data regarding a particular candidate, will typically try and determine whether they can agree with the employee on a potential salary. It is best for managers not to spend too much time touting the good qualities of the business; oversold employees may easily become embittered. Typically, hiring decisions regarding low-level employees can be made fairly quickly. More time will be taken to fill managerial vacancies, and there will usually be a series of interviews to accompany whatever battery of tests the business administers to potential employees. Many companies have established their own selection formulas: whatever combination of psychological tests, interviews, and charts they use to select employees.

Employee Orientation

Orientation is the process through which new employees are introduced into the culture of the company. Most businesses will include a partial orientation in the hiring process, so that employees can determine whether the job is a good fit for them. Once hired, though, employees will receive a full orientation, which usually includes the following: company history and major operations; general company policies and rules; outline of the organizational structure; rules concerning wages and payment, overtime, vacations, and holidays; the economic and recreational services made available by the company, such as insurance or pensions; the system for promotion and transfer; the procedure to follow when the employee has a problem or a suggestion regarding the company.

<u>Informal means of employee orientation</u> -- Of course, no employee will remember everything they are told during a formal orientation. There are several other ways for them to become experienced on the job. In vestibule training, new employees are led through a brief course of training in an environment identical to the one they will be working in. This is a method of orientation often used by factories. On-the-job training is simply when the new employee learns his or her job by performing it. Apprenticeship is a common form of orientation in skilled jobs; here, the new employee is mentored by a veteran employee with long experience in the field. In management positions, orientation may take the form of job rotation, in which employees receive training in several different fields. "Assistant-to" positions give new employees a chance to tag along with

some senior executive and thereby get a feel for the job.

Managerial Control

In order to properly oversee the operations of a business, managers must exercise effective control. Managerial control is simply making the adjustments that allow the business to be successful. The three essential steps of managerial control are the establishment of standards, the comparison of performance to those standards, and all the actions taken to bring performance in line with the standards. Managerial standards should be explicit not only to management but also to the staff. Furthermore, management should always make their assessment of performance at least somewhat transparent, so that employees can understand the criteria of judgment and better remedy any mistakes they might be unconsciously making. It is also important that managers react quickly to improve performance, but without interfering too much in day-to-day operations.

Business Standards

The standards in a business are simply the areas in which performance is assessed. An airline, for example, might set itself standards in sales, customer service, or repair quality, for instance. Clear and verifiable standards are important since managers do not have the ability to oversee every aspect of operations; employees need to have some consistent idea of the company's expectations for them. Effective managers will only set a few important standards for their employees, so that these can be given enough attention. For this reason, it is essential that managers select the few standards that will give them the best indication that their subordinates are dong their jobs well. Standards may be measured in money, quotas, time, speed, quality, or volume.

Performance Appraisals

Every business needs some way to assess the competence and efficiency of its employees. Although it may be universally unpopular, performance appraisal is necessary in every field. From the point of view of management, the point of performance appraisal is to properly allocate resources, to reestablish the focus on the company's goals, and to give employees a venue to express their feelings about their job and about the goals of the company. Oftentimes, the performance appraisal process is more remarkable for what it reveals about the business than about any particular employee. Some managers dislike performance appraisal, because they fail to understand it as a chance to improve the business; nevertheless, it is essential that appraisal systems be clear and precise, so that a company can continue to get the maximum form happy employees.

<u>Employee performance review</u> -- In order for a business to conduct of performance, there must be some sort of easily understandable system of measurement. There are a few easy ways for a business to make this possible. First, management should break everything up into small units. It is also important to make sure that comparisons are being made between similar things, so that an accurate gauge of progress can be discerned. It is also important for management to differentiate between team assignments and individual assignments; in other words, decide what resources are required for each area of operations as well as how productive those areas are. Last, an effective manager will make sure that one person is in charge of every area of operations, and that that person understands the

system of measurement and accountability.

Using company history -- It seems absurd, but many managers continue to try and assess company progress without comparing the present data with the data of the past. In order to really understand how a business is developing, it is crucial to compare the accounting numbers from year to year. Some companies even begin their budgeting for the next year by simply entering all the data from the previous year and then making adjustments. While this method may only work for businesses with consistent operations, every business should revisit the numbers from the previous years when they are conducting performance appraisal. This is one way to ensure that appraisal is conducted objectively and fairly.

Importance of benchmarks -- One way that many businesses assess their performance is by comparing themselves with the best businesses in their field and in the economy in general. This process, known as benchmarking, is effective if it inspires employees to make specific beneficial changes. Managers should avoid, however, setting standards for their business that are unreachable and may become discouraging. In order for benchmarking to be useful, a business should make very specific comparisons, like between customer service departments or between specific accounts. Many businesses try to motivate themselves by competing for the Baldridge Award, a prize given out every year to the American companies with the best marks for quality control.

Productivity Bonus System

Although money is not necessarily the most important factor in selecting a job for everyone, it must be considered by anyone seeking to be self-sufficient. Many manufacturing workers are paid on the piecework or productivity bonus system, meaning that they receive a certain amount of money for every completed task. Often, they are given a certain minimum sum for each hour, and the chance to earn a bonus if they exceed a certain amount of finished products. This system has been seen to dramatically increase production, as employees are much more motivated to work when their rate of pay is determined by production. Receiving just a standard hourly wage does not give the worker much incentive to increase his or her output.

Employee Compensation

Wages, salary, guaranteed annual wage (GAW), and bonus -- Large corporations may use a variety of measures to determine the rate of pay for their employees. Wages are the employee's pay based on hours of work or on the specific units of work that have been finished. A salary, on the other hand, is pay based on time at work, when that time is measured in weeks, months, or years. Salaries are generally paid on a weekly, semi-monthly, or monthly basis, and are typically reserved for managerial positions. A guaranteed annual wage (GAW) is the amount of guaranteed hours of work in a year that a company promises its employees. A GAW may be important in businesses that tend to have varying production demands throughout the year. A bonus is simply anything awarded to an employee for special performance, especially when the money is derived from profits.

Overtime pay, incentive pay, profit sharing, insurance, and paid vacation -- Overtime pay is usually one and one-half times the normal wage, and is paid for hours worked in excess of the normal amount. Usually salaried employees are exempt from overtime pay. Incentive pay is given to employees as a reward fro meeting certain production goals; it is usually offered as a means of stimulating increased productivity. Profit sharing is any system whereby employees are entitled to a certain amount of the company's profits, whether in cash or as contributions to their pension plans. Insurance, in this context, is any group, life, health, or disability insurance paid for by the company. Paid vacations, of course, are time off from work in which the employee continues to receive full pay.

Stock options, savings plans, retirement or pension plans, and additional non-money benefits -- Stock options are chance for employees to purchase company stock for a period of five or ten years at prices set at the time the option is awarded. Obviously, employees hope that the price of the stock will go up after the stock options are handed out. A savings plan is a savings account or pension plan that is sponsored by a company. Often, employers will put money in the account proportional to the amount that the employee deposits. A retirement or pension plan is a company's provision for the retirement of the employee. It is usually based on length of service and pay level. These plans are given in addition to Social Security benefits, and are often financed by company profits. Besides all these forms of compensation, employees may also receive discounts on company products, special gifts at the holidays, or military leaves of absence.

Promotions

The most common means to higher compensation is advancement to a higher position in the company, otherwise known as promotion. Of course, there are social and psychological advantages to promotion besides any increase in pay. Companies have various means of determining when employees will be promoted or given a raise. Some companies use a merit-rating system, in which every employee is evaluated at a certain interval. Employees are assessed for their dependency, initiative, handling of responsibility, appearance, production, use of resources, and the amount of supervision they require. If an employee seems to have demonstrated positive progress in these areas, he or she will receive a raise or promotion. Some critics of this system suggest that it often tends to degenerate into a system of automatic rewards, without the accompanying evaluation.

Seniority System

When union members are allowed to vote on their company's system for promotions and raises, they almost uniformly select the seniority system, in which decisions regarding advancement and elimination of employees are made based on the employee's length of service. Of course, this system does not always work in the best interests of the company; those employees who have been around the longest may not be the most qualified for advancement. However, a seniority system may seem like a good objective alternative to a merit-based system of promotion that they feel is unfair or prejudiced. The seniority system also tends to induce a certain amount of complacency among employees, who may feel that they do not need to do anything but wait for their inevitable promotion.

Peter Principle

The Peter Principle is a somewhat satirical notion about the way promotions work in a bureaucratic organization. It stems from the common mistake made by managers: namely, assuming that because an employee can do one thing well, they will be able to do another, more complicated thing well also. The Peter Principle asserts that individuals who are competent at their work will be promoted again and again, until they eventually reach a position for which they are not qualified. At this point, the organization will have damaged itself, by removing a worker from a position of competence and placed him or her into a position of incompetence. Over and over, the drive for more money and higher status propels workers into jobs for which they are simply not qualified.

Personnel Termination

Termination of employees may take a number of different forms. Many workers are considered terminated because they retire. For the purposes of the company, the money that an individual receives after retiring is money that was earned during the period of service, and has simply been deferred until the employee became inactive. Retirement plans are influenced by the state of the economy, the rate of unemployment, the life expectancy, and the rate of inflation. Another kind of termination occurs when workers voluntarily leave a company to work somewhere else. In the American business community, mobility is much greater than in countries (like Japan) where loyalty to an employer is more carefully cultivated. Termination of employees may also take the form of layoffs, motivated by poor performance or declines in the industry.

Ergonomics

Ergonomics is any special strategy used by a manager to efficiently pair workers with machinery, tools, or other equipment. Ergonomics evolved out of a series of time-and-motion tests conducted by the military, and was originally created to aid marksmanship and pilot control. It attempts to discover and adjust to the strengths and weaknesses of human labor. Some examples of products that have been built with ergonomics in mind are computers, power tools, and chairs. Human factors engineering is the field of technology that develops machines and work environments that suit the physical and mental needs of humans. Human factors engineering and ergonomics aim to reduce the monotony and fatigue of production, as well as to minimize waste and improve productivity.

Nondiscriminatory Discrimination

Screening is always the first part of the recruiting process. Some companies have recruiting officers that travel to universities to interview potential employees. In any case, it is important that the firm have a good set of minimum requirements, and that they do not bother to interview just anyone who is interested in a job. An able recruiter should establish close relationships with people at the place of recruiting, so that he or she will have an available reference for candidates. Usually, resumes are used to screen candidates at first. Business analysts all agree that it is best for a company to have an immediate idea of a candidates weaknesses; being placed in a job for which one is unqualified is as bad for the individual as it is for the company.

Laws and Acts

Civil Rights Act and EEOC -- The United States government has set up some laws to ensure that all citizens are given a fair chance at available jobs. The Civil Rights Act of 1964 decreed that it is illegal to discriminate against candidates based on their race, ethnicity, religion, or gender. Title VII of this act established the Equal Employment Opportunity Commission (EEOC), which has its goal an increase in job opportunities for women and minorities. Since its inception the EEOC has been enhanced by the Equal Pay Act of 1963, the Age Discrimination in Employment Act of 1967, and the Equal Employment Opportunity Act of 1972.

These are laws that apply to business, state and local governments, labor unions, and educational institutions.

Laws affecting employee compensation and benefits -- The Consolidated Omnibus Budget Reconciliation Act (COBRA) requires employers to allow employees who have lost their jobs for certain reasons to continue receiving health insurance at the company rate. The Equal Pay Act prohibits employers from paying two people who perform the same job different wages because of gender. The Fair Labor Standards Act requires employers to pay the minimum wage and to pay overtime wages to all employees that earn them. The Health insurance Portability and Accountability Act of 1996 regulates the health information that employers can require from employees, although it does not strictly forbid employers from viewing employee health records under certain circumstances.

The Family and Medical Leave Act of 1993, Drug Free Workplace Act, and Occupational Safety and Health Act -- The Family and Medical Leave Act was passed in 1993. It enables employees to take up to twelve weeks of unpaid leave for certain family or medical emergencies without risking the loss of their job. This law was created because of the tendency of employers to be rather callous in dealing with employees who have legitimate personal crises. The Drug Free Workplace Act allows employers to discipline or terminate employees who are using or distributing controlled substances in the workplace. The Occupational Safety and Health Act requires employers to meet certain standards regarding safety in the workplace. OSHA also created an agency to survey businesses and ensure that these standards are being maintained.

Employee Rights

There are four main categories of employee rights: rights associated with collective bargaining and unions; rights having to do with working hours and pay; rights having to do with workplace safety and worker's compensation; and rights having to do with discrimination in the workplace. The rights that employees have today have been codified by federal legislation. Before that, however, employee rights were established first by state law, and later by negotiation between unions and employers. Some of the specific rights enjoyed by employees are the rights to distribute union literature, the right to negotiate wages and working conditions in good faith, and the right to work without being treated differently because of race or gender.

Business Contracts

As part of a comprehensive business class students should learn the basics about business contracts. Since contracts are legally binding agreements, it is imperative that they be clear and understandable for all the parties involved. Every good contract has four parts: offer and acceptance, mutuality and consideration, competent parties, and a legal object. The offer will be expressed in writing and must be set in definite terms. Mutuality indicates that some action will be taken by both parties, while consideration indicates that a sum of money will be exchanged. The section regarding competent parties simply establishes that all the signers of the contact are in control of themselves and capable of acting in their own interest. Contracts don't necessarily have to be formal, but in order to be legally valid they have to be understandable and clear.

Students in a business class should get some experience drawing up simple contracts. The most important thing to begin with in composing an effective contract is an accurate idea of the issues and conditions that are being agreed upon, as well as the ability to express these issues and conditions clearly in writing. If necessary, a contract should include a detailed payment schedule, or a clear deadline for services to be rendered, goods to be delivered, or money to be paid. If intellectual property (ideas, software, etc.) is involved in the deal, then the contract should specify the owner of this property. It is absolutely essential that a contract makes very clear the point at which the conditions of the contract will have been fulfilled. There are a number of computer programs currently available to assist in the composition of basic contracts.

Statute of Frauds

The statute of frauds requires certain documents to be put into writing. These documents include real estate titles, leases lasting longer than a year, wills, and some contracts. This law was originally passed by the English Parliament in 1677, and has been present in the United States since its inception. It exists to prevent disputes over important business transactions; by making it mandatory for individuals to sign a written contract in regards to certain issues, the government makes it easier to settle any potential conflict. The statute of frauds is continually modified to include various documents, but it mainly covers four types: contracts to assume someone else's obligation; contracts that cannot be performed within one year; contracts for the sale of land; and contracts for the sale of goods.

Duress

Duress is any actual or threatened violence or incarceration which forces a person to enter into some contractual agreement which they would not otherwise enter. Sometimes, the threat of violence or incarceration may be directed at the family or friends of the person forced into the contract. Individuals may be able to escape from contracts of they can prove that they were moved to originally agree by duress. In business, this may include duress to goods, in which a person is threatened with the destruction of their property if they do not agree to terms. Of course, it can be quite difficult to prove duress, as the plaintiff will have to produce evidence of threats from the defendant, as well as show why the contract would be disadvantageous to him or herself.

Principals and Agents

Investors often grant control over their funds to investment agents, who are supposed to be experts that are bond by law to operate in the best interests of the original investor, or principal. Of course, this does not always happen, and so the principal-agent relationship is notoriously thorny. It is essential that the rights of the agent to act on behalf of the principal be made explicit in some sort of contract. Then, if the agent acts without the authority of the principal, on behalf of the principal, then the agent is required to pay back to the principal any losses or damages. Likewise, if the agent has acted within the scope of authority granted him by the principal, the principal is liable for any expenses the agent incurs while acting on behalf of the principal.

Life Insurance

Life insurance may take a variety of different forms. Whole life insurance requires fixed payments throughout the individual's lifetime, which, along with compound interest, is paid to some beneficiary upon the policyholder's death. Universal life insurance is similar to whole life insurance, except that the insured can vary the amount and the timing of the premium. Variable life insurance is a system in which the premiums are put into an investment portfolio and the amount received by the beneficiary after the death of the policyholder depends on the performance of the portfolio. Term life insurance only applies to a particular period of time.

Forms of Insurance

Besides life insurance, there are a number of other forms of insurance commonly taken out by individuals and businesses. Health insurance helps pay for medical goods and services. Many businesses own insurance to protect them in case of natural disasters, like fire, flood, hail, or tornado. Individuals and businesses are also required to have automotive insurance, to protect themselves and others from injury and damage. Title insurance protects purchasers of real estate from potential losses due to defective titles. Credit insurance protects businesses from losses they stand to suffer if customers are unable to pay their credit debts. Marine insurance is taken out by shipping companies to pay for any loss of cargo or vessels while transporting goods at sea.

Consignment and Factor's Lien

Consignment is the system of sale wherein one business delivers goods to another, on the understanding that the second business will pay for the goods once they have been sold. This is a popular way of doing business for high-end retail stores, such as art galleries, who do not expect to sell all of their merchandise and do not want to get stock with it. Of course, this is a form of transaction that often becomes contentious, and so the government has established legislation indicating when goods must be returned. Ownership of property never actually passed to the company that holds it for sale; it passes directly from the original company to the buyer. A factor's lien gives the second company the right, however, to hang onto the merchandise until payment for it is made to the original owner.

Tort

A tort is simply a legal wrong done to some person for which that person is entitled to some sort of restitution. Intentional torts are any acts that could have been predicted to cause harm to another person, and then do so. These may be torts against the person (like assault), property torts (like trespass), dignitary torts (those that cause harm to another person's reputation, like slander), and economic torts (like fraud). Torts of negligence occur when an individual with a certain responsibility fails to meet that responsibility and thus brings harm to another individual. Torts of nuisance interfere with another individual's use of land. In some countries, strict liability is applied to extremely hazardous activities in which individuals can be held accountable even if they have not been strictly negligent. Legal proceedings in torts, unlike those in criminal cases, are initiated by the plaintiff and not by some public body.

American tort law -- The American legal system divides actionable torts into three types: intentional torts, torts of negligence, and strict liability torts. Intentional torts are those that were made on purpose by the tortfeasor (the person who committed the tort) and include battery, assault, false imprisonment, fraud, defamation of character, and malicious prosecution. Torts of negligence are the most common form of tort in the American legal system. Common examples of this kind of tort are malpractice, emotional distress due to negligence, and product liability. Strict liability torts are brought after injuries resulting from ultrahazardous activities, for which the tortfeasor can be charged even without having been negligent. Most tort claims are heard in state courts.

Business Failure and Bankruptcy

Business failure is typically the result of a lack of planning and market knowledge, though it may be sped along by bad luck. Usually, business failure is preceded by economic failure, in which chances are lost, and earnings are small at best, even if the owners are still able to contribute capital. Persistent economic failure results in financial failure, in which the business is first insolvent (cannot pay its debts) and then bankrupt (has no value in its current form). Although bankruptcy is generally taken to mean the inability to pay one's debts and therefore to continue business, in the United States there are laws in place which guarantee fair treatment to the bankrupt business' creditors, and which may give a second chance to failed businesses that meet certain criteria.

Bankruptcy, Chapter 7, Chapter 11, and Chapter 13 -- The United States has established the Bankruptcy Code to provide for the equitable treatment of creditors and to allow the possibility of resurrection in the event of a business failure. The modern Bankruptcy Code is divided into four Titles, the first of which is commonly referred to because of its categorical description of business failure. Each Title in the Bankruptcy Code is divided into odd-numbered Chapters. In the First Title, Chapter 7 Bankruptcy refers to an arrangement wherein the business owner either pays his debts or sells his property, and gives up his right to continue operations. A business that files for Chapter 11 bankruptcy is attempting to reorganize itself so that it can pay its debts and continue operations. In a Chapter 13 bankruptcy, the debtor arranges a payment plan with his creditors and tries to continue business operations.

Worker's Compensation Laws

Worker's compensation laws are those statutes that require employers to pay workers or the dependents of workers who are injured or become ill on the job. These laws, which are typically enacted at the state level, also establish that employers are liable for illness and injury that occurs in their workplace. Generally, employers will be required to pay medical bills, disability benefits, and lost wages. In exchange, workers are prohibited from suing their employers for any more damages. One important piece of federal legislation relating to worker's compensation is the Occupational Health and Safety Act of 1970, which established standards for safety at various workplaces. Since then, there has also been federal legislation requiring employers to notify employees in advance of any major layoffs.

Union Regulations

There are a number of American laws that affect the ability of American workers to join and participate in organized labor unions. The National Labor Relations Act gives workers the right to join unions, and forbids employers from discriminating against individuals because of their membership in a union. This act does not apply to federal employees, who are governed more strictly by the Federal Labor Relations Act. The Norris-LaGuardia Act of 1932 forbade the government or business from preventing union strikes with anti-trust injunctions. For a long time, officials had used these anti-trust laws to prevent workers from meeting and organizing, much less engaging in work stoppages.

International Trade Law

Since there is no legislative body that governs international trade, the process of ensuring that commercial transactions between businesses from different countries remain equitable is accomplished by a sort of cooperative effort. Most of the precedents for modern trade law have been taken from the maritime laws that governed overseas trade in the past. Jurisdiction is the most important determinant in how a case will be handled; depending on where the alleged offenses were committed, and by whom, cases may be held in countries with wildly different legal systems. Most large American firms that do extensive business overseas have legal teams whose specialty is ensuring that the business does not run afoul of any foreign laws, as being a defendant in a foreign country can be quite expensive.

Employment

Labor force, unemployment rate, and full employment -- The labor force is the total number of employed and unemployed individuals in a society. Unemployed individuals are those who are out of work but are actively seeking work (individuals out of work and not seeking work are voluntarily unemployed and are not considered part of the labor force). The unemployment rate is the percentage of the labor force that is unemployed. Full employment, surprisingly, does not mean that the unemployment rate is zero. Instead, full employment is defined as an unemployment rate of six percent. This is because economists do not believe it is realistic to expect that the unemployment rate will ever drop below this level, even under the best circumstances, because of natural and seasonal causes of unemployment.

Seasonal and frictional unemployment -- Seasonal unemployment is the inevitable result of the presence of industries in which the demand for labor fluctuates during the course of the year. In agriculture, for example, employment increases a great deal during the peak harvest season, and then decreases during the winter. In some cold climates, construction workers may be unemployed throughout the winter months. Frictional unemployment is the result of the huge numbers of people entering and leaving the job market at any given time. There is always a lag time between deciding to look for a job and finding one; during this period the individual is considered frictionally unemployed. Every economy has a bit of frictional unemployment, though some say that the policy of unemployment compensation in the United States encourages more frictional unemployment than is necessary.

Structural unemployment -- Structural unemployment develops when changes in the industry result in a mismatch between the jobs available (and where they are available) and the skills possessed by the workers. This has occurred in the shoe industry in America: workers here no longer have the training to operate the requisite equipment, and demand a higher rate of pay, so jobs have gone overseas. Structural unemployment can last much longer than other forms of unemployment, as workers struggle to acquire new skills. Some people suggest that the government could remedy this problem by helping to pay for structurally unemployed citizens to get the training they need, or for workers to move to locations where they can be paid for the skills they already have.

Cyclical unemployment-- Cyclical unemployment is the lack of jobs that results from the lack of demand in an economy. Essentially, cyclical unemployment is the unemployment left over after all of the unemployment for structural, seasonal, and frictional reasons has been taken out. Since most economic models suggest that the usual combined rate of unemployment by natural causes (that is, structural, seasonal, and frictional unemployment) is six percent, any increase over six percent is considered cyclical unemployment. The government tries to increase aggregate demand and minimize cyclical unemployment through macroeconomic policy; indeed, most of the unemployment data collected by the government is aimed at minimizing cyclical unemployment. Every economy, though, will experience decreases in demand from time to time.

Ethical Behavior

One of the most important missions of the modern business education teacher is to show students what constitutes ethical behavior in the workplace. Put simply, ethical behavior is just good business sense; customers that are lost to unethical behavior are a much bigger concern to a company than any short-term profits that may be gained from the behavior. Companies work hard to earn reputations for ethical behavior because they know it will help them in the market. To this end, they discourage lying to customers, employee theft, and misuse of company time. If a business teacher can instill a good sense for business ethics in his or her students, then he or she has given them perhaps the most valuable tool for success in the contemporary workplace.

<u>Utilizing and maintaining a specific code of ethics in the workplace</u> -- In order to ensure that all employees understand and can abide by the basic principles of business ethics, the manager s of a business should set out a concrete code of ethics for their company. In doing so, they should consider the general principles that will lead to fair business practice in their industry, and then confer with any similar organizations. The managers should then write out a specific code of conduct for employees, using examples from the business itself and making sure to square the code with company policy. Some businesses may find it necessary or advantageous to provide employees with specific training in ethics. Finally, the managers of a business should recognize that ethical decisions are not always easy to make, and therefore they should resolve to continually monitor adherence to the company code, and update the code if necessary.

<u>Some topics that are generally applicable to a code of ethics in the workplace</u> --

Although every business will have a unique set of issues that are relevant to its operations, there are certain topics that are generally applicable to business, and should therefore be covered in any company code of ethics. These include the company policy for handling checks and cash from customers, as well as the forbidding of any preferential pricing for personal friends. Employees should know whether they can accept gifts from suppliers and business associates, as well as how they should deal with shoplifters or damaged merchandise. A company code of ethics usually includes provisions for making accurate advertising promises, handling problems with employee performance, the accounting procedures that will be used for cash sales, and how to deal with the return of purchased merchandise.

<u>The steps in making the right decisions about ethical behavior in the workplace that a business teacher should teach</u> -- Unfortunately, making ethical decisions in the business world is often quite difficult. Business teachers should recognize this fact, and equip their students with a good decision-making process. The first step in the process should be defining the problem; students may often jump to

conclusions about a problem without ever really articulating it to themselves. Next, students should be trained to consider the various alternative solutions to the problem. Making a list on paper is a good way of externalizing choices. After this, students should get in the habit of identifying the consequences of the various proposed solutions. Consequences may be both short-term and long-term; as every businessperson knows, losing a customer in the name of short-term profit is always a bad decision. Finally, students should determine whether they have enough information to make decision, and if not they should have the discipline to acquire the information they need.

Accounting, Economics, and Finance

Capitalism and Free Enterprise

Capitalism is an economic model with the following characteristics: emphasis on private property; the freedom to manipulate private property to derive as much income as possible; competitive and open markets (specifically, markets in which there is no government intervention in the form of taxation or price controls). Although capitalist countries do have governments that provide various collective goods like a military, public education, and health care, and although the government usually sets the basic rules of the economy, most production and consumption is done by private individuals and groups. Free enterprise refers to any situation, whether in a capitalist economy or not, in which individuals and groups are free to use their resources in any way they see fit, without government influence or regulation.

Fiscal Policy

Fiscal policy is created and implemented by the federal government in the hopes of increasing the gross national product, raising employment, and stabilizing price and money. Fiscal policy may be either expansionary or contractionary: expansionary policy is designed to combat a recession and consists of either lowering taxes or increasing government spending, while contractionary policy aims to fight inflation and involves raising taxes and decreasing spending. It should be noted that such actions are an example of discretionary fiscal policy; that is, explicit and purposeful adjustment of the economy rather than reliance on the "invisible hand" of market correction. Any results of fiscal policy are usually registered in the national debt.

Monetary Policy

Monetary policy is the actions of a central bank or currency regulation organization that affect the size of the money supply, and thereby affect interest rates. Monetary policy is designed to restrain inflation, improve the employment rate, and generally stabilize the economy. Monetary policy is either expansionary or contractionary, depending on whether it seeks to enlarge or diminish the money supply. In the United States, monetary policy is carried out by the Fed in three ways: through open market operations, the discount rate, and reserve requirements. In order to halt a recession, the Fed typically tries to expand the money supply; when inflation is too great, the Fed attempts to limit spending by contracting the money supply.

Three ways the monetary policy of the Fed may be promoted -- The monetary policy of the Fed may be promoted in three ways: through open market operations, the discount rate, and the reserve requirements. Open market operations are the most common means of adjusting the money supply, and consist of the government's purchasing and selling government securities (savings bonds, for example) in order to affect the size of bank reserves. If the Fed wants to increase the money supply, it will buy securities, thus putting money into the economy. The discount rate is the rate of interest the Fed charges for loans to banks. Adjustment of this rate will either encourage or discourage bank borrowing. Reserve requirements are the levels of reserve funds that the Fed requires of banks. Adjusting this amount may affect the money supply, although this method is used much less frequently than open market operations or the discount rate.

Federal Reserve System

History -- The First and Second National Banks of the United States are the historical antecedents of the current Federal Reserve System. Alexander Hamilton first advocated the creation of a central national bank to help foster private banks and create a larger store of bank credit, which he believed would stimulate economic growth. This bank would also help carry out the financial responsibilities of Congress and the Treasury. The First National Bank of the United States was created in 1791, but its charter ran out twenty years later, throwing the American economy into turmoil. The Second National Bank (1816-1841) was at first successful in regulating monetary regulation, but was eventually deemed too powerful and a threat to democracy. Its dissolution led to another period of chaos in which state-chartered banks struggled to regulate the monetary system.

In 1908, the United States established a National Monetary Commission to investigate the country's monetary policy. This group recommended the creation of a federal banking system, and the Federal Reserve Act became law in 1913, despite some critics who claimed that a central bank would place too much power in the hands of a small group. The Federal Reserve Act created the Federal Reserve System to provide an elastic supply of currency, a way to give helpful credit to commercial interests (and thus stimulate economic growth), and a supervisor for the nation's banks and financial institutions. After a long process of consultation with various business and government leaders, the Federal Reserve Bank as we know it today opened in 1914.

The Federal Reserve System defined -- The Federal Reserve System is the central bank in the United States, responsible for maintaining stable growth in the economy and creating monetary policy. The "Fed," as it is called, does not deal with individual accounts; rather, it is the bank of private banks and other depository institutions. The Fed also regulates and supervises banks, distributes currency to the public through the banks, facilitates the collection and transfer of checks, and implements some of the regulations of consumer credit legislation. The Federal Reserve System consists of the Board of Governors, the Federal Open Market Committee, twelve Federal Reserve Banks around the country, various branches of these banks, advisory committees, and some member financial institutions.

The highest authority in the Federal Reserve System -- The Board of Governors, which consists of seven members, is the highest authority in the Federal Reserve System. These members, usually renowned economists, are appointed by the President and confirmed by the Senate, and serve terms of fourteen years. The main responsibility of the board is to create and implement monetary policy, although they must also supervise the financial activity of banks, Reserve Banks, bank holding companies, and Federal Reserve System banks. The board decides how much money to loan these institutions, and where to set the rate of interest on these loans. Besides all this, the board oversees any bank mergers and acquisitions for American banks, as well as those international banks which are members. The Board of Governors must report its activities to Congress.

Interstate Commerce Commission

The Interstate Commerce Commission was established in 1887 by the Interstate

Commerce Act. At first, all it did was regulate interstate commerce as it took place by rail or by a combination of water and rail. Now, it regulates railroads, trucks, buses, water carriers, and all the pipelines that are not overseen by the Federal Energy Regulatory Commission. The ICC regulates the rates that carriers charge, and oversees any mergers, acquisitions, and sales of carriers. Besides setting the rules for accounting, the ICC also grants the right to operate a railroad, trucking company, bus line, water carrier, or transportation broker. The ICC makes sure that the public receives the fair rates and reasonable service guaranteed by the Interstate Commerce Act. In this line, the ICC makes sure there is no discrimination, prejudice, or preferential treatment in the transportation industry.

Debt, Deficits, and Surplus

A national debt is created when the federal government spends more money than it takes in. If the government is in debt, it must borrow money, and so the national debt includes not only the borrowed money but the interest that accrues on that money. To pay for this, the government issues Treasury notes, bills, and bonds. The national debt remains if it is not paid that year, and so over time a nation may have an accumulated deficit that is enormous (the United States had in 1995 accumulated $4 trillion in debt since 1969). The United States first began the policy of deficit spending (spending more than what is taken in through taxation) during the Great Depression, in the hopes of stimulating the economy. When the government takes in more money than it is spending, it accumulates a surplus.

Gross Domestic Product

The gross domestic product of a country is the total value of goods and services produced by that country in a given period (usually a year). Measures of GDP are typically used to assess the growth of a nation's economy: a steadily increasing GDP indicates a healthy, expanding economy. In the United States, GDP is calculated as the sum total of four components of aggregate demand: net exports (that is, the total value of exports less the total value of imports), consumption (that is, the total amount spent on durable goods, non-durable goods, and services), investment, and federal, state, and local government purchases. GDP is very similar to gross national product (GNP), except that GDP excludes net income from foreign sources.

Taxes

Tax, taxable income, and exemption -- A tax is any payment demanded by the government to help pay for its operation. The federal government is largely funded by income tax, while the state government earns most of its money from the property and sales taxes. The goal of the tax system is to be equitable both horizontally (people of the same income pay the same amount in taxes) and vertically (people pay an amount of taxes proportional to their income). Taxable income is the amount of personal or corporate income that is left after all deductions, exemptions, and losses have been subtracted. An exemption is an amount of money that, for some reason, is not eligible to be taxed. Many individuals receive tax exemptions for the money they use to pay for dependents.

Itemized deductions -- The government generally allows individuals to avoid being taxed on certain expenses, which when they are listed and calculated on the individual's income tax form are known as itemized deductions. Medical and dental costs may be deductible, if they are greater than 7.5% of income. Interest on a mortgage or on investments may be deductible. Items that are stolen or lost due to a natural disaster may be deductible as well. Other miscellaneous deductions may include the cost of work uniforms, job-search expenses, repayments of Social Security, some legal fees, home office expenses, and education expenses that are related to the individual's job. Individuals cannot deduct political donations, raffle tickets, cosmetic surgery, life insurance, funeral expenses, gifts, tuition, home repairs, and commuting expenses, among other things.

Personal taxation -- Individuals may be subject to a number of taxes as they conduct their business in the United States. The greatest is the income tax, which is collected on both the federal and state levels, and which is determined by the individual's level of income. The income tax is meant to be the tax that most clearly assesses the individual's ability to pay. Individuals may also be subject to a property tax based on buildings and land that they own. Inheritance tax is assessed on any property an individual received upon the death of someone else. Individuals pay a sales tax any time they purchase a good or a service. A capital gains tax is paid on the income received from the sale of capital assets, like stocks or bonds. Social security payments are also a sort of tax levied on the individual, in which money is set aside to ensure the financial security of older workers.

Business taxation -- Corporations, because they are considered as individual entities by the state, are required to pay income tax on their earnings. All other businesses are required to pay property tax on any buildings, land, or equipment that they own. Businesses also pay a regular sales tax on the goods and services that they purchase, and a capital gains tax on the monies made from the sale of capital assets, including securities and real estate. Businesses may be required to pay an excise tax if they sell a certain good (tobacco or gasoline, for instance), although the money for this tax is usually just added on to the price the ultimate consumer has to pay. A value-added tax is a tax that companies must pay on goods as they pass through the stages to becoming a finished product; companies are taxed according to the amount of value that their work has added to the product.

Mixed Economy Goals

The five economic goals of a mixed economy (one in which both markets and the government allocate resources) are full employment, stability, economic growth, efficiency, and equity. Full employment indicates that all the resources, human and otherwise, that could potentially be used are being used. Stability is achieved when an economy is able to avoid large changes in price, production, and rate of employment. An economy that is growing has ever-increasing opportunities for diversified production. Efficiency and equity are the two goals emphasized by micro economics, efficiency being the best possible result from the given amount of resources, and equity being the degree of fairness with which wealth is distributed in the society. Of course, the degree to which any economy realizes these goals will depend on the definition of fairness and efficiency.

Inflation and Deflation

Inflation is the rate of change in the price level. Although most economies exhibit rising price rates every year, there is occasionally a reduction in price level, known as deflation. Inflation does not necessarily mean that every price increases, only that the average price has increased. Demand-pull inflation is when greater demand results in inadequate supply and raised prices. Cost-push inflation results when increases in he cost of production lead to supply shortages across the economy, again leading to a raise in price. The two major problems associated with inflation are economic uncertainty (people are unwilling to make long-term investments because of the perceived instability of the market) and the random distribution of wealth that results when price becomes so variable. Such a distribution of wealth may not be in the best interest of society.

Recession

A recession is typically defined as the economic situation in which a nation's gross domestic product has diminished in each of the last three quarters. A recession often leads to falling prices, which can lead to a depression (an extended recession, basically). On the other hand, a recession may lead to a sharp rise in prices, creating a condition known as stagflation. In most developed economies, recessions occur every five or ten years, although many economists suggest ways that governments can smooth the cycle. Recessions are typically caused either by shocks to the economy or by a downturn in investment because of a lack of consumer confidence. Often, a series of negative events send a national economy into a downward trend that eventually becomes a recession.

Competition

Competition is considered the basis of capitalism and the free market economy. In terms of the market, competition is the process in which different individuals or firms struggle for superior position in a given market for products or services. For the consumer, competition is supposed to keep prices low and encourage a variety of purchasing options. The degree of competition in a given market is determined by five factors: the number of firms in the market, the control any firm or firms exercise over price, they type of product being sold, the barriers to entry for new firms, and the existence of non-price competition)that is, competition over advertising or product characteristics as opposed to price). Depending on these factors, a market may exhibit perfect competition, monopolistic competition, oligopoly, or monopoly.

<u>Perfect competition</u> -- Perfect competition is the state of a market in which there are a number of firms selling the identical product at the same price. In this model, no one firm will have control over the price of the product. New firms will be able to enter such a market easily, as all they will have to do is create a version of the product identical to those already being sold. Each firm will supply only a very small amount of the total industry output. Competition in this model is usually very impersonal (that is, there is no clear rivalry between any two firms) because there are so many firms on the market. At this point, there is no market in the world that can be considered perfectly competitive; rather the idea of perfect competition is used as a reference for considering existing markets.

<u>Monopolistic competition</u> -- In a market displaying monopolistic competition, there are a number of firms (fifty or more) selling slightly different products. The difference between products may be more perceived than actual in this model. Product differentiation is often just a matter of special packaging or advertising. Because there are so many sellers, entry into the market is relatively easy for new firms, and there is very little direct competition between firms. Since there is a degree of difference between products, firms have a little bit of control over price, and will typically produce the quantity of product that maximizes profit at the price they set (known as equilibrium output). This sort of

competition is probably the closest any real market will come to perfect competition.

Oligopolies

In the market structure known as oligopoly, a small number of interdependent firms compete for market shares. Since there are only a few firms in the market, any change in price or output by one of the firms affects all the other firms. It can be very difficult for new firms to enter an oligopolistic market, because they usually depend on ownership of large amounts of raw materials, or access to specialized technology. Examples of oligopolistic market include the auto and steel industries in the United States. Most of the time, the firms in an oligopoly operate on what is known as an economy of scale: that is, the more units they produce, the more the cost per unit goes down. There is always the danger of collusion (when competing firms agree on prices and output to maximize profit) in an oligopoly.

Monopolies

In a monopoly, there is only one firm. Obviously, a firm holding a monopoly has a great deal of control over price; they may charge whatever price maximizes their profit. It is impossible, usually for legal reasons, for another company to enter the market. There are a number of ways in which monopolies arise. One way is through the patenting of a new product to which the inventor has exclusive rights (in the United States, these rights last for seventeen years). Sometimes the government creates monopolies by giving a certain firm exclusive rights to a product. Other times, the market for a product is only sufficient to successfully sustain one firm. This is called a natural monopoly, and is regulated by the government. Monopoly is the exact opposite of perfect competition.

Supply and Demand

Supply and demand are the two factors that determine price. Supply is the desire and ability to sell a certain amount of goods at a certain price, within a given time period. Supply may fluctuate depending on price and the quantity of goods being sold; that is to say, supply is a measure of the goods available at a certain price, not just the quantity of goods in existence. Demand is the willingness to buy a certain quantity of goods at a certain price, in a given time period. A simple economic graph is often drawn to illustrate the relation between supply and demand. In it, the demand curve slopes such that a greater quantity is being demanded when the price is lower, and the supply curve shows that producers will make more goods as the price for those goods rises; the equilibrium point, where these two lines intersect, is the level at which producers will be content to produce a certain amount for a certain price, which consumers will also be willing to pay.

Price Systems

A price system is the system of assigning value to goods that affects the distribution of those goods and services. In order to have a price system, there must be an economy with a money system, so that the value of a good can be consciously changed. In the simplest example of pricing, goods that are in high demand become more valuable (and hence acquire a higher price), and goods that are in abundant supply or are not greatly desired lose price. Prices are continually fluctuating as supply and demand change, and they also tend to gradually rise due to inflation. Price can often be changed artificially by holding goods back from market or flooding the market with a particular good.

Law of Diminishing Returns

The law of diminishing returns is an economic proposition stating that if one aspect of production is increased while all the others remain at the same level, the overall return will decrease after a certain point. For example, if five people are hired to paint a building, they will do so at a certain speed. If anther person is hired, they will be able to finish the job more quickly. However, for each extra painter that is added, the time saved decreases, for the simple reason that each painter now has less total space under his control. For this reason, business managers have to determine at what point they are getting maximum yield, taking into account the wages that they pay their laborers and the amount of work that is finished.

Competing in Foreign Markets

Globalization has made competition in the international market necessary for many corporations. In the past few decades, foreign direct investment has increased tremendously, meaning that national economies are more interrelated than ever. There are three main ways to compete in foreign markets: investment, exporting, and licensing agreements. Investment is common when businesses want to have influence in a country whose raw materials they desire. Exporting is a common way for companies to initially explore the international market, because it offers a relatively low risk if it is done at a minimal level. Licensing agreements are pacts between companies in different countries to market one another's products, or in some other way to engage in mutually beneficial trade.

Balance of Trade

No country wants to be dependent on foreign imports, and so governments impose tariffs, quotas, and other trade barriers in an attempt to aid domestic production. In doing so they are always mindful of the balance of trade: the difference between the value of the nation's exports and its imports. Every country aspires to export more than it imports. For the most part, the United States has had a favorable balance of trade over the past century; however, at some points an increase in military spending, foreign travel, and foreign aid have resulted in an unfavorable balance of payments: the difference between a country's total payments to other countries and the payments that country receives from abroad. Economists are split as to whether this balance of payments needs to be closely minded, or whether the United States would do well to help other, smaller economies.

Comparative Advantage

The economic principle of comparative advantage suggests that every country should produce whatever it can produce most profitably, without trying to emphasize total national self-sufficiency. According to this idea, the nations that operate according to their comparative advantage will get the most out of their people and natural resources. This includes scenarios in which a focus on one profitable good means the country must import goods which it could also make more economically at home. For instance, advocates of this theory argue, doe sit make sense to add a 50% duty to products that Japanese manufacturers can produce for half the cost? Wouldn't it make more sense, they argue, to find those products that American firms can produce more economically and export them?

Labor Unions

A labor union is a group of laborers organized to promote their common interests. Unions are found in most industrialized countries. Their primary goals are to improve compensation and working conditions. Union membership has declined considerably in the United States over the past fifty years; today, only about sixteen percent of the labor force belongs to a union. Of course, the actions taken by unions often set industry standards that affect even non-union laborers. Unions pursue their goals by recruiting new members, negotiating with management, working to promote legislation favorable to their cause, and, if necessary, organizing strikes and work stoppages. Unions often have remarkable political strength, which has occasionally been exploited by their leaders.

Basic Accounting Equation

Assets = Liab + S.H.E

The basic equation of accounting is that assets are equal to the sum of liabilities and capital (sometimes referred to as equity or proprietorship). This equation can be rearranged to show the total value of ownership: assets minus liabilities. Every transaction made by a business results in a change to one of these three categories. If the business borrows money from the bank, for instance, it increases its cash assets and its liabilities. If the business buys a new machine, it has increased its assets, but it has also decreased its cash assets or liabilities, depending on whether the machine was bought with cash or credit. When a business hires employees, its assets increase by whatever amount the new employee will produce, but the business has become liable for whatever it has agreed to pay the employee.

Fact Neccessitating Accounting

The basic fact that necessitates business accounting is that every business owns property, and this property comes with certain rights. The operations of the business necessarily cause changes in the amount and kind of property owned by the business, and the changes can be expressed in terms of dollars and cents. The property owned by a business may be any number of things: manufacturing firms own equipment, land, and buildings, and law firms own books, offices, and office equipment. Every business requires a certain amount of cash to pay the bills. All of this property is referred to as the assets of the business. Every business, no matter how large or small, will need assets in order to operate.

Property Rights

All property entails certain rights and restrictions. When a person or a partnership owns a business, this ownership is registered as net worth, capital, or proprietorship. When a business has borrowed funds in order to sustain operations, the claims of their lenders are known as liabilities. Businesses may also have a liability to their employees, insofar as they must pay their employees at regular intervals. Taxes on property are also considered a liability. In the case of the corporation, property ownership and rights are a bit more complicated. Since the corporation functions as an independent entity in its own right, so it has its own rights and responsibilities. Still, stockholders own the corporation, though they do not personally assume its liabilities. They instead have what is called stockholders' equity, the amount of their original investment plus accumulated profits not paid out in dividends.

Accounts Receivable and Payable

The phrases accounts receivable and accounts payable refer to transactions in which payment is delayed. When a business sells a product to someone today but will not be paid for another thirty days, the amount that the buyer owes is considered an account receivable. Assuming that the increase in accounts receivable is more that the product was worth as an asset in its own right, the business has made a profit, or an increase in capital or proprietorship. On the other hand, businesses may buy materials and agree to pay for them later. Until they are paid for, the materials count as increasing assets (in this case, the business inventory) and increasing the firm's liabilities. Such liabilities are called accounts payable.

Debits and Credits

In accounting, any transaction that increases the assets of a firm or reduces its liabilities or proprietorship is called a debit. Any transaction that decreases assets or increases liabilities or proprietorship is known as a credit. Every business transaction will affect at least two accounts, one being a debit and the other being a credit of an equal amount. One of the main ways that accountants check their books for errors is by adding up all the debits and credits and making sure that the two numbers are equal. Though these terms are often a source of confusion for beginning accounting students, they are really quite easy to use if one simply bears in mind that a credit (or "addition") to a liability account means the business has lost value, and a debit to liabilities means that the business gains value; in other words, the crediting and debiting applies only to the specific account, and not to the business as a whole.

Balance

Every business transaction has a cost and a value; when material is purchased, for instance, assets are increased and either assets (cash) or liabilities (credit) are increased. For this reason, accountants use what is known as double-entry bookkeeping: that is, a system of records wherein every transaction provides a total number of debits equal to the total number of credits. Occasionally, a business may have more liabilities than it has assets, resulting in a decrease in the claims of the ownership. If however, the business' liabilities exceed the net worth of the business, then the business is technically insolvent. If the business can sell enough if its assets to satisfy the immediate claims of creditors and continue operations, it is known as a deficit.

Actual Costs and Sales

One important thing to remember about accounting is that it is always based on actual costs and sales rather than any other measures. For example, if a business purchases some land for a certain amount, and the land has since then doubled in value, the firm still considers the land as having the original value when it performs its accounting. The only adjustment to such an asset is depreciation, the expression of the loss of value due to the wearing out of an asset (for instance a machine, which becomes less and less valuable from year to year). Similarly, a business always registers its actual sales in its accounting documents: even if a product is normally sold at a higher price, the form will only account for the money made in the particular sale at the particular sale price.

Inaccuracies in Traditional Accounting

Though accounting strives to provide an accurate view of the financial status of a business, there are several reasons why its calculations may miss the mark. For one thing, assets often change their value while a business owns them: machines may become obsolete, or land may increase in value. Measuring the depreciation of assets is also an inexact science. Some firms carry a great deal of inventory, and it is difficult to say whether this inventory is worth what the accounting records suggest, because it is impossible to predict whether it will ever be sold, and at what price. Finally, it is very difficult to accurately allocate the costs that will be incurred by a large business. While it is easy to see how much labor and machinery equals a certain amount of product, it is more difficult to say how much insurance or executive salary will equal that same amount of product.

Problems of Inflation

Inflation can cause major problems for accountants, since it can make it impossible for them to accurately predict costs. For instance, a business may assume that it can purchase the same amount of materials at the same price from year to year, but any inflation will make this impossible. This change in price value can make accounting reports quite misleading; some companies, for instance, will report excellent profits that, once inflation is taken into account, turn out to be poor or mediocre. The United States government has tried to remedy this problem by forcing large companies to report the effects of price inflation on accounts to their stockholders. Nevertheless, this is still no better than a crude solution to a very difficult problem.

Balance Sheets

Double-entry bookkeeping appear on what is known as a balance sheet: the accounting statement that describes the relationship between assets, which are indicated on the left side of the sheet, and the claims against those assets made by creditors or owners, indicated on the right. Balance sheets may be quite simple, as in the case of small businesses, or very complex, as for large corporations. Some businesses must use what is known as a consolidated balance sheet to combine their accounts with the accounts of the other companies in which that business has a significant interest. For large corporations, the balance sheet offers an opportunity for stockholders to view the raw data of the business, and interpret its progress.

Time deposits and marketable securities, prepaid expenses, accrued income and other taxes -- Some of the items commonly found on a balance sheet may require a bit of explanation. For instance, the item called time deposits and marketable securities refers to money that has been deposited in a bank and earning interest, as well as investments in government bonds, stocks, or other securities that can be easily exchanged. Timed deposits and marketable securities are added to cash to find the total of assets equivalent to cash. The item prepaid expenses refers to rent and insurance premiums that have already been paid. Accrued income and other taxes refer to taxes on income that are owed to the federal government, state governments, and foreign governments. Generally, these taxes must be paid early in the following year.

Assets -- There are a few important observations to make when assessing a business' balance sheet. First, one should look at cash: it may be stable or rising, but it also may include a rise in short-term borrowings and accounts payable, which might be worrisome to an investor. The item accounts and notes receivable will indicate the progress of sales, as lower sales typically require fewer receivables (goods sold but for which the business has yet to be paid). A balance sheet might also include categories under assets like "construction in progress," indicating that the business is making some kind of transition. One might also want to consider the accountant's estimation of depreciation, to determine whether the business' assets hold the value he or she claims.

Liabilities and equity -- When assessing a business' liabilities on a balance sheet, there are several key areas to check. First, a rise in short-term liabilities might indicate that the business has recently had to borrow a great deal of money to finance some expansion project. If short-term borrowings are low for a large business, investors can rest assured that the business still has the potential to borrow considerable money against accounts receivable should it be necessary. The long-term liabilities indicated on a balance sheet are also important; even if assets clearly cover any liabilities, the interest accrued on long-term debts can damage finances. The figures listed under stockholder's equity indicate when and how many dividends have been paid. Treasury stock is any stock in the corporation that was sold to the public and then repurchased by the corporation; it has the potential to be sold again.

Income Statements

Although the balance sheet is very helpful in assessing the financial status of a business, it cannot indicate exactly what happened during a given year, what sales and expenses were, and what the exact profit was. For this information, accountants use an income statement. The income statement describes in summary form the sales for some period of time (a month, three months, or a year, typically). It then subtracts the expenses incurred by that business during the same period, and gives the resulting amount as either a profit or a loss. For this reason, most people consider the income statement to be the clearest indicator of a business' fortunes. Every business, of course, must begin to turn a profit at some point if it aims to remain operating.

Sales, net sales, and cost of goods sold (cost of production) -- A normal income statement combines several distinct categories. Sales are considered to be the total amount of goods or services that a business has sold in the period. Sales are considered final when the item or service is delivered, even if it has not yet been paid for. Net sales are simply sales less returned merchandise, discounts granted for prompt payment, or reduction in cost for damaged goods. The cost of goods sold, also called the cost of production, is the amount that it took to produce all the goods that were sold. It typically includes the cost of the materials needed to create the goods, the cost of the labor used to make the good, and the overhead costs (electricity, machine maintenance, etc.) associated with making that good.

Gross profit, operating expenses, and income from operations -- The standard income statement has a number of different categories. Gross profit is calculated as the net sales minus the cost of the goods sold (also called cost of production). The operating expenses for a business are any expenses that are not directly related to the production of a good or performance of a service. Some examples of operating expenses are rent, utilities, insurance, depreciation on buildings, and managerial salaries. Income from operations is calculated as gross profit minus operating expenses. This is the company's profit before adjusting for interest payments, income, or expenses that are not directly related to the business (for instance, royalties on patents, income from investments, losses from unpaid sales). It is also the income before income taxes.

Income before income taxes, income taxes, and net income (profit) -- Once sales and expenses have been fully tabulated, the income statement gives a summary of income. Income before income taxes is the profit that the company has made, after adjusting for miscellaneous expenses or income. Because interest expenses are deducted from the total at this point, income before income taxes is usually less than income from operations. Income taxes, of course, are the taxes the business owes to various agencies of the government for the income earned during that particular period. Net income, otherwise known as profit, is the final yield of the business after all expenses and taxes have been considered. This is the amount that is available to pay stockholders in the form of dividends, or to reinvest in the business. A negative amount here represents a loss.

Tracking Cash

For most companies, having available cash is even more important than turning a profit. A company that takes a loss need not suspend operations as long as it has a ready supply of cash. In the opposite way, a business may appear to be quite profitable and yet flounder if it does not have access to cash. For this reason, it is important to get a sense of how much cash a business has available by looking at its balance sheet. If all the assets of the business are represented by machinery and real estate, for instance, the business has a problem. Employees, after all, cannot be paid in machinery! In order to fully assess a business, one must analyze how much cash a business has, as well as how much it is likely to be able to borrow if necessary.

Generating Cash

Some businesses are better at generating and holding onto cash than others. If a business has vast expenses payable in cash, it had better be brining in a lot of cash to offset these expenses. Assuming the business does not invest in other ways, profits generally mean an increase in cash. Cash can also be brought into a business by loans from ownership. An increase in accounts payable is much the same as borrowing cash, because the business gets the materials it need without losing the use of the cash owed for them. Similarly, reducing accounts receivable means increasing cash, as prior customers have finally paid off their purchases. Any large expenditures typically require a reduction in cash, as will a reduction in accounts payable. Reduction of inventory typically means an increase in cash, as products have been sold.

Ratios

Balance sheet and ratio analysis -- For obvious reasons, a number of people may need to assess the financial status of a business. These people may be investors in the business, people who have lent the business money and want to be paid back, or the managers of the business itself. One of the most common ways to quickly judge a balance sheet is to perform a ratio analysis. A ration measures the relationship between two different items, for instance assets and liabilities. Analysts use different ratios to see how businesses compare to one another. Usually, a business will be compared solely with other businesses in the same industry, but one of the advantages of ratio analysis is that it allows businesses of widely differing size and structure to be easily compared.

Current ratio -- The current ratio is one of the most common measurements used to analyze a balance sheet. It is the ratio of current assets to current liabilities. This measure is very important to lenders, and so it is often used by banks and other businesses that allow the business being considered to buy on credit. Typically, lenders are encouraged when a business has twice as many assets as liabilities. This ratio indicates that the business will have no trouble meeting its liabilities, even if its current assets shrink due to the inability to collect accounts receivable or because of a loss of inventory. Current liabilities, of course, will remain constant. The safe amount of assets for a particular business may depend on the form of those assets: assets in the form of machinery are much more difficult to exchange to pay off liabilities.

Acid test (quick ratio) and debt to net worth ratio -- The acid test ratio, also known as the quick ratio, is the ratio of cash and accounts receivable to current liabilities. This ratio excludes inventory, and only includes those assets that can be quickly converted into cash to meet current liabilities. Generally, an acceptable standard for this ratio is one to one. The debt to net worth ratio is the ratio of the total debt to the equity of the stockholders. This is essentially a measure of the money put into the company by the owners compared with the money put into the company by lenders. From the perspective of banks it is healthy for businesses to have debts equal to no more than half of the ownership equity. If the company is especially profitable, however, banks may not be concerned as long as debt is equal to net worth.

Inventory turnover ratio -- The inventory turnover ratio is the ratio of sales to inventory. In other words, it measures the number of times a year that inventory is fully replaced ("turned over"). Inventory is usually one of the larger investments that a business makes, and there is always a danger of assuming a big loss if much inventory goes unsold. Also, it can be very expensive simply to maintain a large inventory. The costs associated with materials, parts, and finished goods usually amount to thirty or forty percent of the inventory's value every year. So, companies that can operate while keeping inventory low stand to gain a considerable amount of money. There is no universally accepted inventory turnover ratio, but for manufacturing firms the ratio shouldn't be below six, meaning that inventory should be turned over about every two months.

Collection Period

Analysts should be able to look at the balance sheet for a business and determine whether the amount of accounts receivable is cause for worry. They can do this by calculating the number of days of sales represented by the accounts receivable. The calculation is done by dividing the sales figure by the value of accounts receivable, to derive the number of times accounts will turn over in a year. This figure is then converted into days to determine the number of days of sales represented by accounts receivable, a total known as the collection period. In most manufacturing businesses, the collection period ranges from 35 to 55 days. If it extends much beyond that, analysts will be concerned that many of these accounts will be uncollectible; if it is much shorter, a strict credit policy may be driving off potential business.

Profit Margin

Gross profit margin -- The gross profit margin is one of the measures taken to analyze the income statements of a company. It is a ratio indicating the percentage that gross profit (deducting cost of services or products but not deducting operating expenses, taxes, and other items) bears to total sales. Essentially, it is the amount that the business has available to pay for whatever expenses are not directly related to the production of a service or product. Most successful manufacturing firms have gross profit margins of about 25 to 35 percent. This is considered to be the most effective way of comparing businesses in the same industry. If a business cannot make a gross profit equal to or better than the industry standard, it is not likely to last for very long.

Pretax profit margin -- Analysts may use the pretax profit margin to assess a business' income statement. The pretax profit margin is the business' profits before taxes as a percentage of sales. This ratio is widely considered to be the true measure of the profitability of a company, because it measures the percentage of each sales dollar that is registered as profits before taxes. Manufacturing firms usually have around eight to ten percent of the sales dollar as their pretax profit margin. Of course, businesses that have a large volume of sales in relation to the amount of investment will typically have lower pretax profit margins. Supermarkets, for instance, which turnover their inventory constantly, have pretax profit margins between one and two percent.

Measuring profitability -- Financial analysts may measure the profitability of a business by looking at the amount the company earns after income taxes. This information is found on the company's income statement. Of course, the standards for this measure will vary from company to company, depending on the special tax restrictions on each. Typically, income taxes amount to about half of net income before taxes, so the percentage of net income to sales after taxes is usually half that of pretax income to sales. In other words, income taxes take about half of the money that a business makes in sales. The percentage of profit after taxes to sales for manufacturing businesses is generally around five percent. The ratio of profit after taxes to net worth assesses what the owners of a company are making from their investment. It is calculated by taking the profits after taxes and dividing them by the net worth of the business.

General Ledger

A general ledger, also known as a nominal ledger, is the central record of accounts for a business that uses double-entry bookkeeping. A general ledger will usually include accounts for fixed assets, current assets, liabilities, profits or losses, income and expenditure, and reserves. The general ledger is essentially a summary of all the financial activity of the company. It takes its data from the general journal, where all of the business transactions are recorded. A proper general ledger should make it possible for the business to see the effects of any transaction on the company's entire financial outlook. Besides just the numerical data for each transaction, the general ledger will include the date of the transaction and a brief description of it.

Calculating Depreciation

Calculating depreciation of equipment is one of the biggest challenges to accuracy in accounting. Depreciation may be classified as general wearing down of equipment, obsolescence, or predictable mechanical failures. It is important to try and assess depreciation accurately because otherwise assets may be overstated. There are several theories on how to calculate depreciation. Straight-line depreciation is the simplest means, in which a company determines how much the equipment may be sold for at some future date and then assumes it will lose equal amounts of value every year until it reaches that price. Declining-balance depreciation is a slightly more sophisticated method: it operates on the assumption that an asset will decline in value most in its first few years of operation. Activity methods of measuring depreciation consider not the length of ownership, but how often the item is used.

Cost of Goods Sold

The cost of goods sold is all of the expenses directly related to producing a particular good for sale. This can include the cost of the materials as well as the labor needed to make the good. The cost of goods sold does not include things like office expenses, shipping, or advertising. The cost of goods sold can be determined by combining all of the costs associated with the creation of a particular good, and then dividing this total by the number of those goods that are sold. The gross profit on that good is then determined by subtracting the cost of goods sold from the sales revenue generated by that good. In order to determine net profit, however, a business also has to subtract all of the indirect expenses that are incurred during operation.

Trial Balance

In accounting, a trial balance is the worksheet on which all of the various balances from the various ledgers are entered into two columns: debit and credit. Trial balances are typically prepared during each financial period, in summation of the closing of the previous ledgers. Accuracy can be determined by whether the total of the debit side is equal to the total of the credit side. Basically, the trial balance is used to pinpoint any errors that have been made during the creation of the ledger. It should be noted, though, that a balanced trial balance does not necessarily indicate and accurate ledger; for example, if a debit and credit are switched by accident, this will not unbalance the ledger, though it will present false data.

Worksheets

A worksheet is an accounting form that is used to collect all of the information from various ledgers onto one sheet of paper. Worksheets typically have either six or eight columns, depending on how much information the business feels obliged to list. A standard six-column worksheet has a list of the business' accounts (that is, the various other firms and individuals that the business has had transactions with, as well as the various incomes and expenses the business has incurred) on the left, and then there are columns where the data from the trial balance, income statement, and balance sheet is entered. Once all of the account information has been entered, the net income can be calculated by adding together all the debits and all the credits, and finding the difference.

Unit Cost

Businesses calculate the average unit cost in order to determine just how much it is costing them to produce a single unit for sale. This number is essentially an average, and is found by adding together all of the manufacturing costs that were incurred during a particular time period, and then dividing this total by the number of units that were produced during that same period. It should be noted that manufacturing costs include the cost of materials and labor, but not other business expenses like employee insurance or executive salaries. Some businesses that have a long-term production process may have to add up a number of partially-competed products as fractions of whole units.

Increases, Decreases and Elasticity

A change in price is usually calculated as a percent, meaning that the difference in price is divided by the original price and multiplied by a hundred. For instance, if a candy bar cost $.75, and then the price increased to $.85, the price increase would be calculated -.1/.85 x 100, which equals a price decrease of about 12%. Change in price is often used to determine price elasticity of demand, the change in demand for a particular product based on changes in its price. Price elasticity of demand is calculated by dividing the percent change in the quantity demanded by the percent change in price. The price elasticity of demand of a certain item depends on how many competing goods exist, the level of consumer income, and whether the good is considered to be a luxury or a necessity.

Simple Interest

It should be very easy to calculate simple interest, which may apply to money deposited in a bank or borrowed from a bank or another lender. Only three factors are needed: principle, rate, and time. The principle is the amount originally deposited or borrowed, the rate is the percent of the principal that is added as interest, and the time is simply the number of years (since the interest rate is usually expressed as an annual rate) the money has been deposited, or the time over which the loan will be repaid. Simple interest, then, is calculated by multiplying these three factors. For example, if $100 dollars has been in the bank for 2 years with a 3% rate of interest, it has now become $106.

Payroll Calculation

When calculating the payroll for a business, financial managers may take into account several factors. First, they will determine the individual's gross pay by multiplying the number of hours worked by the hourly wage. They also add up the individual's total gross pay for that year. The payroll manager will then deduct percentages of the gross pay for the employee's federal and state income taxes, as well as for Social Security and Medicare (FICA). The percentage of pay that is taken for these taxes varies from year to year and can depend on the total gross pay amount. This money is paid on the employee's behalf, so he or she will not have to pay it later in income tax. There may be additional federal and state withholdings of money for various reasons. The amount remaining after all withholdings is the employee's net pay.

Consumer Education

One of the biggest and most immediately important jobs of a business education teacher is to provide some basic consumer education to students. Consumer education enables students to enter the marketplace with a more sophisticated understanding of how to spend their money. It may include learning to budget, learning to discern various marketing ploys, learning to differentiate between products, and learning to do simple consumer calculations. Students will also learn about the typical expenses for adults, and how to go about providing for themselves and their families. Because consumer information changes so rapidly with the market, it is essential that teachers not only provide a set of critical skills that can be used in a variety of circumstances, but that they show their students how to access the wealth of objective data having to do with consumer issues.

Consumer Budget

A consumer budget is a plan for spending and saving money during a particular period of time. Business students should learn how to construct a personal budget so that they can anticipate common personal expenses and keep track of where their money goes. If students are trying to save up their money for a particular purpose (for instance, college tuition), then they should get experience planning a budget that will allow them to reach their goals. A budget will include the student's fixed expenses (those which are consistent every month), variable expenses (those which are always present, but may vary in amount), and discretionary expenses (those that are not strictly necessary but are the result of personal desire).

Consumer Finance companies

Consumer finance companies are small companies that will loan money to individual for virtually any purpose. These loans typically have rather high interest rates, as there is a degree of risk involved for the lender. There is generally either a small amount of money or a piece of property that is used as security. The purpose of the consumer finance company is to give consumers the means to purchase items they might not be able to afford by themselves. These companies are often criticized for their slightly immoral methods, which include sending live checks through the mail which when used become loans, charging extremely high fees on mortgage financing, and failing to alert borrowers that they may be eligible for better terms because of their credit record.

Consumer Information Resources

There is a host of ways to gather the information necessary to be an informed and conscientious participant in the marketplace. Since consumer issues change so rapidly, one of the best places to get current information about scams and consumer rights is on the internet. The Federal Trade Commission publishes a number of free on-line documents that outline basic consumer rights concerning credit, automobiles, telemarketing, investments, and e-commerce. There are also many private sites that offer similar information. Many magazines are designed to serve the consumer, from the general (Consumer Reports) to the very specific (Motorcycle Digest, for instance). The local chamber of commerce is also a reference that students should be familiar with as they become more sophisticated in their consumer behavior.

Bank and Business Relationship

Banks are businesses; they exist to make a profit. That being said, banks also make it possible for business community to exist at all. Besides the obvious service of lending money, banks do many things for businesses. For one, banks provide a safe place for businesses to store cash. Banks also give short-term and long-term loans to businesses, so that the businesses may purchase products and services essential for enhancing their operations. Banks facilitate international transactions by making currency exchanges and working with foreign banks. Banks handle the registration and transfer of company securities, such as stocks and bonds. Banks may also act as a trust department, ensuring assets and contracts. Finally, banks have a wealth of knowledge about financial dealings, which they share with their business clients.

Commercial Banks

Commercial banks are mainly concerned with accepting deposits of money, making funds available to depositors, and lending money. Most commercial banks also have a large savings operation, where it is possible to make time deposits. All commercial banks in the United States are owned by private individuals through the purchase of common stock. Banks that have been incorporated by the federal government are called national banks, and those incorporated by the state government are state banks. Usually, all one needs to start a bank is a minimum amount of money, and the ability to demonstrate to the government that there is a legitimate need for the bank.

Banks must also maintain books that are open to government auditors.

Demand Deposit

A demand deposit is made by an individual or a company and can be withdrawn at any time. Placing a demand deposit is essentially the same thing as opening a checking account, and can be done quite easily. Generally, all a commercial bank will require is a minimum deposit of cash or valid checks from another bank, as well as a copy of the depositor's signature (so that checks can be confirmed and honored). Partnerships can also open accounts of this kind in a commercial bank, but for corporations to place a demand deposit requires a bit more doing. Usually, the board of directors of the corporation has to authorize a resolution permitting the opening of the account, and indicating which corporate officers have the power to draw from it.

Time Deposits

Commercial banks accept a great number of what are called time deposits, which will remain deposited for a long time and collect interest during that period. There are two types of time deposit: savings deposits and certificates of deposit. Typically, savings deposits are made by smaller savers; banks may require some notice before such a deposit is withdrawn, but it is not often necessary for this to be enforced. Savings deposits may only be placed by individual and nonprofit organizations. Certificates of deposit, on the other hand, are available to businesses as well. These deposits must be held by the bank for a certain amount of time, and are usually made in much larger amounts. Sometimes, certificates of deposit are made negotiable, meaning that the bank can sell them to other banks or investors.

Short-Term Loans

The main source of income for commercial banks is making short-term loans to individuals and businesses. The lowest rate of interest, known as the prime rate, is granted to borrowers with impeccable credit ratings, whereas most borrowers must pay considerably more. Such short-term loans may be secured or unsecured, but banks will never lend money to those without well established credit ratings. Banks will usually require unknown borrowers to deposit some collateral, in the form of stocks, bonds, or life insurance policies, as security for the loan. Then, if the borrower does not pay, the bank has permission to sell these things. Unsecured loans are given to individuals and businesses with established credit, and are given on nothing greater than the assumption that it is in the borrower's best interest to pay.

Banks and Monetary Supply

Although banks do not print currency or mint coins, they may still increase the supply of money by allowing checks, which can be used as money, to be drawn against their deposits. So, when a bank loans money, it is registered in the bank's accounts as an asset (notes receivable) and a liability (the amount of the loan), and money has been created. It would seem that banks might run the risk of losing money if the money they loan out goes to other banks, but in the banking system there tends to be an equilibrium of borrowing and depositing. A short example: a town has only one bank and that bank lends a man $100, which he deposits in a checking account. He then pays bills to several merchants, who in turn deposit the money in their accounts at the bank. Banks do keep a certain amount of money in reserve to guard against any momentary shortages of funds.

Deposit Insurance

Because banks cannot both lend money and keep on hand the amount equal to all deposits, there is always the danger that if all the depositors asked for their money back at once, the bank would not have enough to comply. This scenario actually happened in the United States during the Great Depression. To prevent it from happening again, the United States government created what is known as the Federal Deposit Insurance Corporation, to provide insurance to banks on their deposits. Every national bank is required to carry deposit insurance, and most state banks do, as well. Deposit insurance has virtually eliminated any massive runs on a bank's funds; often, though, FDIC policy is to have healthy bank take over the operations of one that has been hit hard by withdrawals.

Savings Banks

Savings banks are less common than commercial banks, and are set up to serve smaller savers. To that end, they pool savings, make investments, and pay to the depositors any interest that the investments earn. Savings banks were originally known as mutual banks because their ownership was by depositors instead of stockholders. Though savings banks are not very prevalent anymore, most large commercial banks have divisions that function in much the same way as a savings bank. Savings banks are not typically used by businesses, because they invest most of their money in government securities and in loans that have been secured by real estate (mortgages, that is). Savings banks often finance the construction if buildings or the purchase of homes.

Savings and Loan Associations

Savings and loan associations bear a number of similarities to savings banks. However, their lending is limited to the mortgages on homes and other real estate. Indeed, they were first created as a way for a community to help pay for individuals to build their homes. Some savings and loan associations are owned by stockholders, and some are mutual companies owned by the savers themselves. Savings and loan associations may pay interest to savers, but they also make profit. The line between savings and loan associations and savings banks has blurred considerably now that savings banks mainly work in real estate as well. Both of these institutions are generally only of use to business in the construction of new buildings.

Life Insurance Companies

Though life insurance companies are not banks in the strict sense, they have become large holders of individual savings. The assets of a life insurance company are earned by selling policies for much more money than the likely cost of death benefits at the time at which they are sold. Indeed, the life insurance premiums paid out by American policyholders are usually about three times the death benefits paid out by insurance companies. Insurance companies typically invest their assets in corporate stock, corporate bonds, and home mortgages. In some circumstances, they also loan money directly to businesses, usually to help finance new factories and warehouses. Insurance companies may also aid businesses by purchasing from them notes and bonds as a long-term loan.

Commercial Finance Companies

Commercial finance companies purchase the accounts receivable of a business at a discount, thereby helping the business to get some immediate return on money that they are owed. Of course, this practice is only successful when the customer pays his or her debt. (otherwise, the original seller must make good the payment). Commercial finance companies also frequently make loans on business inventory, or on machinery and equipment. They typically charge higher interest rates than commercial banks, because higher risk is involved. Commercial finance companies will try to guard their investment by watching closely the way the machinery or equipment is used, and possibly placing restrictions on the way management operates.

Factoring and Commercial Finance

Factoring companies act in a very similar way to commercial finance companies, with one important distinction. Factoring companies purchase accounts receivable from businesses at a discount because, unlike commercial finance companies, they take the loss if the account remains unpaid. Since they are taking a higher risk, they receive a greater discount. Of course, factoring companies are very selective in the accounts that they will purchase. Factoring companies also occasionally lend money to businesses with the business' inventory as security. Factoring companies are usually only used by small companies; larger firms tend to finance their credit through commercial banks. Financing through factors may give a business the reputation of not being solid enough to borrow from commercial banks.

Sales Finance Companies

Individuals buying expensive items from businesses frequently rely on sales finance companies. The companies allow people to pay for major purchases on an installment plan. Sales finance companies are important, because otherwise most dealers of items like televisions, automobiles, or furniture would not have the resources, much less the inclination, to sell many items on credit. So, when customers purchase items on an installment plan, the item purchased acts as security; the sales finance company will repossess the item if the customer does not make payments. The risks involved in running a sales finance company are quite large, so they tend to charge high interest rates. Their prevalence, however, has led most commercial banks to start financing divisions.

Leasing Companies

Businesses and individuals often acquire the use of assets not by purchasing them, but by leasing them. Businesses may lease buildings, equipment, or any other important asset. Leasing companies are formed to facilitate these transactions. Insurance companies often have divisions devoted to leasing to business, and private investors may lease things as well. Banks and other large businesses frequently lease airplanes to airline companies, and real estate leasing companies have been created to lease buildings and land. It should be noted that leasing is not the same thing as banking, though it does remove the need for businesses to borrow from banks. Of course, banks keep an interest in leasing by acting as lessor (party making the lease) to large businesses.

<u>The advantages and disadvantages of leasing</u> -- Leasing is typically more expensive than borrowing money to pay

for a purchase. Lessors require not only interest but money equal to depreciation and to the risk they are taking in the transaction. Businesses continue to lease, however, because they can thereby avoid using cash resource, and because the costs of a lease may be tax-deductible. Furthermore, leasing means that the company can avoid long-term commitments to assets, and avoid being stuck with things they no longer need and can hardly sell. Still, leases amount to a fixed payment schedule that may be difficult for a business to meet, and the business forfeits any improvement in the value of the asset. For instance, if a business leases some land which then skyrockets in value, they share in none of this good fortune.

The Public Market

The public market is the collection of thousands of individuals and groups of investors that buy and sell corporation stocks and bonds. Groups of investors may include pension funds, insurance companies, investment trusts, mutual funds, commercial banks, savings banks, loan companies, businesses that invest in other businesses, government agencies, and investment banks. Indeed many people who have life insurance policies or pensions do not even realize that they have funds invested in American business. Universities, hospitals, churches, and other charitable organizations also frequently invest in business. Most American corporations get their money from the public market, and prefer to do so.

<u>The value of the public market for business</u> -- Obviously, the public market aids business by providing funds for financing operations and growth. The public market provides a number of other services, as well. For one, the ease with which securities can be bought and sold encourages a level of investment hat otherwise would be difficult to imagine. Moreover, the constant sale of securities means that investors will always have a good idea of what their securities are worth. Smaller businesses that do not sell stock may have more difficulty assessing their own worth. Even better, the public market gives business an immediate appraisal of their recent actions; if the public has confidence in the direction the business is moving, the stock's price will rise. In this way, the pubic market acts as a metric for corporate decisions.

Common Stock and Par Value

Corporations may sell either common or preferred stock as shares in ownership. Typically, common stock entails the right to vote on the members of the board of directors, as well as the right to a share in the corporation's profits when dividends are divided, and a share of the corporation's assets should it be liquidated. The share of liquidated assets is divided from the total remaining after creditors and preferred stockholders are paid. Each share of stock has a par value: a dollar amount that is supposed to have been given to the original purchasers of the stock. Of course, stock with a par value of $100 may have an actual value much lower, depending on the fortunes of the corporation. Indeed, many stocks no longer carry a par value, as it is almost impossible to sell common stock for less than the stated par value.

Preferred Stock

Corporations are required to sell common stock, but they may also sell preferred stock if they wish to raise extra funds. The owners of preferred stock have several advantages. They may receive their dividends before the owners of common stock, in the amount of their preference: for instance, many preferred stocks receive eight percent of the par value per share. Preferred stock may be either cumulative or non-cumulative. If it is cumulative, unpaid dividends accumulate from year to year until they are paid in full, thereby obligating corporations to pay preferred stockholders their due before paying common stockholders in years that a dividend is paid Non-cumulative preferred stock does not require the corporation to pay preferred stockholders back after years in which no dividends were paid.

Bonds

Corporate bonds -- Corporations often raise funds by borrowing money, and giving corporate bonds or notes in exchange. Bonds are evidences of debt that a corporation agrees to pay to a particular group of creditors. When issuing bonds, corporations agree with a representative of the lender, called a trustee, as to what the terms of the bond will be. Corporations may promise not to pay dividends should earning dip below a certain level, or they may agree not to borrow any more money without the consent of that lender. Bonds may be held for any length of time, although there is usually a determined time by which they must be repaid. Until a bond is repaid, the lender receives interest, a small percentage of the total amount the corporation has borrowed.

Mortgage bond, collateral trust bond, debenture bond, sinking-fund bond, and convertible bond -- There are a number of different types of bonds. Many lenders may desire some guarantee of repayment, and so many bonds are secured by some piece of valuable property. If this property has a mortgage placed on it, the bond is called a mortgage bond. If stocks and bonds from other companies are held as security of repayment, the bond is called a collateral trust bind. Most bonds are simple debenture bonds, in which the only security offered is the general assets and earnings of the corporation. These bonds are called sinking-fund bonds when the borrowing corporation promises to slowly pay back the bonds. Occasionally, corporations will issue bonds that are eligible to be traded in for common stock at any time: these are called convertible bonds.

Investment Banks

Investment banks do not do any of the things that commercial banks do. Rather, they make money by marketing new issues of stocks and bonds to the general public, pension funds, insurance companies, or other large investing institutions. Investment banks may facilitate the entry of new securities onto the market by underwriting them: that is, buying them all and agreeing to sell them to the public, thus guaranteeing their legitimacy to any prospective buyers. Most of the time, underwritten securities are sold almost immediately after they become available. Occasionally an investment bank will agree to sell securities on a best-efforts basis, meaning that they will try their best to sell but are making no guarantees. Of course, this is not the preferred position for corporations.

How investment banks help business -- Investment banks provide a great service to businesses by making their stock known and available to a broad selection of potential investors. Without investment banks, businesses would be left to sell stock to the people they are in close contact with, or to unknown buyers with uncertain financial histories. Investment banks almost act as department stores, buying inventory from manufacturers and then employing specialized workers to sell it again. For the most part, however, investment banks are too expensive for small companies, who will find it difficult to have much success with a small batch of stock on the public market, anyway. The services of underwriting may be as much for a small issue as for a large one. Furthermore, investment banks prefer to make large issues, so that they can quickly determine the appropriate price for it.

Brokerage Houses

Brokerage houses are organizations that buy and sell securities on behalf of investors. Brokerage houses are essential to the market because they specialize in knowing who owns what stock at what time; if a single investor, for instance, wanted to buy one hundred shares of a certain stock, it could take that investor an extremely long time to find someone who owns that stock and would like to sell. Almost all investment banks also operate as brokers, and most investment banks have divisions handling transactions of already-issued securities. Brokerage houses make their money by charging a commission on purchases and sales. This commission is usually modest for a single share of stock, but it quickly expands with the thousands of transaction made by brokerage houses every day.

Security Exchanges

Security exchanges are locations where members of the exchange come together to buy and sell securities among themselves. To be a member of the exchange is known as "owning a seat" on it. Typically, brokerage houses will own multiple seats on any exchange. The best-known security exchange in the United States is the New York Stock Exchange (NYSE). The general public is forbidden from making transactions on the floor of this and other exchanges in the United States and worldwide. Security exchanges make their money from the charge for membership; they do not themselves engage in the buying and selling of securities. Members are allowed to sell their seats if they choose to do so, as long as the buyer is approved by the exchange.

Security exchange members -- The members of security exchanges typically fall into one of four categories. Commission brokers are the largest group of exchange members. They maintain offices near the exchange and handle transactions both for non-members and for other exchange members, receiving a commission on the transactions they aid. Registered traders buy and sell securities on their own behalf, hoping to make a profit out of avoiding commissions and receiving first-hand information from the exchange floor. Some traders focus on one specific area of security exchange; these traders may work for others or on their own behalf. Odd-lot dealers are those who specialize in making transactions in units of less than a hundred shares. They receive a commission for buying and sharing these smaller lots for other members and non-members.

Listed and Unlisted Stocks

A listed stock is any stock that a stock exchange has authorized to be bought and sold. There are certain requirements that most exchanges have for listed stocks. If a stock is only bought and sold by brokers and small retailers, and not through the facilities of any security exchange, it is considered unlisted stock. It used to be that listed stocks were strongly preferred by investors, because of their supposed stability and because it was easy to find out their selling price. However, it has become increasingly easy to discover the value of unlisted stocks, and so the only real advantage now offered by organized exchanges is some prestige and a minimum listing standard. There is some speculation that the growing efficiency of the over-the-counter market may someday render the exchanges obsolete.

Securities Investors

Any individual entering the stock market will either function as a speculator or as an investor. An investor is one who buys stocks for long-term use, rather than in the hopes of taking advantage of temporary price changes. Investors are usually trying either to ensure the safety of the money they invest (known as the principal), to earn money from the investment by means of dividends or interest, or because they hope to see the investment increase its value. It is rare that the same investment can satisfy all of these conditions at once; that is, the stocks and bonds that have the chance to increase dramatically in value usually carry with them a greater degree of risk, and the safer stocks and bonds are unlikely to accrue much value in a short time.

Safe Investments

For investors looking to ensure the safety of their principal, the best investment is a deposit in a savings bank or the purchase of bank certificates of deposit. There is also a great deal of security in government bonds, though these cannot always be drawn out when an investor would like. The market value of a bond is determined by its interest rate, the current market rate of interest, and the date on which the bond can be redeemed. Investors buy bonds with an eye towards their yield, the amount of interest plus the payment they can expect when the bond is redeemed; if this amount is less than investors can get for other government bonds, it will be difficult for the investor holding the bond to get rid of it.

Annual Return

It is quite common for investors to select their stock and bond purchases in the hopes of getting the highest possible annual return without sacrificing safety. If interest rates are very high in a given year, there will be plenty of bonds and stocks that offer excellent return without putting the principal in jeopardy. Even when interest rates are lower, good public utility stocks often increase steadily throughout the year. For the most part, bond yields will be higher than dividend yields for good stocks. This is because those who invest in stocks usually anticipate that the stock will increase in value as the market improves or as the profits of the company increase. For this reason, they are willing to accept a lower dividend yield.

Investment Increases

Many investors are less concerned with the dividends they will receive than with the potential increase in the value of the company. These investors look for a growth stock or for a bond that can be converted at their discretion into common stock. Oftentimes, stock can be sold for a high price even when it has not paid out any dividends at all. Stable, fast-growing stocks will have a high price/earnings (P/E) ratio, the market price per share divided by the annual earning s per share. If this ratio is high, it reflects a confidence in that company in the market. Price/earnings ratio tends to be self-fulfilling; that is, companies with high ratios tend to continue their success, while those companies with a low P/E ratio may have a difficult time reversing a negative trend.

Company Performance

Obviously, investors are taking a risk when they put money into a company. There is always the chance that the company could go bankrupt, and they could thereby lose their entire investment. Stockholders therefore feel justified in expecting payment for the risk they take as well as for the use of their money. Company managers have a similar interest in getting the highest possible return for their investors; the rate of return on equity (that is, the percentage of earnings after taxes to stockholder's equity) is the way that they determine the successfulness of their company. Indeed, the price/earnings ratio and the rate of return on equity are essentially measuring the same thing, because high profits and continued investment are dependent on one another.

Speculation, Bear and Bull Market

Speculating in securities is trying to make money from the very short-term and temporary fluctuations in the price of stocks and bonds. Depending on supply and demand, security prices are constantly moving up and down; successful speculators are those who can correctly anticipate changes in the attitudes of investors, and therefore predict price movements. They must continually find stock that is either overvalued or undervalued. Of course, it is difficult to make a very large profit on speculation in any one transaction. Instead, speculators hope to accrue their earnings from a long series of mostly correct decisions. Some speculators are able to make money in a bear market (when most stock prices drop), though most find more success in a bull market (when most stock prices go up).

Option Trading

Option trading is a type of security transaction in which options (contracts that give the holder a right to buy or sell certain shares of stock at a certain price over a certain period of time) to buy or sell stock in a company are exchanged. An option to buy shares of tock is known as a call option. An option that requires another buyer to purchase one's stock at a specified price is known as a put option. Option trading allows speculators to gain the rights to much larger pools of stock than they would be able to if they had to buy each share outright. This means that they have the chance to increase their earnings when they guess correctly regarding changes in the market. Those who sell options to speculators benefit, too, in that they receive the price of the options.

Securities and Exchange Commission

The Securities and Exchange Commission is an American federal government agency that protects the interests of the public and investors in regards to the issuing and sale of corporate securities. The SEC is made up of five people appointed by the president. These individuals serve for five years at a time. Over the years, the SEC has influenced the government to pass laws transferring the burden of quality from the buyer to the seller of securities. The SEC closely supervises stock exchanges and brokers to prevent them from taking advantage of less savvy investors. Of course, the work of the SEC does not prevent investors from losing their money; it only seeks to ensure that they do so in a fair manner.

Borrowing on Credit

Credit, from the Latin word meaning "to trust," is the willingness of the seller or lender to allow someone else, be it an individual or a business, to have something now and pay for it later. Unless the borrower has a sterling credit record, the lender will usually require that something else be offered as security, to be given to the lender if the borrower cannot make payments. Companies may use a variety of assets as security when they borrow money on credit. The business may offer securities or accounts receivable, or they may give the lender assurances of assets they hold in warehouses (shown by warehouse receipts), or assets currently in transit (shown by bills of lading). Indeed, anything that could ever be resold is eligible to serve as security.

Promissory Notes

A promissory note, sometimes simply called a note, is a promise made by the borrower to pay back to the lender the sum of money that has been borrowed, along with a specified amount of interest, after a certain amount of time (or on a certain date). Promissory notes are common instruments of credit for businesses borrowing money from banks. Dealers of goods or services may also accept notes instead of money. Promissory notes are often negotiable, meaning that the lender can sell them to someone else, who then has the responsibility of collecting the loan. Some notes are sold with recourse, meaning that the buyer can demand payment from the original lender if the borrower fails to repay the money.

Drafts

One of the more common instruments of credit is the draft, an order made by one party (the drawer) to another party (the drawee), telling it to pay a certain amount to a third party (the payee). Drafts are different from promissory notes in that it is an order, rather than a promise, to pay. Regular checks are considered a form of draft: when an individual consumer writes a check to the supermarket, for instance, he or se is essentially telling his or her bank to pay the supermarket a certain sum. In business, drafts are typically used when the seller doesn't want to give credit to the buyer, and demands payment before the buyer takes possession. This is often the case when the buyer is from a different country, or has an uncertain credit record.

Demand and Time Draft

There are a couple of different drafts that are used as credit instruments. A demand (or sight) draft is one that is payable as soon as the seller (the payee) presents it to the bank (the drawee). Regular bank checks that bear the current date are demand drafts; once an individual has written a check to a retail store, for instance, that check may be immediately deposited. A time draft, on the other hand, is payable at some predetermined future date. Drafts do not even need to be made out to a specific payee; if it is just made out to the bearer, then it can be deposited by anyone that has it. This is done just as an individual might make a check payable to cash. This is often the case when the draft is written by one member of a business and given to another to give to the appropriate, as yet undetermined seller.

Acceptances

Trade (or bank) acceptances are a special form of time draft. They are written up by the seller and sent to the drawee, who then accepts it as binding by signing his or her name. At this point, the acceptance becomes a negotiable document; that is, it can be bought and sold. If the acceptance is taken by a business firm, it is called a trade acceptance. If the bank takes the acceptance, it is called a bank acceptance. For the most part, the use of acceptances is restricted to the sale of goods. Acceptances are easily negotiable when they are accepted by individuals or businesses with excellent credit ratings. In these cases, even the Federal Reserve Banks will buy acceptances on a discount basis.

Certified and Cashier's Checks

Most of the time, businesses will accept a check from an individual or company without any guarantee of its validity, as long as it is for a relatively low amount and is from a reputable bank. However, in many cases the payee needs more reassurance. In these cases, businesses or individuals may acquire certified checks or cashier's checks. To create a certified check, the bank simply stamps the word "certified" on a regular check and immediately deducts the amount from the individual or business' account. It is then apparent to the payee that there are sufficient funds to cover the transaction. Cashier's checks are checks written to the payee by the bank itself, and charged to the individual or business' account. Assuming the bank is reputable, the payee will accept the check.

Lines of Credit

Generally, businesses borrow cash for a short period of time in order to finance accounts receivable, inventories, and other short-term operating costs. If a company needs to borrow funds for a short period of time, it will go to its bank and ask for a line of credit, the right to borrow up to a certain amount of money over a period of time. Assuming that the business is in good standing, the bank will consider it a good credit risk and will grant the credit. Most of the time, there is not any security involved in this kind of arrangement. Of course, the bank will request some kind of summary of the business' accounts, so that it can make an accurate assessment of how much cash the business is likely to need and how much it will likely have available in the future to repay the loan.

Revolving Credit

Sometimes banks will guarantee a line of credit to a business for a long period of time. The bank will charge a slightly higher interest fee for this service, known as revolving credit. The higher interest rate compensates the bank for the inconvenience of keeping a large amount of money ready should the business need it. Banks may also require that a borrowing business keep some minimum amount of money in a deposit account. According to banks, this compensating balance is required because it makes sense for borrowers to also be depositors. It seems more likely, though, that compensating balances are required because they allow banks to charge deceptively high interest: if a business borrows and pays interest $1000, for instance, and has to deposit $150, it is as if they had only borrowed $850.

Present Value Theory

Investment analysts use present value theory to account for the changes in the value of a sum of money over time. The present value is simply the amount of money one has today that will be worth a given amount at some future date given a certain rate of return. If, for instance, one has $620, and one is guaranteed a 10% rate of return every year, then in five years that $620 will be $1000. The present value is $620 and the future value is $1000; investors use this calculation to show how much a given investment is likely to accrue over time, and to illustrate the gains that can be made through sound investment and patience. Even more astounding is the difference between present and future value when compound interest (interest that accrues both on the principal and on the interest already earned) is accrued.

Risk Management

Risk management, for businesses and individuals, is the effort to identify, consider, and make the most efficient defense against various types of risk. In investing, risk management specifically is the practice of assessing the likelihood of loss and making adjustments to ensure that the potential for loss is tolerable to the investor. Some investors may be uncomfortable with great risk, and are willing to sacrifice the chance for great gain to avoid danger. Investors that seek to avoid risk often purchase government bonds, which tend to be relatively stable, rather than corporate securities. If an investor can stand to lose his or her investment, however, he or she might gamble on some potentially lucrative stocks.

Marketing, Customer Service, and Entrepreneurship

Entrepreneurship

Entrepreneurship is the process of collecting and organizing the financial, technological, and managerial resources necessary to start a new business venture with the aim of making a profit. Entrepreneurship is considered to be the foundation of the free market economy; it rewards hard work and innovation. Advocates of free market capitalism suggest that the process of entrepreneurship benefits both the entrepreneur and the society as a whole; the former by the chance for great material gain, and the latter by the creative and diverse product market that is created. Although entrepreneurship is typically thought of as an activity of lone, self-interested individuals, some economists argue that the characteristics of innovation and risk-taking can also be found in dynamic corporations.

Total Marketing Concept

Marketing did not assume its prominence in American business until the middle of the twentieth century. At this point, in order to succeed in a more competitive market it became imperative to tailor every aspect of the business to meet the needs and wants of the customer. Product development, marketing research, product servicing and business forecasting all became part of the marketing department's mission. This idea, that a business must organize itself such that the marketing department has the resources and power to attract customers, is called the total marketing concept, and it is standard practice in business today. Now, marketing activities account for one third to one fourth of the work force, and include such diverse areas as transportation, communications, retailing, and warehousing

Marketing Mix

The marketing mix is the specific combination of tools used by a marketing program to promote a certain product to its market. The marketing mix includes the product mix, the distribution mix, the communications mix, and the service mix. The product mix is the composition, design, and packaging of particular products. The distribution mix is the different methods of storing and transporting goods to the place where they are sold. The communications mix is the sum total of advertising, sales, promotional and market research activities. The service mix is the activities that follow a purchase and strive to ensure customer satisfaction. Marketing executives must try to find the balance in their marketing mix that creates the most profitable scenario for their product.

Copyrights, Trademarks, and Patents

Copyrights are the government's granting of an exclusive right to an individual to produce or sell some product during a certain period of time. Copyrights only protect the particular form in which something is produced; they do not protect any concepts, facts, or processes which may be a part of the product's creation. A trademark is a name or symbol placed on a product that identifies it and forbids other companies from copying it. Any corporate logo is an example of a trademark. A patent is a right granted by the government to certain individuals to be the sole producers and distributors of some good or service that the individual has invented. The system of patenting encourages innovation by guaranteeing the exclusive right to the profits created by some new invention.

Market Segmentation

When marketing executives attempt to remove the threat of competition by marketing their product to an exclusive portion of the population, they are practicing what is known as market segmentation. For instance, a shoe company that specializes in high-quality sandals does not compete with sneaker manufacturers. Market segmentation is particularly successful when businesses tend to sell their product to an intermediate buyer, who collects a number of these diverse lines and sells them to the general public. This can be a dangerous strategy to pursue, though: any shocks to the larger market can devastate a business that only trades in a limited portion of that market, and has no other product lines to fall back on.

Phases of Marketing

The typical marketing process has two distinct phases. First, marketing executives research the market in an attempt to determine exactly what goods and services customers are looking to buy. This may include looking at the past performance of the company or similar companies, conducting surveys or focus groups, or working in product development to anticipate future trends in the market. Next, the company attempts to provide the product to the public at the appropriate time, place, and price. This is much easier said than done: it takes a great deal of research and attention to the market to successfully serve the customer. Advocates of the new focus on marketing suggest that it creates a business community more attuned to consumer needs; critics, however, sense the same hunger for profits alone beneath the seemingly customer-oriented marketing.

Customers

Types -- Although most people think of private citizens when they envision the American consumer, there are actually a number of other kinds of customer that marketing executives must consider when they plan their strategies. Industrial buyers are those that purchase goods with the intent to resell them, either as is or in an altered form. Most complex products, books for instance, are the result of many industrial sales. Commercial buyers are those that don't alter goods before resale. They include hotels, offices, banks, schools, hospitals, and theaters. The things that they buy may be used in production or resold without any change. Governments, perhaps surprisingly to some, are the largest consumer in the United States. They buy everything from office supplies to nuclear warheads.

Determining what customers want -- There are three main ways in which marketing executives try to determine what consumers want. First, they may study the consumer. This can involve surveys or questionnaires, all with the aim of discovering how consumers will respond to a new product or advertisement. Another way of assessing the market is by determining what products would improve the lives of consumers, and then marketing these products. Some companies even go so far as to "manufacture" previously unknown needs among people, and then fulfill those needs. The last approach to market research is to try the product out in a test market; that is, sell it in a limited area in order to gauge whether it is worth the risk of a larger scale of manufacture and marketing.

Intermediate Purchasers

Typically, intermediate purchasers (those who buy things in order to resell them) are more systematic in making their purchases than are final customers. They usually buy things according to a rigid set of rules and are unlikely to be susceptible to flashy marketing. The people that make purchases for intermediate buyers, known as purchasing agents, value stability in the supply source. They frequently buy in large bulk, and appreciate a discount for large purchases or for consistent purchases over a long period of time. The purchasing agent typically works with supply sources to ensure that the product is best suited to his or her business; price, while important, is not always the determining factor in intermediate purchases.

Motivation

Marketers who wish to sell their products to the general public are aware that private buyers are often much less systematic in their purchasing than professional buyers. They may be more easily influenced by emotion. Generally, marketers consider several sources of motivation in consumers. First, the consumer may be moved by the satisfaction of the senses if they enjoy the way a product feels, tastes, looks, smells, or sounds. They may be afraid of what will happen to them if they do not make the purchase (bike helmets, for instance). They may be moved to buy a product that represents the accomplishment of a worthwhile goal, or they may seek to satisfy their curiosity with a particular product. Buyers may also buy something simply because they believe it will change the way they feel about themselves, and the way others view them.

Personal Selling

Personal selling is when an individual salesperson tried to persuade a customer to purchase a product in a face-to-face encounter. One good thing about personal selling is that it can be tailored to the audience. The two main types of personal selling are retail and industrial sales. Retail sales are those made to the final consumer, and takes place mainly in retail stores. In this case, the salesperson may do little more than facilitate the transaction. Retail selling can also include door-to-door sales. A more lucrative form of selling is industrial sales, in which products are sold to another business. This might include selling office equipment to a law form, or tube socks to a department store.

Selling Process

There are several typical steps to a sale. First, potential customers are scouted out, or prospected, by the salesman. Many firms conduct extensive research to identify prospective customers. Next, the salesperson approaches the potential customer and indicates an interest to show them the product. A presentation or demonstration will hopefully follow, in which the product is shown to its best advantage. The salesperson will then handle any objections to the product, and answer any questions. Closing the sale is the negotiation of price and payment plan. Finally, the salesperson will conduct what is known as a follow-up: processing the order, delivering or installing the product, and ensuring that the customer is satisfied with his or her purchase.

Direct Sales

Direct sales, in which an individual tries to make a sale in a personal encounter with a prospective buyer, is a difficult way to be successful in business. Although there is very little of the old-fashioned door-to-door salesmanship at present, telephone solicitation still constitutes a huge industry. Sales managers probably have the toughest jobs in the area of sales. It is their job to keep the sales force energetic and successful. One of the best ways to do this, obviously, is through careful selection and training of the sales force. A sales manager must also pay close attention to the sales market, so that any changes in the character in the market can be met by changes in sales technique. Lastly, an effective sales manager should keep in mind the company's philosophy and make sure it is understood by the sales force.

Advertising

Advertising is the practice of trying to call public attention to a business' products, services, plans, or philosophies by paying to communicate through the media. The most common venues for advertising are television, radio, print media, direct mailings, billboards, or public displays. Advertising is most prevalent in those nations with a free market economy and little censorship. In these places, market power is based on consumer preference, and so businesses must compete vigorously for the consumer's attention. Advertising also has the side effect of financing most of the media outlets in which it runs: most radio and television networks, for instance, are almost entirely paid for by advertising. For this reason, the government must keep a strict eye on the relation between business and the media, to make sure that any information presented as objective is not unduly influenced by business.

Newspaper advertising -- Newspaper advertising remains one of the more popular means of advertising, particularly for local businesses. Those who advertise in newspapers appreciate the flexibility, meaning that they can adjust their ads daily if they so choose. They also know they will have a good idea who is seeing the ad, and they expect that being advertised in the newspaper will confer some kind of prestige in their company. It is very easy for local distributors of a nationally-known product to coordinate their newspaper ads with the television and magazine ads of the national company. Of course, newspaper ads have an extremely short life span; they need to be re-run every day to have any kind of longevity. Also, they are usually read hastily, and sometimes photos do not show up well in them.

Radio advertising -- Radio advertising is immediately available for broadcast, and can be developed for a relatively low cost, so it is a good option for business that are trying to promote a series of events or a special sale. Radio stations typically have a good idea of their audience, so companies will be able to air their commercials on the stations that contain the most of their target audience. There are some drawbacks to radio advertising, however. For one thing, it is easy to miss or to only hear part of, which may prevent the company name from getting across. Radio ads also are very temporary things, and unless they are part of a larger, consistent campaign, they may be quickly forgotten by the general public.

Magazine advertising -- Many larger companies do a great deal of advertising in magazines. They appreciate the ability to select their audience by advertising only in certain publications. Magazine ads also tend to look glamorous, and expensive photography will look much better in this format than in a newspaper. Magazine ads also have a longer life than newspaper ads, and therefore have a greater chance of lodging in the public imagination. On the other hand, magazine ads are relatively inflexible; a campaign that is discovered to be ineffective cannot be removed from the pages of a magazine in which it has already been published. Also, depending on the prestige and readership of the magazine, advertising can be quite expensive.

Outdoor advertising -- Although some communities are trying to diminish the amount of advertising that can be displayed outdoors, many companies still use billboards and other outdoor signs to alert the public about their products and services. Outdoor advertising is an excellent way to quickly communicate simple ideas, and is especially useful for promoting products or services that can be purchased nearby. Since they are a quick way to communicate, outdoor ads are often used for repeating a company slogan. There are some disadvantages to advertising out of doors, however. Besides public distaste for this kind of advertising, there is also concern that the brevity of the message will make it forgettable to too many viewers.

Television advertising-- Television advertising is perhaps the most successful form of promotion, because it allows the company to develop a narrative around their product and guarantees them a large audience. Television ads run repeatedly, so they allow companies to drill their message into the audience. It is also quite easy to take ads on and off the air, so companies can make quick adjustments to their campaigns. There is also a certain prestige that goes with advertising on television. Some of the disadvantages of advertising on television are the fleetingness of the presentation, and the high cost compared to other forms of promotion. There is also evidence that the public more reflexively distrusts television advertising than other forms, and that many viewers do not watch advertisements at all.

Direct mail advertising -- Direct mail advertising is when a company sends brochures or leaflets directly to the homes of potential customers. It is easy to be quite selective when using direct mail businesses know exactly who will be seeing their ads. There is also a great deal of flexibility in this form of promotion, as businesses can remake their ads as often as they please. Direct mail ads can be created and sent in a very brief period of time. Furthermore, direct mail is a great venue of businesses to go into great detail about their products or services. Of course, direct mail is only as effective as the company's mailing list. Other disadvantages of direct mail are general public distrust of so-called "junk" mail, and the rather high cost of direct mail per customer.

Advertising Agencies

With the advent of enormous advertising campaigns, it became impractical for businesses to handle their own advertising, and so this work has been assigned to advertising agencies, which are hired to create and develop particular campaigns. Agencies typically have a creative department that will come up with the theme of the campaign; produce the artwork, jingles, or ad copy; hire the people necessary to accomplish the job; and direct the development of the campaign. Agencies also frequently have a media services group that decides where to run advertisements that will best reach the target audience. The account management department of the advertising agency acts as a liaison between the agency and their client, ensuring satisfaction with the campaign.

Sales Promotions

Formally, sales promotion is the marketing activities that motivate consumer purchasing, other than personal selling, advertising, and publicity. Sales promotion might include distributing samples, planning contests to promote a product, developing store display materials, and designing product deals (like rebates or two-for-one offers). Point-of-purchase display units, like cardboard racks next to the cash register in a supermarket, try to encourage immediate sales. Another common sales promotion device is the newspaper coupon, which offers small discounts.

The cost of these coupons is often shared by the product manufacturer and the retail store that sells the product. Other common sales promotions include company t-shirts, pens, or any other item bearing the name of the company.

Types of Goods

Goods on sale in the marketplace may be considered as belonging to one of four types: seasonal, staple, luxury, or convenience. Seasonal goods are those that are only available at particular times during the year. Examples of seasonal goods may include fruits and vegetables, or holiday decorations. Staple goods are those that are available year-round and are required by just about everybody in a society. They include things like gasoline, milk, and basic clothing. Luxury goods are of the highest quality and price, and are generally not necessary for sustaining life. Many markets of seemingly staple goods may include luxury lines. Convenience goods are those that the customer will have to purchase often and without much effort. Newspapers, hygiene products, and candy bars are all examples of convenience goods.

Retail Trade

Retail trade is that section of the economy that sells goods and services directly to the ultimate consumer. There are over a million retail companies in the United States, offering a wide variety of durable and non-durable merchandise. The United States Census Bureau classifies these businesses by their main product line, so a department store that sells much more clothing than home furnishings will have all its home furnishing sales reported under "clothing." The retail trade has in recent years accounted for approximately one-fifth of all non-farm jobs in America, and most economic analysts expect it will maintain or exceed this proportion in the future. They do say, though, that retail jobs may require an increasing amount of education as products diversify and businesses become more specialized.

Wholesale Trade

Wholesale trade is that part of business in which goods are purchased, and then modified before they are resold. Wholesalers do not sell to the ultimate consumer, although many wholesalers have retail operations that do work directly with consumers. Some of the industries in which wholesalers are important are automobiles, plumbing supplies, electrical supplies, and raw farm produce. Perhaps the most important function of wholesalers is to provide producers with an expanded market in which to sell their products. Many small producers do not have the resources to offer their product to a market outside of their geographic area, but by selling to wholesalers they can make their product available to many more consumers.

Public Relations/Publicity

One form of promotion that is frequently overlooked is public relations (also called publicity). Public relations includes any information about the company that is published or aired without being paid for. For instance, magazine and newspaper writer are often invited to visit corporate headquarters or to tour new factories, to try out new products or attend trade shows. The print or airtime that they then devote to the company and its products is essentially free advertising. Publishers and music companies send free copies of their products to journalists, in the hopes of getting reviewed. Many publicists insist that even negative publicity can be beneficial, if it serves to remind the public of the company.

Promotional Mix

Marketing executives are always trying to find for their product the appropriate promotional mix: that is, the combination of promotional techniques that is right for their product. In doing so, marketers must consider the amount of money available for promotion, the nature of the market, and the nature of the product. The amount of money that a company has for advertising and other sales promotions depends on a number of factors. Typically, a small company will spend a greater percentage of each sales dollar on promotion, though the larger company may spend more altogether. New products will require more promotion. Many companies base promotion funds on the success of the product, and some allocate a specific amount of promotional money for every unit that is produced. The best way to determine promotion allocation is to make specific goals and plan precisely to reach those goals.

Physical Distribution Management

Physical distribution is simply the actual transfer of goods from the producer to the user. For a long time, this was a neglected area of business. However, since physical distribution costs are a major part of most manufacturing budgets these days, it has become important for managers to discover the most efficient way to move their product. Today, the two main goals of a physical distribution manager are to maximize the level of customer service and minimize the total cost to the company. For instance, storage costs may be lower if less inventory is held, though that might cause an increase in transportation and processing costs. Physical distribution managers have to keep in mind the entire history of the product, from production to warehousing to processing to delivery, when they work to create the most efficient system.

Inventory

Control -- Manufacturers must constantly struggle to maintain the proper amount of inventory; it can be just as bad to have too large a stock, and pay high storage costs, as it is to run out of stock prematurely. Therefore, managers must try to determine when inventory must be replenished, and how much should be ordered at a time. There are great opportunities to save money by practicing sound inventory management, eliminating waste, and controlling spending on transportation, storage, and distribution to the market. Inventory managers must ensure that a company has all the materials they need to continue production, but that they do not get stuck with large reserves of some material that has become obsolete. They must also ensure that materials will not deteriorate over time.

Periodic inventory, physical inventory, perpetual inventory, floor stock, and back stock -- Inventory managers use a variety of systems to effectively maintain their stock. The goal of any inventory manager is to ensure that there is enough of a product in stock to meet any sudden demands for it, but that there is not so much around that the company incurs unnecessary costs. Periodic inventory is the system inventory managers use to determine the value of merchandise at periodic intervals by taking a physical count of stock. Perpetual inventory is another way of assessing the value of inventory, this time by using computers to calculate sales, returns, and receipts. Physical inventory is simply the name inventory managers have given to the process of physically counting the items in stock in a certain area at a certain time. Floor stock is inventory that is visible and accessible to consumers, and back stock is stored out of customer sight in a warehouse.

LIFO and FIFO -- Inventory managers have a number of options concerning how best to move their goods. Last-in, first-out (LIFO) is a method of managing inventory in which the most recently acquired items are the first to be sold. This method is supposed to create the lowest ending inventory in a period of rising prices. It is also credited with creating lower taxable income, lower gross profit, and a higher cost of goods sold. First-in, first-out, on the other hand, is the method of managing inventory wherein the items that have been around the longest are the first ones to be sold. In periods characterized by rising prices, this method of managing inventory is said to create a higher ending inventory, lower cost of goods sold, higher gross profit, and a higher taxable income.

Shoplifting and Employee Theft

Shoplifting is defined as any theft of merchandise that is for sale in some retail establishment. Shoplifting is one of the most common crimes, and has a significant effect on retail profits. Usually, store owners have to increase prices in order to off-set money lost due to shoplifting. In 2001, researchers declared that shoplifting was costing the United States' retailers $25 million every day. Some of the stolen goods that are considered to have been shoplifted may actually have been stolen by employees. Although most shoplifters are amateurs, there are known to be various rings of organized shoplifters. Some people even shoplift goods from chain stores in a perverse attempt to criticize the dominance of large retail corporations in American commerce.

Purchasing Agents

Every large company employs people to oversee the purchase of products and materials. These people are generally referred to as purchasing agents, though in retail business they are called buyers, and in the military they are said to be engaged in procurement. Careful purchasing may seem somewhat slow, but if it is done in accordance with a sound system it can save a business a great deal of money. In most companies, the purchasing process begins when an employee fills out a requisition form, be it for raw materials like lumber or steel, or merely for office supplies. At this point, purchasing agents work to discover the most efficient quantity and quality of that good available, and the most economic way to acquire it.

Criteria for Purchasing Decisions

It is crucial that a purchasing agent have the proper specifications for the desired item. When specifications are clear, the purchasing agent can consider options objectively, without having to weigh competing bids from various dealers. More attention can be spent on deriving the best value from the purchase. Of course, the purchasing agent has other things to consider, as well. There is always a cost associated with storing goods. Taxes, any interest the money used for inventory might be accruing, and the chance that the inventory will become obsolete must also be considered. The purchasing agent will also determine the various qualities of service and speed of delivery offered by different vendors. Some industrial buyers allow vendors to bid for their business, whereas retail buyers may visit trade shows to determine their best value. There is always a great deal of money to be made on seemingly insignificant purchasing decisions.

Transportation of Goods

Transportation of goods has been one of the most direct influences on the American economy throughout its history. Innovations like the steam engine and the highway system immediately resulted in better transportation costs for all businesses. Companies that specialize in the transport of goods are called commercial transportation companies. They can be either common or contract carriers. Common carrier are certified and overseen by the federal government if they ship goods over state boundaries and by state governments if they operate within a single state. Common carriers are obliged to serve the general public, and to provide reasonable speed and rates to all businesses without preference. Contract carriers are also regulated by the government, but they perform more specialized jobs for certain businesses, and they are allowed to negotiate their rates with the business itself.

Railroad freight -- Railroads were at one time the dominant means of transporting goods in the United States. They now face intense competition from other modes of transport, but still represent a considerable proportion of business shipping. There are certain terms associated with railroad freight. In-transit privelege refers to the right of shippers to have goods left in a certain location for a period of time, so that they can be modified, and then carried on to their final destination. Diversion of transit refers to the right of the shipper to have goods sent to a different location while they are in transit. Carload rates (that is, the cost of shipping per railroad car) is the most common rates of rail shipment; businesses use cheaper commodity rates when they are consistently shipping the same material to the same palce; the rest of rail cargo moves at either class rates, which are rates determined by certain weight and content criteria, and exception rates, the rates that apply to everything else.

Coordinated systems -- Often, competing modes of transport work together to maximize their various advantages. Some of the more common combinations are "piggyback," the combination of trucks and trains; "birdyback," the combination of trucks and planes; and "fishyback," the combination of boats and trucks. Combined methods of transport are more popular since the advent of containerization, in which materials are stored in large, standard-sized containers that can easily be transferred from one type of transport to another. Containerization not only reduces handling time and expense, but, because the containers can be sealed and locked, reduces theft during transportation as well.

Trucking -- As carriers of freight, trucks are generally more reliable and faster than railroads. Trucks are especially efficient at traversing short distances. For this reason, trucks have taken over from railroads as the preeminent means of moving goods. Although there are only a few rail carriers, there are many different and specialized trucking companies. One advantage of trucks is that they can easily combine goods from several different companies in one load. However, trucks tend to be more susceptible to bad weather than are railroads, and they are more often beset by labor problems. Trucks cannot hold as much as trains, and in fact have their load capacities regulated by the government. Trucking companies have also been hard-hit by rapid increases in the price of gasoline. For these reasons and others, the price of having goods shipped by truck has risen considerably in recent decades.

Watercarriers -- Before the explosion of rail transport, the inland and coastal waterways were once the dominant means of goods transportation. Since then, other methods have risen which are faster and more flexible, but water transport is still a substantial business in America. Shippers of heavy, nonperishable goods like iron ore, grain, and steel often find that transport by barge is most efficient. The primary handicap of water transport is that it can easily be interrupted by ice or fog. For this reason, much water shipping is planned around the changing seasons. There has also been a movement to try and extend the shipping season on the frigid northern lakes and rivers by developing large "icebreaker" vessels to make waterways navigable.

Pipelines -- Pipelines have some obvious advantages and disadvantages as a means of transporting goods. They are excellently suited for carrying liquids, and are a main source of transport for petroleum and natural gas. They are also quite inexpensive to use, much less so than trucks or trains. Because of this, there have been efforts to ship other goods via pipeline: coal, wood, and ore have suspended in water, creating a mixture called slurry, and sent through pipelines. Certain pipelines in the United States have been curtailed because the government deemed they would be too destructive to the railroad business. Obviously, one of the main disadvantages of shipping by pipeline is inflexibility; it is quite expensive to divert a pipeline to more than a couple of destinations. Also, pipelines tend to require a great deal of water.

Airlines -- Air transport generally is the most expensive means of shipping goods. However, shipping by air may lower costs for a firm in other areas, if it allows them to hold a lower inventory, close some warehouses, and decrease the amount of product deterioration. There may also be less need for extensive packaging for air transport, as there tend to be fewer stops and transfers. Not every product is suited to air transport, but businesses that deal in expensive, low-weight goods tend to benefit from shipping by air. Also, highly perishable products like flowers and fruit are often best shipped by air. For a long period, American electronic firms have shipped tiny parts overseas to be quickly put together and sent back; the high number of electronic parts that can be sent at a low weight makes them a viable candidate for air transport.

Deregulation of Transport

Deregulation is the removal of any controls over markets that have been imposed by governments. Deregulation is often designed to make it easier for businesses to enter the market. In the transportation industry, this can be achieved by allowing several companies to operate on one rail line, or by introducing sever penalties for any businesses found to be fixing prices. The immediate benefit of deregulating transport is that more lines become available to consumers, and prices are generally much lower as transport businesses must compete more vigorously for the market. Unfortunately, deregulation can also result in many transport companies operating well below full capacity, thus adding to both pollution and traffic congestion problems.

Storage of Goods

Businesses tend to run into problems with the storage of goods when the demand for a product is inconsistent with the supply. This may be caused by seasonal unavailability of a product, like agricultural products. In order to try and avoid great fluctuations in price, companies may elect to store excess products until demand rises again. In these cases, the managers must consider whether holding products off the market for a while will allow them to be sold at a higher cost, and thereby make back the money spent on storage. Storing excess goods may be especially smart if they are likely to be in great demand at peak periods. It may also be necessary for managers to determine the correct locations to store goods, so that they can be available immediately.

Warehouses -- A warehouse is a building used for storing goods at some point between factory and consumer. Most warehouses used to be in the center of cities, making parking and therefore delivery difficult. Businesses eventually determined that is more efficient to have automated warehouses in the suburbs. The main job of the warehouse is to receive, disassemble, store, transfer, and reassemble goods for delivery. Businesses can make a great deal of money by streamlining the ways they organize inventory in the warehouse and minimize the need for human labor. Warehouses may be either public or private, depending on whether they are leased or owned by the firm. The greatest storage needs are typically at the production end; as the product nears its final destination, the consumer, it usually requires less storage space because it is fully assembled.

Distribution Centers

Distribution centers have only emerged as a way of streamlining distribution in the past few decades. Distribution centers have the basic appearance of warehouses, but they are actually places where goods are reorganized for further shipment. Distribution centers are set up like a funnel: trucks unload products into one side of the facility, and they are recombined to form the loads that exit out the other side. Computerized data processing equipment has made it possible for employees to quickly bring together orders and send them on their way. Distribution centers have enabled companies to base their inventory on orders more than output. They may feature either soft automation (some things may be computerized, but employees must still move goods around) or hard automation (all processing and organizing is done by machine).

Business Technology and Information Systems

Postal Mail

The employees of an office will have to use a number of different forms of mail, depending on their purpose. Many professionals still use the United States Postal Service, otherwise known as "snail mail," because it is reliable and still has an air of authority. Once can also use the special delivery services offered by the Postal Service and by various private delivery services. It is now possible for businesses to create a shipping order on-line, and have the document or package picked up at their office. Typically, the length of time it will take to have the item delivered is guaranteed in the terms of the order. The methods are still very popular in business despite the growing presence of electronic mail.

Fax and Email

Although the fax machine has been somewhat replaced by Internet technology in the past few years, most businesses still maintain fax service and use it often. Faxes are valued for being speedy and for immediately confirming their delivery, so that there is no anxiety over whether the document has arrived intact. Faxes require a cover sheet listing the date, recipient, sender, and total number of pages. E-mail is probably the most popular form of office mail these days. Although it is still seen as somewhat informal, the speed and ease of electronic mail makes it very popular in the business world. One can also attach a more formal document (for instance a word-processing document, a database, or a spreadsheet) to an email message and maintain a more formal appearance.

Workflow

In business, workflow is the management of forms and data, especially when this management is done electronically. In general, workflow is the basic structure of operations. It encompasses how tasks are performed, who performs them, how they are ordered, how information moves throughout the company, and how management oversees the performance of tasks. In modern business, much of this is done using workflow software, which can direct documents to the right employees or store them in a database to which only certain employees have access. Some workflow software includes triggers that notify managers when work is taking too long, or when documents are not being properly accessed. Electronic workflow software, though it is somewhat prone to error, can speed the flow of knowledge through a company considerably.

Flow Charts

Businesses use flow charts as a graphical representation of the set of steps that must be performed in order to accomplish a certain goal. This may include the sequencing of operations, machines, materials, or information. Flow charts are useful because they allow managers to see all of the steps in a particular process and understand the interrelationships between them. The creation of a flow chart typically begins with defining the process to be diagrammed, and settling upon the limits of the chart. Then, the managers select those individuals who will be necessary to supply the information for the creation of the flow chart. Once these individual have conferred and developed a diagram, it is finalized in consultation with managers, who can then use the document to improve processes.

Flow chart symbols -- In order to facilitate the creation of flow charts, there are a number of symbols that are used to represent certain kinds of activities. In a standard flow chart, a round-edged rectangle denotes the starting and ending activities, sometimes referred to as the terminal activities. Each activity or step in the process will be represented by a rectangle. Decisions are represented by a diamond. Usually, the decision that has to be made is written inside the diamond, and the answer that is reached determines the next step. The transition from one step to another is illustrated by flow lines or arrows. When the creation or use of a certain document is required during a process, this is represented in a flow chart by a square with a tab descending from the bottom right corner.

Business Travel

Businesses stand to gain or lose a great deal of money depending on how they organize and schedule business travel. The first key step to planning a business trip is to have a clear itinerary, or set of travel plans. Although time spent on business travel is very valuable, it is important to avoid overloading the traveler's schedule. The itinerary should also allow for some space to allow the traveler to make his or her way in unfamiliar surroundings. Often, a business will contract a travel agent to help with planning an itinerary and the daily agendas. Businesses should also bear in mind any local customs, time changes, currency exchanges, and other factors that will affect the employee's ability to transact the business of the firm while traveling.

Business Meetings

Business meetings are essential for maintaining the flow of information through the company, and for making sure that lines of communication are open between the various members of the team. Face-to-face meetings can also defuse any potential conflict much better than can emails or phone calls. In order for a meeting to be effective, however, there must be an acknowledged agenda, and one that has been circulated well in advance. There must also be one person who is charged with administrating the meeting: that is, keeping control, steering conversation, making sure accurate notes are taken, and following up on the decisions that are made. Meetings may be called for any purpose in business: motivating, team building, setting goals, making decisions, clarifying policy, or just checking in with one another's work.

Priorities and outcomes -- When a business meeting is being planned, the priorities and desired outcomes of the meeting must be taken into consideration. Establishing the priorities of a meeting simply means establishing why the meeting is being called in the first place. A list should be made and ordered by importance; if resolving the prioritized issues is not worth the time that will be spent in the meeting, perhaps it would be best to wait. After determining why a meeting is to be held, it should be decided what the desired outcomes of the meeting will be. Some meetings will aim at making a decision, while others may be held just for the purposes of continuing a discussion. Meetings may be held to describe a new point of company policy, or to listen to a guest speaker.

Sequence and timings -- When the agenda for a business meeting is being planned, the most important items should always be placed first. Anything that absolutely must be covered in the meeting should be among the first things to be discussed. Many business managers also try to avoid putting too many controversial items in row when planning a business meeting; they seek to avoid conflict between attendees. In a similar fashion, the meeting planner should determine how long the meeting will need to be, and about how much time should be devoted to each particular item. Long meetings will need to be furnished with a break so that participants can maintain their attention. Many business managers have discovered that "working lunches" tend to add too much time to meetings and make it hard for participants to stay focused.

Date, time, and venue -- When planning a business meeting, one should try to select the date, time, and venue that are most congenial to the participants and appropriate to the task of the meeting. A meeting's date should cause as little disruption for the participants as possible. This is especially important to consider when calling people from different departments of a business, who may be operating on different schedules. Many meeting planners have decided that long meetings should either be held at the beginning or the end of the work day, so that travel time can be minimized. Finally, it is essential that the venue for a meeting have ample seating, whatever technological aids will be required, access to refreshments, and that it be a reasonable distance from the workspace of all who will be required to attend.

Public Speaking

There are a few basic strategies for public speaking that can allow even the shyest individual to represent themselves well in front of a crowd. First, it is essential to know both the room and the audience. This makes it possible to tailor one's speech and manner so that they will be appropriate. Next, a speaker should know his or her material well. It is always a good idea to try and relax before speaking. Many speakers find that it helps them to visualize their speech beforehand. During a speech, one should never apologize for being nervous or for any other problems; simply try to remedy these problems as quickly as possible. Finally, a good public speaker will concentrate on his or her message rather than on him or herself.

Speaking aids -- There are a variety of technological aids currently available to aid in public speaking. Probably the most popular of these is the PowerPoint computer software, which allows the user to create elaborate slide systems that can be projected onto a large screen to provide an outline for a speech. The same equipment that is used to project PowerPoint presentations can be used to project web page or word processing documents, as well. Many speakers enhance their speeches with audio or video footage, which can be manipulated and presented using basic computer software. Besides these more advanced forms of equipment, many speakers still use such old-fashioned props as overhead and slide projectors.

Telephone Calls

Defusing customer complaints and placing telephone calls -- Since an individual's first contact with a business may be over the phone, it is essential that employees are schooled in proper telephone etiquette. When an employee (a receptionist, for example) answers the phone for someone else, he or she should always identify him or herself and the company he or she represents. Then, he or she should always ask how the other person could be helped. It is important not to make commitments on behalf of other people; in other words, one should say that one will pass on the message rather than saying that one's superior will call back at a particular time. Finally, it is very important to always take accurate and legible messages that include a time, date, the reason for the call, the degree of urgency, the company the caller represents, and any other relevant information.

Proper telephone etiquitte when answering calls for others -- It is essential that students learn the proper way to defuse customer complaints and place calls. First, one must listen carefully as the customer outlines his or her complaint. One should remain calm and respectful, agreeing with the customer when appropriate, but never explicitly disagreeing. One should never interrupt or blame the customer for any problems. One should always apologize personally (this is more meaningful than apologizing on behalf of the company) and act quickly to remedy the situation. When placing a call, one should always plan the call and place it oneself. At the beginning of any phone call, one should briefly identify oneself and one's business, and describe the reason for the call in summary.

Tips concerning the qualities of a good voice and a good phone image when conducting business via telephone -- There are some general tips that students can learn to immediately improve their manner on the telephone. As far as one's voice, one should always strive for distinctness, so that every word can be understood. One should also try to cultivate warmth, naturalness, expressiveness, and pleasantness. Many writers on the subject recommend adopting a lower, mellower pitch to one's voice; they claim that this style of speech is more soothing to customers. In order to create a good image on the phone, employees should avoid using slang or chewing gum. They should never slam the phone down or fail to introduce themselves and offer a few courteous words. Last, and perhaps most important, employees should always keep the promises they make on the telephone.

Basic Office Equipment

There are a few basic items of office equipment that every business is likely to have. Perhaps the most important piece of office equipment these days is the computer. Computers are now used for word-processing, scanning, mailing documents, and developing presentations. Offices will almost certainly have a photocopier and a printer. They will most likely be equipped with a fax machine. Larger businesses may have a network server, which connects all of the computers in the business to one network and organizes their internet access. If a business is likely to have a lot of meetings, it will probably own some sort of video projector, so that employees can display slides as they make a presentation.

Resumes

Composing -- A resume may be the most important document that students will ever compose in their lives, so it is essential that business teachers give them the skills to construct thoughtful and effective ones. It is essential first of all that students have an idea of who the target audience is for their resume. If they are applying for a babysitting job, for instance, they would want to highlight different aspects of their background than if they were applying for an internship with their local congressman. A student should think of the resume as a marketing tool, in which the product being sold is him or herself. To this end, a resume should make clear the unique and positive attributes of the student, without going into too much detail. After all, a resume aims to earn an interview, not necessarily a job. Too many resumes are overloaded with accomplishments, to the point where they are either unbelievable or unreadable.

Key stylistic points of language and grammar -- There are a few stylistic points that students should keep in mind when they are composing a resume. First, they should always use short, bulleted statements rather than lengthy descriptions. After all, they can expect that their potential employer is going to be looking over a large number of resumes, and so they need to make the information immediately accessible. A resume should try to use as many "action" words as possible, rather than using forms of "to be" or passive verbs. If the student is applying for a job in a particular field, then it may help to demonstrate some knowledge of the terminology associated with that field, as well as to display any experience doing the kind of work that will be required. Finally, and most obviously, a resume must contain no grammatical or spelling errors!

Looking forward -- One of the quirky things about writing a resume is that, even though it lists your past achievements, it is actually supposed to be a document about your future. That is, an effective resume should be designed to suggest your ability to do whatever work you are aiming to do, rather than show your past successes in their best light. So, the accomplishments that you list should be those that will be the most impressive to your desired employer, not those that you happen to think are noteworthy. A good resume should always lead off with a statement of purpose, so that whoever reads it knows immediately what you would like to be doing. Then, you should design the rest of the resume as if it were an advertisement for yourself, showing how you can fill the role you desire.

Avoiding overabundance -- Some students will have been a part of many organizations, received many awards, and just generally have acquired a number of tings to list on a resume. They should be discouraged from including everything. A proper resume will take its cues from its statement of purpose; in other words, if a certain achievement doesn't support your desire to do the work you are aiming for, it has no place on your resume. Including too much information will only confuse whoever reads the resume, and may result in that person not reading it any further. This may be of particular concern if you are applying for a job for which you feel overqualified. Many times, individuals in desperate need of a job apply for positions that are below their level of training. They may feel concerned that their full resume will put off potential employers; it is perfectly alright in such a case to omit certain data, as long as the resume remains truthful and doesn't contain any large gaps in the employment history.

Including job descriptions -- Too often, resumes include long, detailed descriptions of the duties and responsibilities the applicant held at a previous job. For the most part, these summaries should be avoided in favor of lists of achievements at that job. The main reason for this is that a simple job description does not convey to the resume reader that the applicant is particularly good at his or her job; in many cases, it may simply tell the reader things about a certain job that he or she already knew or could have guessed. It is much better to alert the reader to whatever success you may have had in a previous position, or to indicate any special privileges or duties that would not normally be considered part of the job.

Avoiding irrelevant information -- In order for a resume to net the desired job, it should be oriented to promote the idea that you are capable of performing that job. In other words, you should avoid bragging about skills you no longer wish to use, or describing jobs you no longer wish to perform. Say, for instance, that you had a managerial job in a restaurant in which you were frequently called upon to wash dishes; it would be foolish to apply for another managerial position by mentioning how great your dish-washing skills are. This is not to say that one should lie about one's job history, but simply that one should only advertise what one has an interest in providing to a future employer. Nondisclosure (that is, not mentioning something) is not the same things as lying.

Avoiding lies -- One of the most important things a student can learn about composing a resume is how foolish it is to ever lie on one. Resume lies can take a number of forms, from misrepresenting your duties and position at a former job to claiming to have degrees that you haven't obtained. No form of misrepresentation is acceptable on a resume; besides being immoral, it is bound to catch up with you. The advent of high-powered search engines has made it quite easy for companies to check up on the claims that their applicants make, and any candidate who lies on their resume can be assured that if it is discovered during the selection process they will be disqualified, and if it is discovered after they have been hired they will most likely be terminated.

Job objective -- Every resume should begin with a job objective. The job objective sets the tone for the rest of the resume by answering three key questions: what position you are seeking to find, who should be reading your application materials, and how to interpret your resume. In order for this to work, of course, a job objective must be clear and precise. One should not say something like, "I want to improve myself and work as part of a cohesive team." Of course this may be true, but a potential employer needs to hear exactly what you want to do for his or her company, so that he or she can be start visualizing you in that position as he or she reads the rest of the resume. A strong objective, with action verbs and precise terminology, immediately separates a quality resume from the pack.

Summary of qualifications -- After a job objective is given, an effective resume will provide a brief Summary of Qualifications; that is, a list of the three or four best reasons for you to be considered for the job. This is the place to mention whatever you consider to be the most impressive, and most relevant, attribute that you have. This might include your experience, your credentials, your particular expertise, your work ethic, or your personality. Note that a summary of qualifications does not have to reference specific achievements. This is not to say, however, that it should be general. On the contrary, you should take this opportunity to highlight any skills that make you different from every other applicant, and worthy of special consideration.

Work history -- The work history section of a resume is your opportunity to showcase whatever experience and training you have already acquired, so long as it is pertinent to the job for which you are applying. Even if a job you have had is not directly relevant to your desired job, however, it is a good idea to briefly list it so as to avoid giving the impression that you have been unemployed for long periods. If there are gaps in your employment record, it is a good idea to indicate that you were not just lying about during this period by entering something like "student" or "personal travel," and then giving a brief summary. Job candidates should avoid mentioning rehabilitation, unemployment, or personal illness unless it is absolutely necessary.

Promotions and job changes -- If you have been promoted at a past job, the work history section of your resume is the right place to indicate it. Future employers will naturally be impressed by candidates who have apparently thrived in their past jobs. In order to effectively show these promotions, you can create separate entries for each position you have held—just make sure to list the name of the company for each, so that people reading your resume won't think you simply changed businesses often. If in fact you have worked for a number of companies over a brief period of time, you should try to minimize the impression of flightiness this might give by simply listing the employment agency you were working with, or indicating that you were performing strictly contractual work by including a title like "consultant" or "contractor."

Presenting achievements -- Every resume should include a list of whatever achievements either indicate particular skills relevant to the job or general personal qualities that will be appreciated in an employee. In fact, a successful resume will simply frame every job description in terms of achievements; that is, instead of describing responsibilities held and tasks performed, a good resume will list skills acquired and advances made. The idea that you are trying to convey by listing achievements is that you have the skills to do the job, you enjoy and are proud of these skills, and you hope to do more of the same in the future. For this reason, it is a good idea to downplay any achievements that may seem irrelevant to the job for which you are applying, and especially those which may make it seem as if you are overqualified.

Cover letter -- In order for a letter of application (or cover letter) to have the desired effect, it must be tailored to its audience. This means finding out the name and title of the person who will read the letter, even if it requires a bit of research to discover this information. A proper cover letter should also give the reader a bit of insight into the author; including some personal experience or anecdotes is a good way to distinguish one's letter from the rest. In this line, it is important to try and disguise whatever letter form the author may be using. Many applicants are helped by using available models of application letters, but it should never be apparent to the reader that a cover letter "formula" is being used. A cover letter should always strive to represent the individuality of the person it represents.

Catching the reader's attention -- Since business managers will read many letters of application, business students need to be equipped with some tools to help their letters stand out from the pack. The most important place to distinguish oneself is in the opening paragraph. Rather than use some formulaic introduction, students should be encouraged to pique the reader's interest with an anecdote, or a clever way of mentioning how the job came to his or her attention. Certainly, a letter of application should stay on the subject, but too many students damage their chances for employment by merely filling in the blanks of some cover letter model. Instead of doing this, the savvy applicant will indirectly demonstrate his or her intelligence and familiarity with the company without boring the reader with empty praise or false modesty.

Letter of application -- There are a few essential tips that concern the composition of all letters of application, and that any business class should be sure to impart to students. First, a cover letter should always refer the reader to the applicant's application, or to any other documents that may be contained in the same envelope. A cover letter should always end with a clear and courteous offer for an interview, and should of course include the same contact information as the resume. It goes without saying that any letters of application should be scrutinized closely for spelling and grammatical errors. An accomplished cover letter will be professional without being boring and interesting without being too casual. Students should be encouraged to always have a friend or mentor read their cover letters before submission.

Job Interviews

Preparation -- In order to be fully prepared for a job interview, a candidate must have considered three areas. First, the candidate must have a general understanding of his or her own skill, strengths, and weaknesses. This is essential so that he or she can decide whether the job is truly an appropriate one for him or her. Next, the candidate must have prepared for the questions he or she is likely to be asked, both those that are standard to a job interview (for instance, why he or she would like the job, or what he or she already knows about the company) and those that are unique to the company. So that these last questions may be answered effectively, the candidate should also have spent some time researching the business as well as the job that is available. If possible, it is good to know a bit about the person who will be conducting the interview.

Objectives -- Too often, students assume that a job interview is always given with an eye towards getting a particular job. While this may be the usual case, it is also perfectly appropriate to interview for a job so that one can discover more about it, as well as about one's place in the job market. Many time, individuals will interview for a number of jobs they have no intention of taking, for the sole reason of polishing their interview skills. It is important to decide before an interview just exactly what your objectives are. One danger that candidates run when they interview only to seek information, however, is that they will discover mid-interview that they would like the job and they have not done adequate preparatory work for the interview. For this reason, it is best to always be as well-prepared as possible, and settle the question of objective before the interview begins.

Listening skills -- One common misunderstanding of job interviews is that they are simply opportunities to go through a rehearsed monologue of one's skills and achievements. In actuality, one's ability to listen well may be more impressive to a potential employer. The candidate should make sure not to interrupt the interviewer, or fill in blanks in their sentences. If one is not sure about something the interviewer has said, it is always better to ask for clarification than to pretend comprehension. Too often, candidates are so focused on what they intend to say that they do not pay adequate attention to the tone and nuance of the interviewer; a well-prepared candidate should never have to worry about forgetting his or her lines.

Areas that are appropriate for a job candidate to inquire about -- Any candidate who hasn't got any questions about the employer during the interview is, whether intentionally or not, conveying the idea that he or she does not really care about the company. A candidate should always inquire about a few key areas. First, who are the business' chief competitors, and how does the business distinguish itself? What is the leadership structure of the business, and how long has the present leadership been in place? What particular issues or problems is the business dealing with at present? Does the company have a particular set of values? What is the "culture" of the company? Have there been any major changes in the business or in the industry as a whole that will affect the business in the near future? Questions like these convey to a potential employer that the candidate has a real interest in the business.

Acquiring information in preparation for a job interview-- Once an individual has scheduled an interview with a particular company, he or she should seek to find out as much about that company as possible. There are a number of ways to go about this. First, he or she can simply ask the company to send along any brochures or promotional literature that might be helpful. He or she might also try to contact other businesses that work with the company, to ask them their opinions. A very simple way to procure some information is to do an internet search of the company, or to search at the local library for articles about the business. Finally, one can make use of one's own business network, to try and discern what the reputation of the business is in the local community.

Google!

Closed questions -- In a job interview, closed questions should be the easiest to answer, although they may not necessarily be the most pleasant. Closed questions are those that require just a one or two word answer. Such questions might include whether the candidate has a college degree, what their grade point average was, or whether they have ever done similar work before. Usually, these questions are asked simply to verify information that is listed in an individual's resume, or to introduce lines of conversation that will then be developed more fully. As a candidate, one should avoid elaborating too fully on these kinds of questions, particularly if such elaboration might be seen as making excuses or qualifying negative aspects of a resume. One should simply answer these questions and move on.

Open questions -- Open questions are those that require more than just a simple one-word answer. An open question might invite a candidate to describe a past work experience, or to detail what it is about the company that interests him or her. These are good questions for well-prepared candidates, because they give him or her a chance to accentuate positive aspects of his or her resume, as well as to avoid mentioning qualities that might be viewed less favorably. One of the common dangers of these questions, however, is that they may lead to vague responses. If the candidate feels unsure exactly how to answer an open question, there is nothing wrong with politely asking the interviewer to narrow it down, or breaking it down him or herself into some simpler parts.

Leading questions -- Leading questions are those which the interviewer poses with an eye towards introducing some further line of conversation. Leading questions can be very dangerous for a candidate if he or she is not well prepared. As an example, an interviewer might insinuate that one of your previous bosses was unfair or incompetent. While this may or may not be true, sometimes interviewers will use such a line of questioning to determine whether a job candidate is likely to be overly critical of authority, or to pass the buck. The best thing to do in an introductory interview is to try and remain diplomatic when presented with opportunities to be critical. A good candidate will not suggest that he or she is incapable of criticizing others, but will always emphasize his or her own responsibility as the most important concern.

Appropriate clothing -- Perhaps the most important thing a job candidate can do is present a positive image with his or her dress. Although what is appropriate clothing will vary from job to job, it is generally agreed that a successful candidate will ensure that no aspect of his or her appearance will be uncommon for people in that profession. This may seem a rather soulless idea, but one should remember that the point of a job interview is to convey the impression that one can easily assume the role and responsibilities of the job. Even if one is supremely qualified otherwise, it will be difficult to convince a potential employer of this if one's first impression is wildly outside the norm. In a similar line, it is crucial that a candidate have performed the appropriate hygiene regimen before the interview; bad breath and body odor can kill job chances before the interview even starts.

Screening interview stage -- The first in the series of job interviews is the screening interview. During their screening interviews, a company is just trying to narrow down a large field of potential candidates. These interviews may not be performed by the same individuals that will conduct later interviews, and they may even be performed over the phone. For this reason, candidates should always be prepared for a screening interview. This means having a copy of one's resume and cover letter close to the phone, and being able to provide succinct answers to basic questions. The main point of a screening interview is to ensure that candidates have the basic qualifications and skills to be further considered for vacancies.

Selection and confirmation stage -- After the initial screening interview, a candidate should assume that his or her basic skills and achievements are known by the company. So, in the next interview (known as a selection interview), the goals should be to make clear what other skills the candidate will be able to bring to the business. If the selection interview goes well, there will be a final interview, the confirmation interview. In some cases, the confirmation interview may be simply a formality, in which the top executives get a chance to meet candidates who have already been approved for hire by the human resources department. Candidates who make it to a confirmation interview should just try and be polite, and not try too hard to sell themselves.

Mechanization

Mechanization is the use of a machine to do work that had formerly been done by a human being or an animal. Although mechanization has occurred in human societies for thousands of years in one way or another, it increased exponentially during the Industrial Revolution of the mid-nineteenth century. Whereas in 1850 the average laborer put in seventy hours a week and produced about 27 cents worth of goods an hour, by 1950 the average worker was spending forty hours a week helping machines create goods worth around three dollars an hour. Although many people have been critical of mechanization, and suggested that it will eliminate jobs for people. It has actually been seen to increase jobs in most industries.

Automation

Automation is simply the next step after mechanization; it refers to the state in which machines operate themselves. Automated machines can stop and start themselves, and may be programmed to perform a variety of functions at their own discretion. Automated machines can even check themselves periodically to ensure their proper function. Automation tends to reduce labor costs for business, but rather than diminishing the overall demand for human labor, it has actually increased it by creating new fields for work. Although there have occasionally been short-term layoffs in industries that become automated, the overall trend for employment in automated societies appears to be positive.

Standardization

Standardization is the process through which machine parts are made interchangeable, and it therefore becomes easier to produce a consistent product. Although we take standardization for granted in modern society, it was not always the case that the purchaser of a particular product could expect the same thing every time. Eli Whitney, who is famous for developing the cotton gin, also discovered that he could manufacture rifles much more efficiently if he standardized his machines. Managerial standardization is less well known than product standardization, but basically follows the same line of thought. It simply means maintaining the same systems, processes, and methods of running a certain kind of business. Accounting procedures, for instance, are basically the same everywhere, making it easy for accountants to communicate and transfer from one job to another.

Specialization

Specialization means dividing a particular job up into its various components, an allowing one worker to specialize in each. Although this idea has been around for centuries, it has been taken to another level by factory managers. Industrial engineers in the modern era may divide up the manufacture of a product by process, workers, geographical location, or chronology. They may plan to develop certain parts of their operation in places where it is most cost-effective, or in the places where the workers are already skilled in the appropriate ways. They must also have plans in place for any errors or insufficiencies that may occur. The United States, because of its diverse geography, offers great opportunities for specialization.

Production Managers

Production is simply combining land, labor, tools, and materials to make a product. A production manager, then, is one who tries to organize and administrate this process so that it will be efficient and profitable. The first step in the production management is planning. A production manager lists all the materials and processes, and decides what personnel and facilities will be necessary. Next, the production manager will construct a routing scheme, in which he or she determines when certain tasks need to be done, and if some can be done at the same time. He or she will then construct a schedule, to arrange the sequence of steps, and make sure enough time is allotted for each. Following a schedule is extremely important, as is the production manager's control over the operation: if he or she is unable to ensure that the schedule is viable and appropriate, production will become chaotic.

Service Industry Managers

The past few decade have seen the United States emerge from an industrial economy to one that is more heavily based on service industries. Of course, manufacturing concerns like scheduling, routing, and planning are still very important to service industry operators. Moreover, it is even more important for service industry managers to set an appropriate price for their work, because it is more difficult to gauge the value of an intangible service. For this reason, workers in service industries often have a hard time justifying an increase in price or to accurately consider their production scheme. Most economists agree that service industries are likely to dominate the future economy, as automation continues to free human resources for other work.

Service Industry Characteristics

The businesses that are considered part of the service industry have a few things in common. For one thing, they do not have an inventory of completed products in stock. Doctors, for instance, to not have healed patients in a warehouse! Most service businesses are small proprietorships, perhaps because there is typically a small initial; investment required to start these businesses. Often, service businesses can only serve a restricted area, as the presence of an employee may be necessary. In these businesses, skill is more important than capital, because repeat business is more dependent on how the service is performed than on anything else. In service industries, labor is usually the largest expense, and the product, be it entertainment, maintenance, or health care, may be quite intangible.

Productivity Declines

Although the United States has long been a leader in technological innovation, there are certain statistical measures that indicate to economists a slip in American productivity. When federal grants for research and development decrease, for instance, it is typically a sign that less money is being allocated to the development of new business methods. Private spending on basic research has also declined in recent years, and an increasing proportion of the patents given out by the United States government have been to foreign inventors. This is unfortunate, as research has shown that firms that spend a great deal on research tend to have much more efficient employees. Some economists believe that economic troubles have made it more difficult for American firms to justify spending on potentially unfruitful research.

Improving Productivity

Productivity is simply the comparison of the time and resources that go into a job with what is produced. Obviously, everybody would like to be more productive in their work, and every nation would like their industries to be more productive. There are three basic ways to improve productivity. The first way is to work harder, or rather to work smarter by considering how best to approach a problem and solve it quickly. Another way to increase productivity is to invent a tool that helps you work faster or better. The last way to increase productivity is to rearrange the task so that it becomes easier, or so that it can be performed better. Most competition among business is simply a struggle to obtain the best possible measure of productivity.

Current Research

Many teachers find it useful to include in their curriculum any modern research and topics that can help enliven their subject matter for students. There are always new studies of business behavior being published in magazines, journals, newspapers, and on the internet, and it is wise for students not only to have access to this information, but to have learned the proper way to interpret it. Business teachers should strive to inculcate the same sort of skills in regards to research as they do in their consumer education program; that is, students should be trained to determine the quality of research, the source of that research, the potential interest of the source in presenting information of a certain type, and the usefulness of the research to the student.

Vocational Education

Vocational education is the training of individuals to perform certain jobs. Often, large communities will have separate schools whose sole purpose is to cultivate workplace skills. These schools may work in conjunction with local industries to tailor the students' education to the anticipated job market. Vocational classes and schools may also offer cooperative training opportunities, in which students gain first-hand experience in their field of interest. As industrial work becomes more and more specialized, companies are requiring extensive vocational training and on-the-job experience for their employees. Public vocational education is designed to enhance the entire life of the worker; to this end, non-vocational classes are required so that students can earn a secondary degree as they gain work skills and experience.

Competency-Based Instruction

Most vocational classrooms now feature what is known as competency-based instruction. Loosely defined, competency-based instruction is a style of teaching in which progress is determined by students' mastery of skills rather than some arbitrary time limit. For example, in a business class, the teacher will ensure that every student is reasonably adept at making a basic budget before moving on. In a teacher-based classroom, a certain number of days would be allotted to each subject, and the teacher would adhere to this schedule whether students learned or not. Research has shown that a more learner-focused style of instruction, like competency-based instruction, ensures that students will retain the most of the curriculum. Teachers using competency-based instruction methods will be required to issue periodic assessments, so that they can gauge whether students have mastered a particular concept or skill.

Computer Technology

There is a wide range of uses for computer technology in business classes. Using computers, students may improve their visual presentations, hone their skills of enquiry, perform any number of business simulations, and gain access to a wealth of information that is pertinent to the course material. For teachers, computers can provide the latest business information, enhance presentation through the use of programs like PowerPoint, and serve as a virtual forum for students to access course information and discuss concepts outside of the time and space restrictions of the class. Many teachers develop their own course web pages, on which they provide course outlines, copies of important forms, further discussion of difficult concepts, grades and assignments, and any news pertaining to the course.

Some considerations regarding the use of computer technology in a business class -- In deciding when and how to use technology in a business class, teachers should bear in mind a few things. First, they should consider their degree of access to equipment. It is important that there be enough equipment for all students to remain involved throughout the course of the program. Teachers should also consider the amount of time available for the activity; most teachers have found that short, specific activities encourage the best use of time and equipment. It is important that teachers take into account their students' experience with the technology to be used, so that there is no delay and confusion over how to do the work. In this same line, teachers should have a back-up plan in case of technical malfunction. Finally, the teacher should ensure that students will be monitored, and that, particularly when the internet is involved, that all the subject matter will be appropriate to the age group.

Organizations and Literature

In order to take full advantage of the resources available to the modern business teacher, it is important for prospective teachers to familiarize themselves with the appropriate organizations and literature. The

National Business Education Association and its affiliate, the National Association for Business Teacher Education, provide a host of on-line and print publications to serve business instructors. The website for the NBEA also provides an on-line bookstore that allows business teachers to procure the most recent texts on business and vocational education. There are also a number of other free sources if valuable information on the internet, including the federal government's Department of Education homepage.

Promoting Business Education

Teachers should be familiar with some ways of promoting their classes to the local community, so that they can develop helpful relationships with local businesses. One good way to do this is by interacting with the community advisory councils from local businesses and municipal groups. These are committees whose only purpose is to discover ways in which the business can create positive connections with their community. Obviously, a great way for them to do this is by setting up relationships with local schools, and so they can become a wonderful resource for business teachers. Through partnerships with community advisory councils, business teachers can set up mentoring, job-shadowing, or internship programs, organize class trips, or simply acquire useful information about contemporary business practices.

Available Resources

In an effort to promote their programs and to establish relationships with local businesses, business teachers should avail themselves of every possible resource. One good way to access the outside community is to create a business class newsletter. This kind of document can be created with any basic desktop publishing program, and sent home with students or through the mail to local businesses. Often, the parents of business students are leaders in the business community themselves, and will be glad to help out if the class' needs are made clear. Business teachers may also find it helpful to advertise their requests for community involvement in the school newspaper, the school bulletin, or the newsletter for the local parent-teacher association

Classroom Equipment

Most business classes currently have a broad array of technology available to them. Teachers should anticipate having several computers (if not one for every student), a printer, a scanner, a television with VCR and DVD player, and a projector. Typically, all of the computers will have broadband access to the internet, so students can receive up-to-the-minute information. Students will probably also have access to graphing calculators, which can be used to demonstrate economic concepts as well as to calculate accounting data. Some teachers may want to make use of the telephones that most classrooms are equipped with in order to help their students with proper telephone etiquette.

Simulations

In the past, business classes have relied mainly on case studies to give students some experience looking at real-world applications of business concepts. Unfortunately, business case studies have some drawbacks: they don't allow students to experience events as they happen, they don't allow students to make business decisions themselves, and they don't allow students to test out what might have happened if different decisions had been made. It is a great aid to study, then, that computer simulations have been created. Business simulation software enables students to act out any number of scenarios, immediately see the results of their decisions, and adjust all kinds of variables to see their effects on business. Many teachers have discovered that this is an excellent way to show students how business concepts apply to real economic exchange.

Student Organizations

FBLA-PBL

Future Business Leaders of America- Phi Beta Lambda is a non-profit education association that works to prepare students for careers in business. The Association is divided into four parts: high school students; middle-school students; postsecondary students; and business people, teachers, and parents who support the mission of the group. FBLA was founded in 1940 and added Phi Beta Lambda as an independent division in 1958. The organization is funded by membership dues, corporate contributions, conference fees, and grants. Two of the most important FBLA-PBL meetings are the Institute for Leaders, a four-day seminar at the state and local level that aims to educate students about entrepreneurship and communication, and the National Fall Leadership Conference, an annual gathering of educators and business leaders.

DECA

The Delta Epsilon Chi Association, more commonly known as DECA, is an organization aimed at promoting marketing skills in students. DECA works specifically to aid the development of marketing in areas like hospitality, finance, sales, business administration, and entrepreneurship. To this end, it provides students with technical training, academic help, and conferences on employability skills and human relations. More broadly, DECA strives to build self-esteem in students by involving them in community service and giving them leadership experience. DECA publishes a number of journals and newsletters, holds frequent conferences around the country, hosts competitive events, and provides classroom resources to teachers and students.

Junior Achievement Program

Junior Achievement is a combination of teachers, parents, and volunteers that seek to educate children about free enterprise, economics, and business. Junior Achievement runs programs for children all they away from elementary school through high school, in the hopes of preparing students for their future participation in the business world. At the high school level, Junior Achievement focuses on four areas: economics, personal finance, business and entrepreneurship, and work preparation. JA also offers a number of scholarships for students who have completed JA programs and plan on studying business or economics in college. JA is a non-profit organization funded by the contributions of corporations and individuals.

Business Professionals of America

The Business Professionals of America is an organization devoted to helping high school students successfully enter the business community. It was created after the passing of the 1963 law expanding the role of vocational education in American schools. The BPA conducts a number of programs and conferences aimed at advancing business education. The Work place Skills Assessment Program is held all over the country, and gives students a chance to see how they measure up to other people in the job market. The BPA also offers a number of scholarships and leadership awards to students who distinguish themselves. Every year, the BPA holds a National Leadership Conference to set goals for the year and discuss how best to promote the organization's agenda.

Vocational Acts

The Vocational Education Act of 1963 and the 1968 amendments to the Vocational Education Act of 1963 -- The Vocational Education Act of 1963, also called the Carl D. Perkins Act of 1963, broadened the government's conception of vocational education. It established some procedures to provide part-time employment to students, and established a federal advisory council on vocational education. It also set aside some federal money for the construction of local vocational schools. This act also established some work-study programs enabling students to get real-life experience while earning some school credit. Some amendments were made to this act in 1968, including some direct support for cooperative education and a renewed emphasis on postsecondary education. The amendments also included new provisions for funding an expanded vocational curriculum.

The Carl D Perkins Vocational Education Act of 1984 and the Carl D Perkins Vocational and Applied Technology Act of 1990 -- The Carl D. Perkins Act of 1984 was issued in the hopes of improving the basic skills of the labor force and preparing students for the job market by enhancing vocational education. Specifically, the Perkins Act sought to establish equal opportunities for adults in vocational education, and to aid in the introduction of new technologies in vocational instruction. In order to meet its objectives, the Perkins Act set aside money for research into vocational education, as well as money to ensure access to vocational studies for people with disabilities, adults in need of retraining, single parents, and ex-convicts. This act was enhanced in 1990 with the issuing of the Perkins Vocational and Applied Technology Act. This act sought to integrate academic and vocational studies, as well as to fund better technology in vocational classrooms and better cooperation between the business and education communities.

Business Education Objectives

Business education has a host of applications for students. Although it is typically assumed to be only relevant for people who are planning to make or sell goods or services for a living, the skills that are essential to business are also used by charities, governments, and farmers, just to name a few. Students may reconsider their future plans after learning a bit about business, especially if they live in an area with seemingly narrow career choices. Business studies will acclimate students to the set of standards they will be held to in their future life as a contributing member of the economy. Moreover, the skills in manipulating numbers and creating and analyzing various graphs and charts will serve students well in many different endeavors.

School Advisory Council

A school's advisory council can help a great deal in fostering a positive environment for business classes. First, business teachers can use the advisory council as a sounding board for new ideas regarding curricula. The school advisory council may also have connections to the local business community that can be helpful for business teachers. By communicating well with the advisory council, business teachers can ensure that their equipment needs are known. An advisory council can also officiate any disputes that may arise between members of a business department, business teachers and the administration, and business teachers and their students.

Developing Business Programs

In order to put together an appropriate business education program, a teacher must conduct a needs assessment and determine what material needs to be covered, what changes need to be made in students, and what the costs will be of achieving those changes. The first step in conducting a needs assessment is performing a gap analysis; in other words, comparing the performance of the school's business department with the standard set by other schools. In order to do this effectively, the department head has to be aware of the technologies that the school already has, those that they will need, and the other strengths and weaknesses of the school. This may result in the purchase of new equipment, some new training for teachers, and perhaps a new philosophy for the department as a whole.

<u>Appropriate needs assessment for a business education program</u> -- In order to construct an appropriate needs assessment, a business education department head needs to first conduct a gap analysis. After this is done, though, he or she needs to identify priorities for the department and rank them in importance. Sometimes a cost-benefit analysis is helpful in figuring out which are the most important actions that the department can take. Next, teachers will try to identify whatever problems may be keeping the department from reaching its potential. Possible problems might include under-trained staff or a failure to make department goals clear. Finally, the effective needs assessment will identify solutions to these problems, as well as any chance for improvement in other areas. The completed needs assessment provides a basis on which the whole department can work in the future.

Developing Teaching Plans

A teacher cannot be effective without properly planning every aspect of class. Good plans give a teacher confidence, security, and a definite direction in class. Teachers that are successful planners typically follow four steps when they plan an activity. First, the have a total understanding of the activity: what it will involve, what it is designed to teach, what potential problems it might have. Next, the teacher imagines its implementation in the classroom, and makes whatever modifications to the environment are necessary. Then, the teacher evaluates the strengths and weaknesses of his or her class, and alters the activity to suit them. Finally, an effective teacher will create a mental image of the finished activity, and imagine exactly how it will be accomplished.

Long-Range Plans

For teachers, long-range plans are those that stretch out over a grading period, a semester, or a school year. They typically are closely related to state curriculum standards. Usually, a teacher will start a long-range plan by studying a calendar to determine exactly how many instructional hours will be available. Next, the teacher should consider which activities are most appropriate for which time of year. Many teacher use long-range plans to decide how they will try to develop a certain theme throughout the school year. These long-range plans will be frequently referred to when teachers are developing their weekly and daily lesson plans. Long-range plans serve as a sort of point of orientation for the rest of the planning process.

Weekly Schedules

Every teacher needs to compose a weekly schedule in order to ensure that progress is maintained. Most teachers use their long-range plans to determine the amount of progress they need to make from week to week. In making weekly plans, teachers should consider which activities are appropriate for classes at the beginning of the day, and which are more appropriate for those after lunch and later. Next, teachers should consider how much direct instructional time will be necessary to give students the abilities to complete any assignments. Many beginning teachers run their weekly plans by more experienced colleagues to make sure that they are viable. The weekly schedule serves as the basic framework for the daily lesson plan.

Daily Lesson Plans

Effective teaching always includes composing clear, detailed, and well-considered daily lesson plans. Many schools place such a high value on daily plans that they require teachers to show their plans to the principal every week. A good daily lesson plan should include the specific content and activities that will be covered in each class period. It will also detail whatever procedures, assignments, student groupings, and materials will be necessary to meet the day's objectives. The composition of a lesson plan is a good chance for a teacher to consider whether his or her plan has an appropriate balance, and whether they are right for a particular class. In other words, plans should be made with the results of recent assessment in mind.

Lesson plans are essential to maintaining an organized class and making sure that all of the goals of the syllabus are attained. Just as businesses create detailed budgets to ensure that there is a clear path to their objectives, so must teachers plan every class in advance to ensure success. When drawing up lesson plans, a teacher should consider several things. First, he or she must have a clear idea of what content is to be covered. Second, he or she should know the time and resources available, as well as the ability level of the students. Third, the teacher should have an idea of what teaching method is most appropriate to deliver that particular lesson. Finally, the teacher should make sure that the lesson has a clear introduction, and an end that brings the material together and gives the student an idea of what they need to remember.

Maximizing Instruction Time

Too many teachers allow time to be wasted in class and cheat their students out of valuable instructional time. There are a few basic ways to remedy this problem. For one thing, teachers can minimize the amount of time students are given to socialize at the beginning or end of class. Next, teachers can try to make transitions between activities as smooth as possible by having the necessary materials ready at the beginning of class. Many teachers try to avoid giving students too much seatwork that could just as easily be completed out of class. Also, teachers should have a clear policy on restroom breaks, so that their time is not wasted by constant requests to be excused.

Managing Time

Teachers are always being pulled in several different directions, and sometimes they may feel that the responsibilities they have outside the classroom are making it difficult for them to meet their teaching goals. There are a few good ways to avoid this problem. First, teacher should list and prioritize their responsibilities, so that they do not get caught up in performing insignificant tasks. If necessary, teachers should avoid being drawn into committee and volunteer work organized by the school administration. Teachers should always have quiet space in which they can concentrate. Also, managing time effectively means abandoning perfectionism and procrastination. Setting firm time limits for open-ended tasks is a good way to avoid spending too much time on things less important than teaching.

First Day of School

The first day of the new school year is a nerve-wracking event for any teacher, much less a first-year professional. In order to make the first day a success, a teacher should arrive early and make sure that everything is ready for the arrival of students. Most teachers write their names on the board, and post a schedule so that students will know what to expect. Some teachers find it helpful to have an activity laid out for students when they come in, so that they will be immediately drawn into the flow of the class. Finally, and most importantly perhaps, teachers should just relax: if they have planned properly, the first day of school should be an exciting and hopeful day.

A teacher always wants to make the right first impression at the beginning of every school year. It is a good idea to greet students individually as they come in, and start the year with some ice-breaking activity. The first day of school is also the right time to acquaint the students with the class rules and goals, as well as to give them a brief idea of your background and expectations. Some teachers use the first day of school to develop a contract with students. If all of this is accomplished with time left in the period, it may be a good idea to review some of the previous year's material with students, or to outline in brief the topics the course will cover. Some teachers use the first day to try and stir up some enthusiasm for the subject matter by previewing some exciting topics or activities.

Navigating First Weeks

The first few weeks can make or break a school year, so it is crucial to maintain effective control over activities. A good teacher will make sure to be firm and consistent in enforcing the rules; if students get the impression early in the year that they can get away with disobedience, they will bedevil their teacher for the rest of the course. Frequent assessment should be a feature of the first few weeks, so that the teacher can get a sense of what skills students already possess, and what they need to improve upon. The first few weeks are the time to drill into students the routines of the class, as well as the things that they will need to bring to class each day. In order to make the first few weeks of class a positive foundation for the rest of the year, students should be closely supervised as much as possible.

Syllabus

A syllabus is essential for effectively organizing and administrating a business class. Preparing a clear and detailed syllabus before the start of the school year allows teachers to be sure that all of the essential areas will be covered, that there will be enough variety among assignments to hold the interest of the class, and to make sure that all the students will understand the program and the expectations. A proper syllabus should include a defined aim for the course, clear assessment objectives, an outline of the assessment structure (that is, how students will be examined), the content of the curriculum, and a grading scale. The grading scale should include a sufficient description of the quality of work that merits each letter grade.

Assessment Objectives

An effective syllabus will adequately describe the assessment objectives for the class. The assessment objectives are the skills that the class will be trying to develop in the student. In business education classes, there are considered to be four basic assessment objectives. The first is knowledge and understanding, meaning that the student should be able to recall the basic facts and concepts of the course. The second objective is application, the ability of the student to take the facts and concepts he or she has learned and apply them to the appropriate situations. The third objective is analysis, the ability of the student to select, order, and interpret information, whether in the form of text, chart, or number. Finally, students should be assessed on their ability to evaluate material; that is, to develop and justify arguments based on the content of the course.

General Structure

Although there is no one way to order the material of a business course, some ways seem to make more sense than others. For instance, most teachers will want to begin the course with an overview of the general themes of the course, so that students will have an idea of the structure of the course and will be prepared for its various transitions. Most teachers cover the nature of business activity, the types of businesses, and the objectives of various businesses early in the year. From there, it makes sense to move on to organizational structure and then to close studies of the various divisions within a large business: accounting, marketing, and so on. From there, the class may want to move to a larger view of business within the context of the whole economy, and to a consideration of macroeconomic trends.

Differentiation

In business classes that consist of students with varying abilities, it is crucial that a teacher practice differentiation: that is, distinguishing between students and adjusting the class material to engage all of them. This of course is a great responsibility for a teacher: more time must be spent planning, and teachers must guard against settling for lessons that appeal strictly to the middle level of the class. Besides differentiating between students, teachers must also differentiate between classes. Some classes may have a different "character" than others, depending on the time of day when they are held and their composition. Differentiation is especially important in business classes because they are frequently available to all students, regardless of aptitude.

Student vs. Teacher-Centered

An effective business class will have a mixture of student-centered and teacher-centered instruction. It is important for students to acquire a base of knowledge before they try to apply it, and teacher-centered instructional methods will tend to be more appropriate for this. Although the lecture is the traditional form of teacher-centered instruction, teachers may also use textbooks, newspapers, the internet, or CD-ROMs to accomplish this goal. After this, it is desirable to move on to activities in which the students are required to do something with the knowledge they have acquired. Group discussions, individual problem-solving exercises, and case studies are all student-centered instruction methods that force students to analyze and evaluate situations based on what they have learned.

Worksheet Design

Worksheets are a typical way to underscore key points in a reading assignment and ensure that students understand the basic material covered in a business class. Traditional worksheets may require students to fill in a blank, answer a multiple-choice question, or provide a short written answer. When designing worksheets, teachers should consider whether the language used is likely to be understood by all the members of the class. Also, teachers should try to vary the difficulty of the questions, so that there will be some way to discern the differentiation among the students. It is also important that the teacher have a clear idea of what material is to be covered by the worksheet, and makes sure that the worksheet fully and fairly covers the material.

Assignments

Business teachers will typically assign students a task or series of tasks to solidify and assess learning. Class assignments encourage students to manipulate and analyze course material. When making assignments, teachers should make sure to have a clear idea of what knowledge they are seeking to reinforce. Assignments should have varying degrees of difficulty, such that the least able students can attempt everything and the most able students will feel challenged. If research is required to complete the assignment, the teacher should have established the means for the students to perform this research. Finally, teachers should always grade every particular part of an assignment separately, so that students will have a better idea of what is expected of them, and also in what areas they need to improve.

Performing investigative assignments -- Teachers should encourage students to apply their knowledge by performing investigative assignments involving research. Investigations are especially useful in reinforcing difficult concepts: students can try to apply their knowledge of a subject to a real-life example, record their findings, and hopefully enhance their overall understanding of the concept. For example, a teacher might have students investigate the marketing mix of a familiar product. For a short assignment, students might isolate one aspect of marketing for a major product (say, price control), and discuss how it is adjusted to meet market demands. A longer assignment might require students to investigate all the aspects of the product's marketing mix, and describe how the business adjusts them to achieve its goals.

A teacher should keep a few things in mind when developing an investigative assignment for his or her class. First, it is better to assign several short tasks than one long task; students are more likely to become confused and flustered by long and unclear assignments. Also, the teacher should leave some of the questions open-ended, so that students can distinguish themselves by their enthusiasm and understanding. Teachers might consider whether a particular investigation would be better carries out by a group or by an individual. Some investigations are more beneficial when students have a chance to talk amongst themselves, whereas in others it may be essential that a student handle every element him or herself. Teachers should make clear requirements about the way the investigation should be presented; it is wise to vary the format throughout the course, so that students gain experience giving speeches, writing reports, and creating visual presentations.

Teaching Methods

Case studies -- Business teachers can effectively use case studies to solidify conceptual knowledge that has been taught in a particular unit. In a case study, the teacher provides specific information, and students are required to analyze and evaluate the information. For example, students might be presented with a business plan and asked to describe its strengths and weaknesses. When developing case studies, a business teacher should make sure that the information is comprehensible to all the members of the class, and that no untaught concepts are required to perform an adequate analysis. It is also important to limit the amount of information given: too much data may confuse students and detract from the power of the exercise. Finally, teachers should ensure that there are some areas of the assignment that require creative thought, rather than simply recitation of the course material.

Role plays -- In a role play, students are required to assume the roles of the various parties in a debate or discussion. This kind of instruction is especially useful for subjects in which it is important that students understand and empathize with the parties concerned; in a discussion of industrial layoffs, for instance, it might be helpful for students to see the pressures acting on both the management and the laborers. It is very important that students are well prepared for their roles, and that the subject of the role play is appropriate for the age group and the progress that has been made in the course. Lastly, teachers should take great care to emphasize that students are merely acting out roles, and that any disagreements should not be personal.

Class discussion -- Class discussion is an effective teaching method when going over difficult concepts or covering material on which there are varying viewpoints. Sometimes, teachers might want to organize discussion by giving an agenda or a list of questions to be collectively answered, while other times teachers may want to allow the conversation to flow where it will. One of the main concerns in a large class is that some students will dominate discussion, while others will remain silent. Teachers may want to make participation mandatory to remedy this, or they may want to divide the class up into smaller discussion groups. Teachers may also find class discussion more profitable if they plan ahead by providing students with a list of the topics to be discussed before the day of the discussion.

Group work -- Group work may be an effective way of encouraging students to master difficult material, because it forces them to describe the material to one another and agree on concepts. Group work also helps develop social skills and the ability to debate objectively and fairly. Teachers may want to select the groups themselves, to ensure that there is the desired distribution of males and females, of high and low ability students, and so that any disruptive students will not be grouped together. It is essential that groups be held responsible for presenting their work either to the teacher or to the rest of the class, so that time is not wasted. Also, teachers will want to set a series of small goals for groups rather than one large one, so that students are continually required to demonstrate progress in their work.

The development of synthesizing and presenting information to an audience is achieved -- It is important that students in a business class work to develop their skill at synthesizing and presenting information to an audience, as this will be necessary in the business world. Teachers may want to assign group presentations at first, if he or she feels students will be extremely uncomfortable speaking in front of the class. It is essential to provide a clear list of what is expected in the presentation. If multimedia equipment, such as televisions or video projectors, is necessary, the teacher should ensure that these are available to students. Students should probably be required to produce a handout accompanying their worksheet, in order to encourage an organized presentation as well as to aid the audience. Evaluation of presentations must be detailed and precise, so that students will know where they need to improve.

Games and simulations -- Games and simulations are an excellent way for students to model complicated business processes and thereby better understand some difficult concepts. Moreover, they are a fun way to conclude a unit while still ensuring that students have mastered the material. There are plenty of games available that deal with running a simulated business. Differentiation is key when assigning games to a class; teachers want to avoid creating unfair teams or creating situations in which some students will be embarrassed. On the other hand, game situations are more likely to encourage cooperation among students of different ability, as they strive to win a contest. As with other activities, it is essential that directions are clear and exact, so that controversy and confusion can be avoided.

Assessments

Formative assessment -- Formative assessment is the testing carried out by the teacher during the course of the school term. Its aim is to ensure that students understand the material, as well as to diagnose any gaps in their understanding. It should provide a clear view of the varying ability levels of the members of the class, and it should indicate some ways in which the teacher needs to improve his or her instruction. Formative assessment should often result in a different means of presenting information, or more time spent with troublesome material. It is a good idea to include self-assessment and peer-assessment, so that students can indicate how they feel about their progress in the course and alert the teacher to any problems in morale.

Summative assessment -- Summative assessment is carried out less frequently by the teacher; it is appropriate for checking knowledge at the end of a unit of study or at the end of the course. Whereas formative assessment is an assessment for learning, in that it helps the teacher to make positive adjustments to the course, summative assessment is an assessment of learning. It is likely that the means of summative assessment will be affected by the performance of students on formative assessments. It is important that summative assessments provide a comprehensive evaluation of students' mastery of the material, such that every area of knowledge is questioned and every skill is tested. Also, summative assessment should include questions of varying difficulty, so that students can distinguish themselves.

Oral questioning -- One easy way for teachers to conduct a formative assessment in class is to briefly quiz students on the material covered. Indeed, whether it is to be done for a grade or not, it is generally useful to recapitulate the previous day's lesson at the beginning of class. Oftentimes, this can be best accomplished by allowing students to articulate the material, and to critique one another's understanding. Some probing questions from the teacher can ensure that the recent material is understood in the context of the material that has already been learned. It is not always necessary to formally grade students on their participation or performance in an informal question-and-answer session; the main thing is to develop an idea of the students' progress.

Written comments on class assignments -- Perhaps the most important kind of formative assessment a teacher can provide is helpful written comments on student papers. This is the place for teachers to clarify the strengths and weaknesses of the student's work, as well as to generally assess the student's progress in the class. Moreover, this is the perfect venue in which to differentiate between students; in order to keep all of the students motivated, teachers must set different standards for them, and indicate these standards in their comments. Comments should always be positive and supportive, but not at the expense of being constructive: simply assigning a letter grade is inadequate. The important thing when commenting on student work is to indicate areas for improvement without alienating or embarrassing the student.

Self-assessment and peer assessment -- It is always a good idea to incorporate some self-assessment and peer assessment into a business class, so that students will be encouraged to think about their own progress relative to the progress of the class, as well as to stay focused on the goals of the course. Interestingly, students are usually much harder on themselves in their evaluations that they are on their fellow students. In order for self-assessment to be successful, the teacher must have clearly outlined the learning objectives of each activity. Furthermore, the teacher must have provided adequate constructive criticism, so that students will have a clear idea of where they stand. Sometimes, it may be useful to design a specific assessment checklist so that students will not resort to vague praise or criticism.

Department Head

The head of a business department occupies an important mediating role between teachers and school administrators. Along with the school's principals, he or she will be responsible for developing the aims of the school and crafting policy that fits the curriculum. As the head of the business department, he or she will be charged with making sure that all of the business teachers understand and employ the school policy, and that the business department cooperates with other departments to achieve school-wide goals. The department head is responsible for making sure that the staff is properly trained, and that all necessary technology is provided by the school. The department head will also be required to handle disputes between business teachers and their students, as well as any conflicts between teachers themselves.

Equipment Needs

A business department will typically require a few technological items in order to give students proper exposure to the methods currently employed in the business community. Obviously, a business department will need to have computer access, do that students can perform business simulations and get current information of economic and business topics. Most classrooms will need to be equipped with a video projector, so that students can practice creating and delivering Power Point presentations. It may be useful for every room to have a television with VCR and DVD player, so that instructors can take advantage of the many visual resources available for business education.

Staffing Needs

Assembling the proper staff for a business department can be a challenging task for the school administration and the department head. In order to adequately determine how many teachers will be required, the school officials will need to predict how many students are likely to register for business classes. Officials will then take this number and, based on the number of students they allow in a single class, determine the number of teachers required. Schools will often try to hire teachers with differing areas of expertise; for instance, a school may hire one teacher with a background in economics and another with a background in business law. If the department is large enough, the school may need to hire a secretary to help the department head and act as a liaison between the department and the main office.

Budgeting

Typically, the budget for a business department is developed by the head of the business department in consultation with the business teachers and the school administration. This collaborative process usually starts with the business leader making a list of the equipment and supplies that he or she feels will be necessary for the upcoming school year. Then, he or she shares the list with the faculty and encourages them to make suggestions and to prioritize the requests. Then, the department head presents the budget proposal to the school administration, who will decide which of the department requests can be fulfilled. Sometimes, the administration will provide a limit to spending to the department head before the creation of a budget proposal.

Classroom Management

There are a few things that a beginning teacher needs to do in order to be properly prepared for the start of the school year. It is always a good idea to familiarize yourself with the school layout, and to introduce yourself to as many of your colleagues as possible. Also, you should meet the staff: secretaries, custodians, and counselors. These people can help make your transition successful. It is also a good idea to read the school policy manual and the state curriculum standards. A beginning teacher should become familiar with the school's philosophy and goals by reading whatever promotional literature is available. Finally, a beginning teacher should have a detailed schedule for his or her first day on the job.

Arranging the classroom space -- The physical arrangement of a classroom will be best when it suits the style of the teacher. If most classes are going to be lectures, then it makes sense to arrange all the desks in rows facing the front of the room. If students are going to spend a lot of time working in small groups, then it is better to group desks together. Large group discussions are best held in a room in which desks have been arranged so that they face one another. It is also important for a teacher to create a generally welcoming environment in their classroom, by posting picture, laying some rugs, or setting out some plants. The point of arranging your classroom is to make it the place most conducive to meeting your goals, so you should avoid things that will be distracting or unpleasant to some students.

Creating a positive environment -- In order for teachers to engage the minds of their students at the highest level, they have to first make sure that certain lesser needs are taken care of. Lighting, for instance, is important for creating a good classroom environment. Some kids may prefer bright light to dim light, so it is a good idea to include areas that receive different amounts of light. It is not a bad idea for there to be some open space in one section of the classroom, so that kids can move around a bit if they get restless. Many teachers have some softer furniture in their classrooms, so that students can get comfortable and focus on their work. Last but not least, teachers should try to determine what temperature is most popular in the classroom, and encourage students to bring whatever clothing they will need to be comfortable at that temperature.

Basic rules of conduct -- Just as a business posts its internal rules for employees, so do teachers need to post a set of basic rules for students to follow when they are in class. The most important and all-encompassing of these rules is simply to treat others the way you would like to be treated. Students should also be told to respect the property and personal space of their teacher and fellow students, and to keep their hands off of one another. Students should never laugh at one another. Students should be responsible for their own learning, and work together to create an environment in which they can be successful. This includes being on time for class each day, and handing in all assignments on time.

Managing Paperwork

Most beginning teachers are overwhelmed at first by the amount of record-keeping and procedural paperwork they are required to fill out every day. The barrage of paper coming at a teacher can include attendance reports, lesson plans, lunch counts, report cards, homework, class reports, etc. There are a few good way to avoid being bogged down by paperwork. First, teachers can minimize their grading by having students grade one another for small assignments. Students can even be encouraged to make up their own worksheets. Many teachers try to use a lot of small quizzes to assess their students, so that they do not get caught up in grading large assignments. Teachers can even administer oral exams to their students, and thereby remove the need for paper altogether.

Grading Papers

Grading papers can be one of the more time-consuming tasks for any teacher. There are a few ways to alleviate the burden of grading. One method that many teachers use is marking incorrect answers with an "O," so that when the student corrects the answer the teacher can just add a "K" to indicate approval. Most teachers use one chart to keep track of all the student grades, so that they can keep them well-organized. Students can often be enlisted to grade one another on short or insignificant assignments, and this may even be an effective learning strategy in some cases. Finally, many teachers use a variety of different ink colors to tell themselves whether a paper is late, or on-time, or to tell themselves how much of it has been graded.

Parents and Teacher Relationships

Teachers too rarely make use of students' parents, or run into problems later in they year as a result of not communicating properly with them. It is important to start off every school year by sending a letter home with your students. This note should generally welcome the student to your class, and also give out your contact information. Also, this is a great chance to make any requests for equipment or help that you might have. Some teachers ask parents to send them a list of their child's strengths and weaknesses. It is always a good idea to inform parents at the beginning of the year about your policies on homework, grading, and assessment. Also, an early note is a good chance to mention whatever supplies the students will need for class.

Career Advice and Counseling

One of the common tasks of a business teacher is to provide students with career advice and counseling. Because of a business teacher's area of expertise, students have a right to expect that teachers will be able to dispense valuable information about careers. In order to do so, a business teacher must stay apprised of changes in the job market, and must be knowledgeable on the responsibilities and functions of various professions. This is not to say that a business teacher must be an expert on every career; on the contrary, one of the most valuable functions a teacher may perform is directing students to on-line or text resources on a certain profession, or setting up a meeting between a student and a member of the community currently working in the student's area of interest.

Job-Shadowing

Job-shadowing is one of the many ways that students can gain some experience in the workplace. In job-shadowing, a student simply follows along with a worker in the field in which they are interested as that worker goes through a normal day. Through shadowing a real worker, students can learn first-hand what skills they will need to hold a certain job and what exactly a job entails. Sometimes, students may discover that they are not as interested in a particular job as they originally thought. For instance, a research study showed that students that originally were interested in fire-fighting often changed their minds once they realized the real, day-to-day life it would involve. One of the limitations of job-shadowing is that students only observe; they do not actually practice any job skills.

Employment Trends

The particular trends in the job market will always be unique to the part of the country in which a business teacher is working, so there is no substitute for staying aware of the employment situation by monitoring the local news and classified ads. That being said, a general trend in the United States over the past few decades has been the loss of manufacturing jobs, coupled with a rise in the demand for technology workers. The service industries in the United States have also seen a sharp raise in employment in recent years. Students can be assured that careers in computer technology will continue to be lucrative and easy to acquire. Students should also be prepared, however, to move to a different location in order to find the career they desire.

Proper Keyboarding Techniques

In order to keyboard properly, there a few basic pointers to keep in mind. First, it is a good idea to clear your workspace of everything that is not essential to the task at hand. You should sit all the way back in your chair, with your back straight and your feet flat in the floor. It is a good idea to place your elbows close to your body, and to have your forearms parallel to the keyboard. You should keep your wrists low, so that they just clear the keyboard. Your body should be positioned so that it is in line with the J-key. You should hold your head straight up, facing the book. With your left hand, you should place your fingertips on the A, S, D, and F keys, and the fingers of your right hand should be on the J, K, and L keys. Your right thumb should be poised above the space bar.

In order to survive in the computer-driven business world, students will have to acquire basic keyboarding skills. While many business classes do not explicitly focus on keyboarding, every class should force students to complete a number of assignments that require word-processing throughout the school year, so that they can develop their keyboarding skills. There are a multitude of texts and computer programs to assist students in this endeavor. Unless a student is interested in becoming a secretary or in pursuing some line of work in which rapid typing is essential, the emphasis should always be on accuracy rather than speed. Students should be encouraged to review and revise their own work rather than rely on the spell-check function.

Macros

A macro is used by a computer to allow one to perform with one keystroke a commonly-performed command that would normally take several keystrokes. Word processing programs often allow the use of macros for editing and formatting. Many users also create macros to insert often-used elements into their documents, for instance tables with a certain number of columns or of a certain size. Typically, word processing programs will have a recorder so that users can enter the commands which they want for their macro to accomplish, and then decide which keystroke will set into motion this action. Users of some programs can create a space for macros on the toolbar, so that they can be enacted with the click of a button.

Production of Business Information

Most businesses rely exclusively on computer systems for the creation of documents and graphics. Whereas before, typewriters were often used to compose short documents, word-processing programs are almost always used these days. Moreover, businesses now have at their disposal sophisticated software packages that allow them to create text documents, databases, spreadsheets, digital graphics, and video footage. Scanners and optical recognition software allow businesses to quickly turn paper documents into electronic format. Most of this software can be operated from a portable computer, so the production of business documents is not limited to a physical office any longer.

Special Office Needs

In the medical and legal fields, huge numbers of documents must be created every day, which necessitates some special services. Specifically, doctors and lawyers rely on transcription service, whether in-house or external, to assist in the creation of records. Oftentimes, a professional will dictate information into a voice recorder, which a transcriptionist then converts into written form. Increasingly, these documents are stored in electronic form, making it possible for them to be easily organized and accessed. Software has also been developed which can take simple voice entries and convert them to text, which can then be proofread and edited by a knowledgeable professional.

Developing Business Statistics

Most businesses rely on statistics to help them chart their past performance and determine the proper actions to take in the future. In fact, one of the fastest-growing areas of the economy is the business analysis sector. Companies in this line of work collect information about a business and compare it with published records of other businesses, to help their client determine how they shape up and how they can improve. The government also keeps extensive records of business statistics, for the purpose of making economic decisions. Increasingly, sophisticated software makes it possible for businesses to predict with a high degree of accuracy their productivity and general financial picture.

Business Software

Businesses use a variety of different software packages to help them accomplish tasks quickly and accurately. Most businesses use some variation of the Office XP package, which includes programs for word processing, spreadsheets, databases, and PowerPoint presentations. Businesses may also use more sophisticated spreadsheet programs, like Excel, or more advanced graphics programs. The accounting department in a business may have special software to help them keep track of financial records, and there are many payroll programs to help monitor employee payment. May businesses have their own unique computer programs designed to help workflow or to manage inventory.

Specialized software -- Some businesses may need to access certain information because of their unique function. Medical and legal businesses, for example, often use sophisticated transcription software to give them access to records and references. Many businesses that used to have extensive filing systems, where hard copies were kept, now keep all of their records electronically. They are then, of course, susceptible to the dangers of a computer malfunction; for this reason, most small businesses have some sort of backup disk where duplicate copies of records are kept. Large businesses often have a contract with their computer provider to create a duplicate computer system in case of some malfunction to the operating system.

Word Processing

Word processing is defined as the use of computers to compose, store, edit, and publish text. Before the advent of word processing, business documentation was an incredibly tedious job. Word processors are most typically used for producing memos and letters, and thus facilitating the flow of information around an office. However, they are also useful for constructing databases, spreadsheets and charts. Studies have indicated that the introduction of word processors has encouraged people to write more, if perhaps not better. There appears to be a tendency to adopt a more conversational tone in word processing than is always appropriate for business communications. There are a few health concerns related to frequent use of word processors, including eyestrain and carpal-tunnel syndrome.

Four different ways to create a new document -- There are four different ways to begin a new document in Word. One way is to simply start up the Word program; the program will open with a blank document. Another way is to click on the button for New Blank Document in the Standard toolbar. Yet another way to create a blank document is to click File, then New while you are in Word. Finally, you can press Control + N. If you would like to use a document template (a blank document with paragraphs and headings already formatted), simply create a new document and then click on the General Templates icon, bringing up the Templates dialog box. You will then be provided with a list of templates from which you can choose.

Two most common ways to enter text into a document -- The two most common ways to enter text into a document are by typing it in or by importing it from another document. Typing is fairly easy in Word, because the AutoCorrect feature alerts the user to potential misspellings and misuses of grammar. Word will correct the spelling of obviously misspelled words, but it will also ask you about words that it believes may be misspelled, and it can learn new words, too. Importing text from another document is a simple process, also: simply use the Copy from the menu or toolbar and move the text from the display window of the original program to the display window of the Word document. It may be necessary when using some programs to save the original text in a new format that is acceptable to Word.

Four main ways to view -- Word gives you a few different ways to look at your document, depending on what you are trying to accomplish. There are four main ways that you can look at a basic document, all of which are accessible from the View menu. The Normal mode is appropriate for periods of typing: it allows you to work on an essentially clean screen without any headers or footers. When you view your document in Web layout, you are seeing what it will look like as a Web page. Print layout has a similar function: it shows you what your document will look like when it is printed. Outline format is fairly self-explanatory; it is the appropriate view for creating an outline to organize data and text.

Scroll bars, screen magnification, and paragraph marks used -- Sometime may want to open up a little space i Word document by removing the horizontal and vertical scroll bars. this, click Tools, then Options, to dis the Options dialog box. Under the v tab, uncheck the boxes for the two s bars and click OK. If you would like change the magnification of the scre click View, and then Zoom, to displa Zoom dialog box. A number of percentages will be displayed, along a setting for Page Width, which will the line of text however long the Wo window is at present. Sometimes, yo may want a visual representation of spacing or the paragraph marks in your document. You can display or hide these by clicking on the paragraph symbol (a backwards P with two vertical lines) on the toolbar.

Standard toolbar -- In order to prevent the user from having to constantly access the menu to perform tasks, Word has developed the Standard toolbar to make a number of common functions accessible by a simple mouse click. The Standard toolbar contains Word's most frequently used commands, beginning with New Blank Document (symbolized by a white sheet of paper), Open (an open file folder, Save (a floppy diskette), E-mail (an envelope and letter), Search (magnifying glass on document with Windows symbol), Print (printer), Preview (magnifying glass on blank document), Spelling and Grammar check (check mark and ABC), Cut (scissors), Copy (two documents), Paste (jar of paste), Format Painter (paintbrush), Undo (arrow looping left), and Redo (arrow looping right).

The buttons that come after the Redo command button on the Standard toolbar, working left to right -- Word has a large and various toolbar, allowing the user to accomplish a number of different tasks ... Working ... at come ... sert ... d infinity ... ur-part ... (graph ... sert ... ph ... ns (two ... g (A with ... ap ... with blue ... marks ... lay ... setting), ... Buttons

Go to Word & learn buttons & Placements & functions!

Do w/ Book in front of me!

Buttons on the formatting toolbar -- In order to facilitate the accomplishment of formatting tasks in Word, the program has a comprehensive toolbar that allows the user to perform tasks with the click of a mouse. The buttons on this toolbar are, from left to right: Style (a display window names the current text style), Font (similar display window), Font Size (display window), Bold (bold B), Italics (italicized I), Underline (underlined U), Align Left, Align Right, and Justify (all symbolized by a representation of their format), Line Spacing (up and down arrows and horizontal lines), Numbering (1, 2, and 3 next to text), Bullets (blue squares next to text), Decrease Indent (arrow moving text left), Increase Indent (arrow moving text right), Outside Border (square), Highlight (highlighter), Font

Color (A with red underline), and More Buttons (small down arrow).

Tabs on the ruler -- In Word, the ruler is the numbered bar along the side of the document that defines the margins and the tabs of the document. You can use the ruler to change the margins or the indenture. To hide or display the ruler, click View, then Ruler. There are five different tabs that are displayed on the ruler. The left tab, which resembles an L, moves the text to the right edge of the page as you type. The center tab, which looks like an upside-down T, centers the text around the tab. The right tab, which looks like a backward L, moves text towards the left edge of the page. The decimal tab, which looks like an inverted T with a dot next to it), aligns all of the numbers in a column by the decimal point. The bar tab, which looks like a straight vertical line, draws a vertical line on the document.

How to use the indents -- The Tab Selection button in Word has a couple of different options to allow the user to indent paragraphs to their specifications. The First Line Indent icon, which looks like an inverted house, allows you to set the left margin of the first line in every paragraph. The Hanging Indent icon is a big U on the Tab Selection button, and a house above the Left Indent button on the ruler. It allows the user to set the left margin for every line by the first in a paragraph. There are also two other indentation options on the ruler, represented by the Left and Right Indent icons. These allow you to define the left and right margins of every line in a particular paragraph. It should be noted that the ruler can only display one indent per paragraph.

Ways to move through a document -- There are a few different ways to navigate through a Word document. The quickest way is usually just to use the mouse. The vertical scroll bar on the right side of the screen allows you to quickly scroll up or down (the single arrows) or to move up or down a page at a time (the double arrows). The keyboard can also be used to navigate a Word document: the arrows move the cursor, obviously, but by pressing Ctrl + the up or down arrow you can jump up or down a paragraph at a time. When you know exactly where you want to go in a document, it may be most efficient to use the Go To command. This command can take you to specific line number, page number, or bookmark, simply by pressing Ctrl + G.

Selecting text with a mouse -- In order to work with text in a Word document, you first have to know how to select that text with the mouse or keyboard. The easiest way to select text is simply by dragging the mouse: just drag the mouse from one end of the desired text to the other, with the left button of the mouse held down. There are some more sophisticated ways to select text with a mouse in Word: double-clicking at the beginning of a word selects that word and the space after it; holding down the Ctrl key and clicking inside a sentence will select that entire sentence; triple-clicking inside a paragraph will select that entire paragraph; clicking to the far left of a line of the first word in a line will select that whole line; double-clicking to the far left of a paragraph will select the entire paragraph.

Selecting text with a keyboard -- Sometimes, it may be more convenient or precise to select text using the keyboard rather than the mouse. There are a few basic key commands for selecting text that every user should know. Pressing Shift + the right or left arrow selects the character to the right or left of the cursor. Shift +Home selects all of the current line to the left of the cursor, while Shift + End selects all of the text to the right of the cursor. Shift + Page Up or Page Down selects a screenful of text either up or down from the cursor. Ctrl + Shift + the right or left arrow selects the word to the right or left of the cursor, while Ctrl + Shift + Home or End selects all of the text from the cursor to either the beginning or end of the document. Ctrl + A selects the entire document.

Deleting text -- There are two keys that can be used to delete text in a Word document. The Backspace key will delete characters to the left of the cursor, while the Delete key will eliminate characters to the right of the cursor. One way in which words are often accidentally deleted is by a mistaken press of the Insert key. This key will shift the computer from Insert mode, in which new typing in the middle of a document will push the old typing to the right, to Overtype mode, in which new type goes over whatever had been there before. If you would like to undo an accidental or ill-advised deletion, simply click Edit, then Undo, or just click the Undo icon (an arrow looping left) in the Standard toolbar. This command will reverse whatever was your last command.

Copying text -- Sometimes, you may want to duplicate part of a document, or move chunks of text from one area of a document to another. To do this, first select the text that you would like to manipulate. Then you may either cut or copy the selected text: cutting will remove the text from this location, whereas copying will keep the text where it is while allowing you to place it elsewhere in the document as well. Both these tasks can be performed by right-clicking on the selected text and choosing from the pop-up menu. Now, move the cursor to the spot where you would like to place the text and Paste it, either by right-clicking and choosing Paste, or be clicking the Paste icon in the Standard toolbar.

Search/replace and spell check -- There are a few basic word processing commands that every business student needs to be familiar with. The search/replace command enables the user to find a particular word or phrase when it is used in a document, and then replace it with another word. The search function is particularly useful for finding common misspellings, or overused words. Spell check is another command that students will find to be very useful. It simply orders the word processing program to go through the document looking for any misspelled words. There is always a danger, of course, that students will rely too heavily on the spell check command. The computer may identify unfamiliar words as misspelled, and may recommend new spellings that deviate from the word the student originally intended.

Spell check and grammar check -- The Word program will alert you when it feels that you may have made a mistake in spelling or grammar. A green wavy line indicates a possible grammar error, while a wavy red line indicates a possible mistake in spelling. To address these problems, right-click the mouse while the pointer is over the word or sentence in question. At this point, a pop-up box will appear in which Word describes the problem it sees and suggests a solution. For spelling mistakes, you may agree with Word's suggested spellings, or you may indicate to Word that the word is spelled correctly, but is simply unknown to the computer. On questions of grammar, you may accept the solution offered by Word, you may make your own changes in a display box and enter them into the document, or you may tell Word to ignore the error.

Find and replace text -- One of the useful features of the Word program is that it allows you to find a particular word and phrase every time it appears in a document. To find a word, click Edit, then

Find, or simply press Ctrl + F. At this point, a Find and Replace dialog box will appear. Enter the word or phrase that you are looking for into the Find What box, or you can click on the down arrow to see a list of your recent searches. After you press Find Next, the program will find the first instance in the text. Then, if you would like to replace the text, enter the new text into the Replace With box. By clicking Find Next, you will substitute the text. If you are absolutely certain it is appropriate, you may select Replace All to have every instance of the original text replaced.

Adjusting fonts -- One of the ways you can personalize your documents is by adjusting the font: that is, the appearance of each letter. Word is equipped with a wide array of fonts, which can be accessed by clicking the Font list box on the Formatting toolbar. It should be noted that choosing a font will have an effect on the size of the type; some fonts demand to be shown in a large format, whereas others are more appropriate for small print. For the most part, business documents will be in either Times New Roman or MS Sans Serif. To change the font of a particular section of text, simply highlight the text, click the Font list box on the Formatting toolbar, and select your font. You will also want to adjust the font size by clicking on the Font Size list box on the same toolbar.

Aligning text -- Word allows you to choose how you would like to align the text of your document. Although most documents should be aligned to the left, it is sometimes appropriate to set up a group of words in another way. Word gives you four options for aligning text: left-align, center-align, right-align, and justify. When text is left-aligned, the left margin will be a straight line, while the right line will be uneven. In a right-aligned document, the format is exactly the opposite. In a centered text, each line is centered in the middle of the page, so that both the right and left margins will be uneven. When text is justified, both the left and right margins are straight; words may need to be somewhat unnaturally spaced to achieve this. All of these can be accessed from the Formatting toolbar.

Indenting text and Format Painter -- It may occasionally be a good idea to indent a certain chunk of text in a Word document, perhaps to set it off from the rest of the text. In academic papers, long quotations are often indented to distinguish them from the work of the author. In order to do this, first select the text you would like to indent; Word will indent an entire paragraph even if you only highlight a section. Then, click the Indent or Decrease Indent buttons to move the text to either the right or the left. If you are pleased with the formatting on a particular piece of text, and would like to have the same formatting on another piece of text, you may do so by using the Format Painter on the Formatting toolbar. To do this, highlight the first batch of text and click the paintbrush icon on the toolbar; then, select the text you would like to format.

Formatting templates -- Rather than force you to make every formatting decision on a document, Word is equipped with a few shortcuts that allow you to easily select some commonly used formats. There are three main decisions that a user must make when settling on a formatting template: themes, style templates, and styles in general. By adjusting the theme, the user is adjusting the color and appearance of any numbers, bullets, horizontal lines, or background of a document. The style templates are simple formats for common documents, like fax cover pages, resumes, and business letters. By adjusting the style, the user is altering the format for particular paragraphs, including the margins, font size, and any underlining.

Theme dialog box -- Word allows the user to adjust the decorative appearance of a document, otherwise known as the theme. To choose a theme, click on Format, then Theme, calling up the Theme dialog box. Once there, you can select a theme from the Choose a Theme list (Word will provide you with a sample of that theme when you click on it). By checking various boxes, you may add or remove colors in the document, add or remove graphics to make the document more lively, and add or remove a background picture. Once you have settled on a theme, clicking OK will apply it to your document. Altering the theme of a Word document does not make any substantial change to the content; it is only appropriate when you are interested in making an attractive presentation.

Using a style template -- If you are creating a common sort of document in Word, you may want to use a style template. There are style templates available for faxes, memos, proposals, cover letters, resumes, and other frequently-used documents. To select a style template, simply click on Format, and then Theme. Once the Theme dialog box appears, click on the Style Gallery button, which will display the Style Gallery dialog box. Here, you can scroll through and select one of the common style templates. By clicking Document, you can see what your present document will look like with the selected format; clicking Example will show you how a generic document looks in the selected format; clicking Style Samples will create an array of the various styles that make up that template.

Formatting paragraphs with different styles -- When you alter the Style of a Word document, you are altering the general appearance of the text, including the font and the size of the type. To select a style, simply utilize the Style box on the Formatting toolbar. First, move the cursor to whatever paragraph you would like to be affected by the formatting. If you haven't typed anything, Word will format whatever you type next. Some of the commonly-used formats are for a signature, for a subject heading, for a numbered list, or for a return address. Simply click on the style you would like to use and Word will format it immediately. This is a useful method of formatting if you are composing a simple business document but do not want to use a comprehensive style template to affect every aspect.

List set up -- At some point, you may want to use Word to create a list for work or for your personal life. You can make two different kinds of lists: numbered or bulleted. In order to set up a list, first select the text you would like to have made into a list. If you do not select nay text, Word will simply turn whatever text you type next into a list. Click Format, then Bullets and Numbering, which will bring up the Bullets and Numbering dialog box. This box will provide a number of numbered or bulleted list types from which you can choose. Once you have selected the type of list you prefer, clicking OK will immediately convert the text into that list format. If you don't really care what style of list Word uses, just click the Numbering or Bullets icon in the Formatting toolbar and start typing. This will tell Word to start a list in the default format.

Headers and footers -- Users of Word can make their documents look more sophisticated by adding headers and footers containing the publication title, chapter title, page number, or author's name. Adding headers and footers allows you to include this helpful information without having to type it on every page. To view the headers and footers, either click View, then Header and Footer, or View, then Print Layout. To add a header or footer, select View, the Header and Footer, to display the Header and Footer text box. You can then type whatever text you would like, or click a button to have Word display the date, page number, or number of pages. You can also toggle between Header and Footer on this screen.

Page numbering -- If you simply tell Word to number the pages in a document, it will print an Arabic numeral (that is, 1, 2, 3...) on each page. You may want to modify the numbering, however, to begin at a certain page or to be expressed in Roman numerals or letters. To do this, you have to use the Page Number Format button on the Header and Footer toolbar. First, select View, then Header and Footer, calling up the Header and Footer toolbar. Next, highlight the page numbers that appear in either the Header or Footer text box. Click on the Format Page Number button to bring up the Page Number Format dialog box. The options in this box will allow you to select a page numbering style, or to designate where you would like the page numbering to begin.

Inserting graphics -- There are several different ways to insert graphics into a Word document. By using the Clip Art feature, you can insert any picture from the Clip Art gallery. You can also insert graphics by calling up those that have been stored in files from other programs. Using the AutoShapes command will draw one of many generic shapes in the document. Using WordArt gives you the chance to create text that appears in different colors and shapes. You can also use the New Drawing command to create original drawings from geometric shapes, lines, and WordArt. Word gives you the option to add digital images that have been created by a scanner or a digital camera. The Chart command allows you to add a chart or graph to represent data.

Clip-art -- Clip-art is ready-made imagery that can be easily inserted into a Word document. Office XP will organize all of the clip-art in various programs into a comprehensive Media Gallery. Before you can start adding clip-art to your documents, you have to tell the Media Gallery which folders you would like to search for art. After you click Insert, then Picture, then Clip Art, the Add Clips to Gallery button will appear. By clicking on the Options button, an Auto Import Settings button will emerge, which will display all of the folders in which Media Gallery can search for pictures. Once you have selected all of the appropriate folders you can click Catalog and the Media gallery will organize your clip-art.

Adding clip-art to a text document is an easy way to enhance the appearance. To do so, first select Insert, then Picture, then Clip Art. This will bring up the Insert Clip Art window. From there, you can type a few words into the Search text box that describe the kind of clip art that you would like to use. Once you have selected the image you would like to display, move the cursor to the point in the Word document where you would like to insert the graphic. Then, click the down arrow next to the image, calling up a short menu. From this menu, click Insert. Once you have confirmed that your chosen graphic has been inserted into the document, you may close the Insert Clip Art window.

Inserting already existing graphic files and Auto Shapes -- Word makes it quite easy to insert your own graphics into a Word document. All you have to do is place the cursor where you would like to insert the image, and then select Insert, then Picture, then From File. After the Insert Picture dialog box appears, find the file you would like to insert and click Insert. Word also has a set of basic shapes (square, circles, ovals) that you can insert into a document. To place these Auto Shapes into your document, move the cursor to the appropriate location and click Insert, then picture, then Auto Shapes. This will bring up an Auto Shapes toolbar, from which you can select an image. Then, move the mouse back to the right spot, hold down the left button, and drag the mouse over to indicate how large you would like the graphic to be.

Manipulating pictures -- Sometimes, a graphic that is inserted into a text document may have the unpleasant effect of covering up the text underneath. To remedy this situation, click on the picture and hit the right mouse button, calling up a pop-up menu. Select Format, and when the Format dialog box appears, go to the Layout tab. Select a style of text wrapping from the available options, and click OK. If you need to move a picture within a document, just click on the picture, so that the handles become evident around it. Then, hold down the left mouse button as you drag the mouse pointer to the place where you would like the graphic to appear. Releasing the left mouse button will place the graphic in the desired location.

Checking formatting -- Formatting a document in Word can be a tricky process, so it is never a bad idea to take a look at your work before you print your document. If you notice an area of text that is incorrect, you can check its formatting by using the Reveal Formatting pane. To access this pane, highlight the text you are interested in adjusting and click Format, then Reveal Formatting. This will bring up the reveal Formatting pane. Here, you can select Show All Formatting Marks, which will allow you to see every single space and paragraph mark in your document. If necessary, you can make adjustments to Alignment, Font, or other formatting aspects by clicking on the appropriate link. Clicking on the Close box will cause the Reveal Formatting pane to disappear.

Mail merge -- The Mail Merge feature in Word allows you to send a standard letter to a list of different people or businesses. To do so, click Tools, then Mail Merge, bringing up the Mail Merge Helper dialog box. If your document is already set up, you can go ahead and click on Data Source (otherwise, use the Main document feature to set up). The Create Data Source dialog box will open, allowing you to enter what information you would like to include for each recipient. When you are satisfied with the various fields, click on Save As, then List, and Word will proceed to letting you enter the data for each of your recipients. Once you have finished entering all of the data, just go to the Insert Merge Field menu and place the various fields where you would like them. When you print the document, the computer should print a different copy for each recipient.

Saving a document -- To save a document in Word, you can simply press Ctrl + S, click the Save button on the Standard toolbar, or click File, then Save. If you are saving a document for the first time, you will be asked to enter a name for the file. Sometimes, you may want to save a document under a new name or as a different type of file. To do this, simply open the document and then click File, then Save As. Type a new name for your file in the File Name box, or select a new file type from the list in the Save as Type box. This may be appropriate of you are going to have to use the file in another program, like WordPerfect. File names cannot contain slashes, backslashes, question marks, quotation marks, colons, or semicolons.

The backup feature -- For users who feel that their system may be unstable, Word has included an easy way to create an automatic backup copy of a document. This backup feature will create a duplicate copy of a document every time it is saved. The backup copy will be called "Backup of [file name]," and will be stored in the same folder as the original document. To turn on the backup feature, select the Tool menu, and then click on Options. This will call up the Options dialog box. Here, click on the Save tab and, once there, make sure that there is a check mark in the Always Create Backup Copy box. Creating a backup file may allow you to retrieve data in the event of a computer crash.

Printing -- When you think that you are ready to print a completed Word document, it is always a good idea to use the Print Preview first. To do this, select File, then Print Preview. A display window will be created, in which you can survey the document to ensure that it is ready to be printed. Before printing, you may want to define the page margins and paper size; this can be done by accessing the Page Setup dialog box under the File menu. Once you are ready to print, click on File, then Print (or just press Ctrl + P), to bring up the Print dialog box. Make sure that the printer selected is the right one, and that the computer is set to print whatever pages you require. You can also adjust the number of copies that will be printed. Once you are satisfied with the print settings, clicking on OK will begin printing.

Proofreading symbols -- Proofreaders in the United States have developed a set of simple symbols and abbreviations that allow them to quickly annotate documents and indicate changes that need to be made. Some of the most common of these are as follows: a caret, which looks like a vertical "greater than" symbol (means insert something here); a number sign (insert a space); slash (delete), eq + number sign (space evenly); stet (let stand); tr (transpose); [(set farther to the left);] (set farther to right); = (align horizontally); // (align vertically); paragraph symbol (start a new paragraph); cap (put into capital letters); sp (spelling error); OK? (note to author, asking "Is this what you meant?").

Works

Starting a database --There are a couple of different ways to start a database in Works. The first way is to double-click the Works shortcut on the desktop screen, and then click the Database icon at the top of the screen. The other way is to click Start, and then select Programs, Microsoft Works, and Microsoft Works Database. Once the program starts, you will be asked to select from between a blank database, a template, and an existing database. If you want to define each field in your new database, you should select blank database. If you would like to pick from a list of pre-existing databases, simply select template. If you would like to make adjustments or additions to a database that you have already constructed, select existing database.

Controls on the Works database window -- The main window in the Works database program has a number of elements that can be adjusted. The menu is simply the menu system found in all other Works programs. The toolbar has a number of the menu options available for instant access. The editing window shows all of the data values contained in a record, and allows the user to alter them. The list of records will appear only in List view. In this format, each row represents a single record. The Zoom control allows the user to magnify or shrink the scale of the database. The status bar gives you help in the event that you make an abnormal entry, and also tells you whether you have the Caps Lock and Num Lock buttons depressed.

The steps involved in creating the first field -- Works provides a wizard dialog box system to help you begin a new database. The first step is to type the name of the first field in the Field Name box. It then allows you to enter the format for that field; that is, whether the field will contain numbers, words, or something else. This enables Works to alert you if you make an abnormal entry later in the database. You may be asked whether data fields should include a default value, if there is likely to be a certain value that is used most of the time in that field. Once all this is done, you can click the Add button. Works will then enter a column on the database for the field you have just created, and will clear the dialog box so that you can begin working on a new field.

Editing -- One of the best things about a database is that it is extremely easy to modify information that is proved to be incorrect. You may use either List or Form view to make changes. First, simply navigate to the record that needs to be changed. In List view, this is done by scrolling; in Form view, you may either search for the record or use the Record box. Then, click on the field that needs to be changed and press F2. At this point, the program will switch to Edit mode. Then, enter the new data value, and press enter to save the changes to the data value and update the field. It should be noted that the user can correct fields as well as specific values in Works; by selecting Insert Field, a new field can be entered between already existing fields.

Finding and organizing records -- There are a couple of different ways to find and organize records in a Works database. To sort records, one just has to click Record, then Sort Records. At this point, Works will show a dialog box, from which the user can select what criteria he or she would like the records to be sorted by (for example, last name, descending order, ascending order). The beauty of the computer database is that it can instantly sort data, so the user can try out a number of different arrangements depending on his or her interest. If he or she just wants to find a particular record, this can be done by clicking Edit, then Find, to display the Find dialog box. Then, the user simply types the text that he or she is looking for and Works will locate it.

Creating database reports -- Databases can not only store and display data, they are also capable of producing database reports. Creating a report in Works is a simple process. First, click Tools, then Report Creator. This will call up the first screen of the Report Creator. Enter a name for the new report and select OK to continue, bringing up the Report Creator dialog box. Then choose whether the report should be presented in Portrait or Landscape format. Next, select the fields that you would like to be included in the report. Then, use the Sorting tab to determine how you would like the data to be arranged. Then, enter any summaries of data that you would like the program to make, as for instance if you would like certain values to be added together. At this point, you can generate the report by clicking Report view.

Printing databases -- Sometimes it is handy to have a hard copy of a particular database you have created in Works. You can print out lists of records, you can print out the records as forms, or you can print out any reports that you have generated. It is always a good idea to click File, then Print, rather than just clicking the Print icon in the toolbar, so that you can double-check that the print settings are appropriate. Once you have selected File, then Print, a Print dialog box will be displayed. In this dialog, you can specify what kind of document you would like as well as any specifications that should be made and the number of copies that you would like to have printed. This dialog box can also be accessed by pressing Control and P at the same time.

Spreadsheets -- Spreadsheets are computer files in which numbers can be manipulated and put into graphical form. Many business teachers find them especially useful when teaching basic accounting principles. One of the advantages of computer spreadsheet programs is that numbers can be changed easily, allowing students to construct various hypothetical situations. For example, a teacher might ask students to develop basic profit and loss accounts for a business, and then see how varying amounts of sales and production costs affect the final profit or loss. Students can implement simple formulae on spreadsheets, such that data can be plugged in and an answer immediately given. Spreadsheets, then, are a great way to help students master the fundamentals of some rather dry accounting subjects.

Starting a spreadsheet -- Spreadsheets are invaluable for any number of tasks, from arranging a budget to making financial forecasts. The spreadsheet program in Works is generally considered to be simpler than Excel, and therefore a better learning tool for introductory business students. In order to start a spreadsheet in Works, you may double-click the Works shortcut on the desktop to run the Task Launcher. Then, click the Spreadsheet icon at the top of the screen. Another way to access the program is by double-clicking a Works Spreadsheet document in Explorer, or on your desktop. A third way is to click Start, then Programs, then Works, then Works Spreadsheet. Instead of pressing Start, one can always press one of the Windows keys on the keyboard.

Features of the spreadsheet window -- The spreadsheet window in Works has a few features that even the casual user should be familiar with. The menu, at the top of the screen, includes all the commands typical of a Works program. The toolbar, and there is only one for spreadsheet applications, allows the user to access certain commands without going to the menu. The editing window, at the bottom of the screen, has all of the spreadsheet cells into which will be entered numbers, text, graphics, or formulas. The row and column header buttons select entire rows at a time, and allow you to adjust the dimensions. The Zoom control allows the user to magnify or shrink the screen. The status bar informs you of possible commands, as well as letting you know of the Caps Lock and Num Lock buttons are selected.

Navigating and entering data -- There are a number of shortcut keys that can be used in Works, to prevent the user from having to constantly shift between keyboard and mouse. The essential keyboard commands for spreadsheet use are the arrows (move the cursor from cell to cell), Home (moves the cursor to the beginning of the row), Ctrl + Home (moves the cursor to the beginning of the worksheet), Ctrl + End (moves the cursor to the last cell in the worksheet that contains a value), Page Up and Page Down (move the cursor from screen to screen), Enter (moves the cursor one cell down), Tab (moves the cursor one cell to the right), Shift + Enter (moves the cursor one cell up), Shift + Tab (moves the cursor one cell to the left), and Ctrl + Arrow key (moves the cursor to the last cell in any range that contains data.

Selecting and editing cells -- Most of the time, it is most efficient to use the mouse to select cells in the Works spreadsheet. In order to select a single cell, simply click on that cell. In order to select a range of cells, click on a cell at one end of the range and drag the mouse in the appropriate direction. In order to select a columns of cells, simply click on the alphabetic heading button at the top of the column. In order to select a row of cells, just click the numeric heading button on the left side of the row. After the appropriate cell or range has been selected, the contents can be edited by simply deleting them, adding text or numbers to them, or copying data from another cell into the selected one.

Choosing a number format -- When a user works with the number format in a spreadsheet, he or she is adjusting how a cell will display numbers; for instance, whether they will be registered as a percent, a dollar amount, or a date. In order to adjust a number format, the user should first select the cell, row, or column that will be affected. Then, click Format, then Number, to display the Format Cells dialog box. Once this dialog box is displayed, the user can type in the kind of formatting that he or she would like to implement. Works will provide an example of the selected style so that the user can confirm their selection. Then, he or she can click OK to apply this formatting style.

Changing cell alignment -- When working with a Works spreadsheet, the user may want to adjust the horizontal or vertical alignment of the text or the numbers in certain cells. In order to do so, first select the cell, row, or column that you desire to format. Then, click Format, then Alignment, to call up the Alignment tab of the Format Cells dialog box. Next, select the desired horizontal and vertical position within the cells. Unless adjustments are made, text will be flushed left and numbers will be flushed right. The user also may want to ensure that Works does not wrap any text values that do not fit on a single line; this can be done by unchecking Wrap Text within a Cell. Once the user is satisfied with his or her new alignments, clicking OK will apply the new formatting.

Changing text format -- Sometimes, a spreadsheet user may want to distinguish the contents of some cells, or create title headings for certain rows or columns. These functions can be performed by adjusting the text format. To do this, first select the cell, row, or column that is to be reformatted. Then, select the Format, then Font button to call up the Font tab of the Format Cells dialog box. Next, from the Select Font list, you can choose the appropriate font and style. At this point, you may also select the size of text, the color, and the presence of any underlining or striking-through. A newly created format can be made the automatic format by selecting the Set as Default button. Once you are satisfied with the text format, clicking OK applies it.

Formatting borders -- Sometimes, when you want to draw attention to a certain cell, row, or column, it is a good idea to alter the borders that surround it. This can be easily done in Works by first selecting the area that you would like to format, and then clicking Format, then Border, to call up the Border tab of the Format Cells dialog box. Next, you can select the color of the border by picking one from a scrolling list. You may also adjust the line type, to make the line surrounding the border thicker or thinner as desired. By clicking the Border Location buttons, you can determine whether you would like a standard outline border, an inside grid, or no border at all. If you would like to design a border of your own, you can do this by adjusting the Border Location buttons; the results will be shown in a display window.

Adjusting shading -- Some spreadsheet authors like to indicate the various sections of a spreadsheet by shading them variously. Adjusting the shading of a spreadsheet is quite simple. First, highlight whatever cell, row, or column you would like to adjust. Then, click

Format, then Shading, to call up the Shading tab of the Format Cells dialog box. From this dialog box, you may select a color from a list, or choose Automatic to have Works select a contrasting color for you. You may then click on the color to create any pattern that you would like. Once you have decided on a color and pattern, and are satisfied with the look displayed in the Preview window, you may apply the shading by clicking OK.

Making easy calculations -- One of the most important applications of a spreadsheet is its ability to calculate values when you enter in simple formulas with which it can work. Formulas in Works will always begin with an equal sign; so, as a simple example, the formula to divide cell A1 by cell B1 would be =A1/B1. Because more complex formulas can be quite difficult to create, Works has included a helpful device called Easy Calc. To access Easy Calc, simply visit it in the menu under Tools or click the little calculator in the toolbar. Then, select the function you would like to have performed, and the cells that will be used in the calculation. Then, indicate where you would like the results of the calculation to be displayed. At this point, clicking on Finish will create the formula and enter it into the spreadsheet.

Adding a chart -- Often, it is useful to create a visual representation of the data that is contained in your spreadsheet. In order to do this, first select whatever group of cells you would like to be included in the chart. Then, click Tools, then Create New Chart, to display the New Chart dialog box. After that, you can click on the thumbnail that represents the kind of chart that you would like to create, and a Preview window will show you how your finished chart will look. Then, type a title for your chart and adjust the border by enabling the Show Border check box. By clicking on the Advanced Options tab, you may make any other fine-tunings you would like to your chart. Once you are finished, clicking OK creates and displays the chart.

Printing -- Many times, a spreadsheet author will want to have a hard copy of their documents that they can have on file or distribute to colleagues or students. It is always a good idea to first click Print Preview under the File menu so that you can get an idea of what the document will look like once it has been printed. That way, you can go back and make adjustments if you are not satisfied. You can print from this screen, or you can click the Print icon on the toolbar or select the print option in the File menu. If you would like instead to send the spreadsheet to another person via email, you can do so by clicking File, the Send, and attaching the document to your message. This is a great way to save paper.

Reprographics

Reprographics is simply the reproduction of printed materials using high-speed printers and printing presses. Reprographic services may be needed by all businesses, but especially by those in the fields of construction, engineering, and architecture, in which large-scale plans may need to be reproduced many times with a high degree of clarity. Today, the top reprographic firms offer digital reproduction of fine art, digital photography reproduction, quick, massive commercial printing, and help with the construction of point-of-purchase displays. Moreover, reprographic firms help facilitate the transfer of reproduced documents by helping with delivery and logistics.

Processing Mail

Despite the growing popularity of electronic document transfer, there is still a great need for equipment to aid businesses in processing physical mail. Most businesses that handle a high volume of mail are likely to have a mail sorter and possibly a mail opener. A mail sorter is programmed to separate mail into various departments, making it possible to expedite it around the company. Businesses that have to send out a great deal of mail are likely to have a letter sealer, an automatic addresser for mass mailings, a postage machine, and postage scales. With these latter two devices, a business can measure and pay their own postage on large packages, and apply a sticker to the outgoing package indicating that postage has been paid.

Simulation Productivity

Recently, software has been developed that allows businesses to simulate their operations, and thereby get a better idea of what their productivity is likely to be and where they can make improvements. In simulation modeling, a small computer model is created using all the known elements of the operational system, and then it is run so that the business managers can observe it. Simulation software is most commonly used to model manufacturing operations, since it is easy to predict all of the variables in a simple manufacturing task. However, system models are being increasingly implemented by other sectors of the economy, including the service industry. Many health care providers currently employ simulation software to help them achieve their productivity goals.

Computer Hardware

In the world of computers, hardware is any machinery or equipment. A computer requires both hardware and software to function. Hardware is distinguished by being physically tangible, and includes accessories like floppy disk drives, hard drives, CD-ROM drives, sound cards, video cards, modems, keyboards, mice, monitors, and printers. The quality of a computer's hardware affects how well its software can operate. Computers with larger hard drives, for instance, can store more information and handle more work. Computers with larger RAM can juggle more tasks simultaneously. A fast CPU allows the computer to process information and run programs more quickly. A business teacher should make sure that students are familiar with the basic types of computer hardware.

Computer Software

Computer software is the set of instructions delivered to the computer's hardware (the physical machinery of the computer) that allows the computer to accomplish certain tasks. A series of instructions that performs a particular task is known as a program. For most general types of computer users, there are three types of software. Platform software is the basic set of programs that allow a user to interact with the computer. This includes operating systems, device drivers, and the basic input-output system. Application software is special task programs, like word processors or video games. Typically, application software must be purchased separately from a computer. User-written software includes things like spreadsheet templates, word-processing macros, and other small programs created by the user to speed up work.

Analog and Digital

When something is referred to as being analog, it means that it is a representation that in some way resembles the thing that it represents. For example, and analog watch represents the motion of the planet by the revolution of a hand around some central axis; an analog telephone turns the vibrations of the human voice into electrical vibrations with a similar shape. For a long time, technology basically consisted of analog devices. In recent decades, however, there has been a trend towards making devices digital in their operations. Digital equipment makes a numerical representation of the original: the time becomes a series of numbers rather than the motions of hands, and the human voice is encoded in a dense collection of numerical data. Digital information is much easier to process, record, and replicate.

Bits and Bytes

A bit, or binary digit, is the smallest unit of computer storage. It is either a one or a zero, the two elements that make up binary code. Physically, a bit is simply a transistor, a magnetic domain on a disk, a high or low voltage in a circuit, or a reflective spot on a compact disk. Bits are used as a measure of how much data a computer can process or transmit, or as a measure of the computer's memory capacity. When bits are referred to in this latter sense, they are usually described in terms of bytes, groups of eight bits. A byte, or binary table, is meant to be the smallest unit of storage that can be considered by a computer. Business teachers should ensure that their students are up to date on the memory and processing speed requirements for all of the software that they are likely to need to accomplish their work.

Peripheral Devices

A peripheral device is any component of a computer, excluding the motherboard, CPU, or working memory. Peripherals may include disks, monitors, keyboards, mice, printers, scanners, tape drives, microphones, speakers, cameras, and many other things. Peripherals are added to a computer to expand its capabilities. Typically, peripheral devices are seen as optional, although many would argue that a keyboard is fairly necessary. Business teachers should be able to provide for their students some experience working with the more common peripherals that may be of use, like scanners and tape drives. Most businesses use scanners for creating advertisements, among other things, and almost every business has some sort of back-up tape system to ensure that important information is protected.

Floppy and Hard Disks

Information may be stored on a computer on either a floppy or hard disk. A floppy disk is a reusable magnetic medium that is generally obsolete these days. Most businesses use CD-ROMs of they have a need for portable, tangible data storage media. For the most part, though, businesses rely on their hard disk drives for the storage of data. Hard disk drives are made from aluminum or glass platter coated with a magnetic material, on which large amounts of data can be stored. It is much faster to retrieve information from hard disk drives than from floppy. In the past decade, the size and speed of hard drives has improved to the point that, along with the easy file transferability made possible by the internet, they have essentially made floppy disks unnecessary.

Modems

A modem is a computer device that sends information, usually digital data, over some network connection. The word modem is a combination of the words modulator and demodulator. Older, analog modems take digital data and convert them into audio tones that can be transferred over a telephone line. More common these days are cable and DSL modems, which use different means to transmit a greater amount of data at a higher speed. Cable modems connect with the internet through an Ethernet port, which have a much greater bandwidth than a normal telephone port.

DSL (digital subscriber line) modems are tailored to download information extremely quickly, although they may be slow in uploading.

Bandwidth

When internet experts are discussing bandwidth, they are simply referring to the amount of data that a system can transmit at a given time. High bandwidth means that a computer can transmit data very quickly, or can transmit multiple streams of data at the same time. Typically, bandwidth is only as good as the weakest link in the network chain. In digital systems, bandwidth is typically measured in bits per second (bps). The term bandwidth should not lead one to assume that is only applies to systems connected to the internet by a cable; bandwidth also applies to wireless connections.

Ports

A serial port is a socket on a computer that is used to transfer data one bit at a time. Serial ports have been used to connect modems, mice, printers, keyboards, and other external devices to a computer. The serial port has recently been overshadowed, however, by parallel and USB ports. Parallel ports operate in a similar manner to serial ports, with the exception that they can transfer eight bits (one byte) of data at a time. Most current computers have at least one parallel port for a printer, scanner, or other external device. Increasingly more popular, however, are USB ports. USB (universal serial bus) ports can transfer 12 megabytes of data every second. They are quickly becoming the standard way of hooking up printers and modems.

Digital Cameras

A digital camera transmits pictures directly to a computer or records them onto a disk without using film. Digital cameras have largely overtaken regular cameras as the preferred way to perform basic photographic functions. The main consideration regarding digital cameras is the number of pixels contained in the image (a pixel is a graphical dot that makes up an image). The image on a TV screen is about 400 x 600 pixels, whereas a good 35mm slide is about 2000 x 3000 pixels. A digital camera generally falls somewhere in between these two. A digital camera can usually store hundred of images at a time, which can be transferred to a computer via a USB port. Digital images can also be previewed on an LCD screen found on the back of most digital cameras.

Intranet and TCP/IP

An intranet is any network that functions in a manner similar to the internet, but is restricted to a certain pool of users. Intranets may or may not be connected to the internet at large. These smaller networks are extremely popular in business; companies frequently use them to set up channels for distributing information throughout their organization. This is possible both because inexpensive servers have become available in recent years, and because the development of TCP/IP software has made it possible to easily set up networks. TCP/IP is a protocol for communications that establishes a standard mode of address that allows different computers to interact with one another. TCP/IP stands for transmission control protocol/ internet protocol.

ROM

ROM stands for read-only memory. This, as the name indicates, is memory on a computer that can be read but cannot be altered. A computer will hold onto information stored in ROM even when the power is turned off. The user or the computer manufacturer only needs place information in ROM one time; it will remain there forever. For this reason, ROM memory space is mainly used for the storage of the most essential programs for running the computer, those which are unlikely to require frequent updating. At present, most ROMs look much like random access memory chips. Although ROM is increasingly becoming obsolete in favor of external storage devices, many computers, video-game systems, and other computer-based technology still rely on ROM to maintain important data.

RAM

RAM stands for random access memory. It is pronounced in the same way as the term for a male sheep. A computer's RAM is composed of small memory chips linked to the motherboard of the computer. Whenever a computer user accesses a particular program from the hard drive, it is moved from the hard drive to the RAM, as it is much faster for a computer to read data from RAM than from the permanent hard drive. It makes sense, then, that the more RAM a computer has, the more large and complex programs it will be able to run at the same time. RAM can be thought of as a sort of short-term memory; if your computer can hold a number of tasks present at the same time, it will be able to function more effectively. Many experts say that adding RAM to a computer is better than improving CPU.

CD-ROM

CD-ROM stands for compact disc- read only memory. This is a data storage format wherein text, graphics, and audio files can be stored on a plastic disc. CD-ROMs use a different format for recording data than do audio CDs. Most computers have a CD-ROM connected to the motherboard. CD-ROMs can hold 650 MB of data, which is about the same as 250,000 pages of text. The data is encoded at microscopic size, which is why so much can be placed on each disc. The data is recorded in binary code, as a series of bumps entered onto the surface of the plastic disc; a laser then "reads" these bumps through reflection and transmits the data. There are a great number of business programs and simulations available in CD-ROM format.

CPU

CPU stands for central processing unit. Put simply, it is the part of a computer that actually does the "computing." Most computers have their entire CPU stored on a single chip. A CPU's operation consists of the actions of its two main components: the control unit and the various execution units. A control unit is the circuitry that finds and analyzes each instruction in a certain program. The execution units are those that perform the tasks in a program. Although many computer dealers mistakenly call the entire computer case on a desktop computer the CPU, it is actually only that part of the computer which performs the tasks of adding, subtracting, moving, retrieving, and so on. The rest of the space in a desktop computer's tower is devoted to memory, disc drives, and various other hardware.

LAN and Ethernet

The acronym LAN stands for Local Area Network, and is pronounced like "land" without the "d." A LAN is any small computer network, typically one that is restricted to a certain building, office, university, or home. Most businesses have their own LAN, which they find enables their employees to share information more easily. These are most often Ethernet connections, meaning that they connect through a port on the compute that looks like a phone jack except slightly wider. An Ethernet port can be used to connect a computer to another computer, to a LAN network, or simply to an external modem. Ethernet connections are able to transfer data much more quickly that connections that use a regular telephone jack. Many companies are now, however, getting rid of Ethernet-based LANs in favor of wireless networks.

Internet Address Parts

Individuals may access content on the Internet by typing the appropriate URL into the location bar. A URL, or uniform resource locator, is the web page's address, and has a few different parts. Let us take as an example the URL http://www.example.com. Here, the "http:" signifies which protocol is used to read this page. In this case, it is the HyperText Transfer Protocol. The "www" stands for World Wide Web, and is the name of the host computer on which the data is stored. Most computers that are hooked up to the internet simply have "www" here, although they need not. The next bit, "example.com," is the domain name, indicating that the page "example" is coming from a commercial site. Other domain designators are "edu" for education, "org" for organization, and "gov" for government sites.

Internet Terminology

Browser, bookmarks, and server -- In the context of the Internet, a browser is a program that mediates content for a computer user. In order to visit a particular internet site, one simply types its address into the browser's location field. Most browsers have a home page that serves as an index to the various sites on the internet. Most browsers allow the user to create bookmarks, immediate links to their favorite sites on the Internet. An Internet server is a computer that is connected to a network and is used by multiple individuals. Individuals who wish to run web pages allow their computers to be servers for that page; other computers that are connected to the network can access the web page by briefly accessing the server computer.

Bandwidth, cache, Common Gateway Interface (CGI), cookies, and Internet Protocol (IP) address -- In the context of the Internet, bandwidth is the measurement of how quickly data can be passed from one computer to another. It may be measured either in Kilobits per second (Kbps) or Megabits per second (Mbps). A cache is a place, either on one's computer or on computers operated by one's service provider, where copies of previously accessed web pages are stored so that they may be quickly brought up again. The Common Gateway Interface (CGI) is the set of rules that allow an Internet browser to interact with a program on the web server. Cookies are small text files that a user downloads to his or her computer, and which may be used to track the user's behavior or to allow for customized browsing. An Internet Protocol (IP) address is a numerical tag that each computer has, so that it can be identified on the Internet.

Domain names, File Transfer Protocol (FTP), firewall, HyperText Markup Language (HTML) -- On the Internet, a domain name is simply a unique title that distinguishes one or more IP addresses. Domain names are used for sending e-mail and as addresses for web pages. File Transfer Protocol (FTP) is a means of transferring files from one computer to another over the Internet. Although FTP is the most popular means of transferring files, it is not entirely safe; passwords and file contents may be intercepted. A firewall is any software or hardware that monitors and controls the information moving in and out of a computer network. Firewalls are meant to protect computers from being accessed by unauthorized users. HyperText Markup Language (HTML) is the basic language of the Internet; every web page is written in this language, which uses simple tags to divide sections of documents.

HyperText Transfer Protocol (HTTP), Internet Service Provider (ISP), plug-in, and server -- HyperText Transfer Protocol (HTTP) is the most common example of the procedure computers use to communicate with one another on the Internet. An Internet Service Provider (ISP) is an organization that enables users to access the Internet. Typically, users are charged for this privilege. Mark up is the process through which document are turned into web pages by inserting HTML tags. On the Internet, a plug-in is a program that enables a computer to access a broader array of content. Common plug-ins allow computers to access certain kinds of video and audio files. A server is a computer on the Internet that provides information for other computers. Servers might enable other users to view web pages or send email.

Cybersquatting

As the Internet has become a more viable arena for business, certain questionable business practices have evolved as well. Cybersquatting is when an individual registers a domain name with the express purpose of reselling it later for a profit. In these cases, the individual selects a domain name that they anticipate will become desired either because of its similarity to a familiar brand or its connection to an area of business. In 1999, the United States passed the Anti-Cybersquatting Consumer Protection Act, which allows trademark-holders to receive damages from cybersquatters who have registered trade names or similar names in an attempt to extort money from the business. This law has not entirely eliminated the practice of cyber squatting, but it has made it more difficult to do successfully.

Page Hijacking

Now that the Internet has become the medium for such a large proportion of American business, it is important for business teachers to inform their students of the various scams that make it somewhat dangerous. The phrase page hijacking refers to a host of dirty tricks, most of which result in a surfer being directed to a web page that he or she had not intended to visit. One common means of doing this is to change the user's home page in his or her default settings, and thereby cause the user to visit some other site every time he or she starts up the browser. Page hijacking may also refer to the practice of copying Internet content from one page to another, so that search engines will refer users to the second page, on which the hijacker then enters other information.

Phishing

Phishing is one of the many forms of Internet scamming that has cropped up as more business is transacted on-line. Specifically, phishing is a form of identity theft in which a website is created which claims to represent a legitimate business, but in actuality is a front so that criminals can acquire personal data from would-be buyers. Some of the more successful phishers have set up web pages that look like those of a major bank, then sends emails from that site to account holders asking for personal information. If the individuals are foolish enough to provide that information, the scammer can then access their bank accounts. Some phishers are sophisticated enough to simply change the programming code underlying a business' website so that visitors are redirected to a fake site, with neither the business nor the visitor ever knowing.

Practice Test

1. A command economy is characterized by:
    a. A *laissez-faire* approach by the government
    b. A moderate amount of government intervention in the economy
    c. Businesses commanding all aspects of the economy
    d. The government controlling prices and production

2. Which of the following is not a responsibility of the Securities and Exchange Commission (SEC)?
    a. Regulating securities
    b. Investigating insider trading
    c. Setting interest rates
    d. Processing applications for initial public offerings (IPOs)

3. In marketing, the demand for a product is directly influenced by:
    a. Customers' desire for a product
    b. Customers' ability to obtain a product
    c. Availability of a product
    d. Both A and B

4. The Sarbanes-Oxley Act of 2002:
    a. Vastly reduced the financial reporting obligations that corporations face
    b. Deregulated public utilities
    c. Was intended to fight corporate and accounting fraud
    d. Reduced tariffs on trade among North American countries

5. An employee earns $2,000.00 per month in gross pay, but pays $104.36 for health insurance, 9% in federal taxes, 3% for state taxes, and 2% for local taxes. What is the employee's net pay?
    a. $2,000.00
    b. $1,615.64
    c. $1,820.00
    d. $1,720.00

6. A market in which product availability exceeds demand is called a:
    a. Free market
    b. Seller's market
    c. Buyer's market
    d. Black market

7. Which of the following is not a part of Maslow's hierarchy of needs?
    a. Self-actualization
    b. Esteem
    c. Safety
    d. Supply and demand

8. Which of the following countries is not part of NAFTA?
   a. Mexico
   b. United States
   c. Canada
   d. China

9. A consumer's credit score is directly influenced by which of the following factors?
   a. Debt repayment history
   b. Employment history over the last five years
   c. Marital status
   d. Income level

10. Upon which organization does the international community primarily rely to deal with claims of unfair protectionism by one country against another?
   a. North Atlantic Treaty Organization (NATO)
   b. World Trade Organization (WTO)
   c. Organization of Petroleum Exporting Countries (OPEC)
   d. International Red Cross (IRC)

11. A homeowner is attempting to choose between several mortgage loans for a $200,000 home. Which of the following would have the lowest monthly payment?
   a. A 30-year fixed rate mortgage at 6%
   b. A 15-year fixed rate mortgage at 7%
   c. A 30-year fixed rate mortgage at 12%
   d. A 15-year fixed rate mortgage at 12%

12. The biggest factor that leads American companies to manufacture their products overseas in developing countries like China and India is:
   a. Higher quality of craftsmanship
   b. Lower labor costs
   c. Decreased transportation costs
   d. Effective legal systems

13. Which of the following correctly summarizes the accounting equation for a sole proprietorship?
   a. Assets = Liabilities + Owners' equity
   b. Liabilities = Assets + Owners' equity
   c. Owner's equity = Assets + Liabilities
   d. Revenue = Assets – Liabilities

14. In order to present a business plan to a group of potential investors, a businessperson would most likely use which software?
   a. Powerpoint
   b. Quickbooks
   c. Peoplesoft
   d. Excel

15. In order to start an online business, and individual would need all but which of the following:
    a. A business model
    b. A website
    c. An email address
    d. A fax machine

16. Which of the following types of assets would not be subject to depreciation?
    a. Heavy equipment
    b. Computers
    c. Real estate
    d. Company vehicles

17. When itemizing deductions on a federal tax return, an individual taxpayer may be able to deduct all but which of the following?
    a. Interest paid on a mortgage
    b. Charitable donations
    c. Losses from theft
    d. Groceries

18. Which of the following terms best describes a situation where an individual enters into an agreement with a company to use the company's business model within a given territory, usually in exchange for a fee?
    a. Sole proprietorship
    b. Limited liability corporation
    c. Franchise
    d. Incorporation

19. The par value of a bond is the:
    a. Average interest rate paid by a given type of bond over subsequent issues
    b. Amount of time until the bond matures
    c. Amount paid when the bond matures
    d. Amount of interest that the bond pays

20. Which of the following best describes Congress' purpose in setting up Freddie Mac in 1970?
    a. Expanding opportunities for home ownership
    b. Deregulating the credit market
    c. Improving regulation of the Internet
    d. Creating a place for small businesses to get loans

21. Which of the following countries would be considered an emerging market?
    a. Japan
    b. India
    c. Britain
    d. Canada

22. If the exchange rate between the Euro (€) and the U.S. dollar ($) is $2.5 to € 1, how many dollars would it take to purchase a plane ticket that costs € 1580.00?
    a. $39,500.00
    b. $3,950.00
    c. $395.00
    d. $632.00

23. If the U.S. Federal Reserve concludes that there is a significant risk of inflation, it will most likely:
    a. Raise interest rates
    b. Lower interest rates
    c. Keep interest rates the same
    d. Decrease bond yields

24. A combination of slow economic growth and high inflation is called:
    a. Inflationary pressure
    b. Deflation
    c. Stagflation
    d. Disinflation

25. A shareholder owns 200 shares of stock XYZ at $58 each. If there is a 2-1 stock split, how many shares will that shareholder have, and what will the new share price be?
    a. 100 shares at $116 per share
    b. 200 shares at $116 per share
    c. 400 shares at $29 per share
    d. 400 shares at $58 per share

26. Which of the following is not true of stock dividends?
    a. They are usually taxable
    b. They are offered voluntarily by companies in order to make their stock more attractive
    c. Their amount and frequency are determined directly by shareholders at large
    d. They may be discontinued or reduced at any time

27. If a stock has a high P/E ratio, this means that:
    a. The stock's price is low considering the value of the company's earnings
    b. The stock pays a high dividend based on its earnings per share
    c. The stock's price is high considering the value of its earnings per share
    d. The company's earnings per share are high

28. An individual who is about to retire and wants to earn interest without risking his or her principal would most likely be advised to invest in:
    a. Value stocks
    b. An index fund
    c. A mutual fund
    d. U.S. Treasury bonds

29. A company that is included in the Dow Jones Industrial Average most likely to be:
    a. A well-known corporation with a large market capitalization
    b. A foreign company
    c. A start-up that was recently listed on the stock exchange
    d. A small- to mid-sized technology company

Table 1

	Investor A	Investor B	Investor C	Investor D
Stocks	20%	85%	70%	50%
Bonds	70%	10%	20%	50%
Cash	10%	5%	10%	0%

30. Which of the investors in Table 1 has the portfolio that is exposed to the greatest amount of risk?
    a. Investor A
    b. Investor B
    c. Investor C
    d. Investor D

31. Refer again to Table 1. If Investor D's stocks have an average return of 8.8% during the year, and Investor D's bonds have an average return of 5.2%, what is the average overall return on Investor D's portfolio?
    a. 14%
    b. 7%
    c. 5.6%
    d. Cannot be determined

32. If one is planning to start a small business, which should one do first?
    a. Obtain a business loan
    b. Find a partner
    c. Assess one's personal financial situation
    d. Choose a location for one's business

33. Frank is 33 years old and married, with 2 children. He has $40,000 in his retirement account, which is earning an average of 5% annually, and $10,000 in his personal savings account, which is earning 2% annually. He is current with his mortgage, and has $50,000 left to pay at a rate of 6%. Frank also has $30,000 in credit card debt with an average rate of 13%. If Frank wants to increase his chances of retiring comfortably, what would the best way be for him to spend a Christmas bonus of $10,000?
    a. Put it in his retirement account
    b. Put it in his savings account
    c. Use half to pay down his mortgage and save the other half
    d. Use all of it to pay down his credit card debt

34. If a country is a net exporter, this means that:
    a. The value of the goods that it imports exceeds the value of the goods that it exports
    b. The value of the goods that it exports exceeds the value of the goods that it imports
    c. It exports consumer products
    d. It has high tariffs
35. If a government implements an import tariff on consumer electronics, what is it most likely trying to accomplish?
    a. It is trying to protect its domestic consumer electronics industry from competition
    b. It is trying to decrease the cost of imported consumer electronics
    c. It is trying to discourage domestic companies from producing consumer electronics
    d. It is trying to increase competition and lower prices in the consumer electronics industry

36. If a potential business owner projects that she will need to invest $100,000 in equipment to start a dry cleaning business, and the business' monthly expenses on rent, insurance, labor costs, and other incidentals is $5,000, how many months will it take for her to earn back her initial investment if the average monthly gross revenue is $8,000?
    a. Less than 9 months
    b. Less than 20 months
    c. Less than 34 months
    d. None of the above

Table 2

	Sticker price of the car	**Down payment**	**Monthly payment**	**Term of loan**
Option A	**$8,000**	**$0**	**$330**	**36 months**
Option B	**$8,000**	**$3,000**	**$160**	**60 months**
Option C	**$15,000**	**$0**	**$250**	**60 months**
Option D	**$15,000**	**$5,000**	**$400**	**36 months**

37. Refer to Table 2 above. A family wants to buy a new car, and is trying to decide between four different car and car loan options. Which of the loans would require them to pay the least amount of money overall, including the down payment and the monthly payments?
    a. Option A
    b. Option B
    c. Option C
    d. Option D

38. Which of the four options listed in Table 2 would require the family to pay the least amount of interest, total?
    a. Option A
    b. Option B
    c. Option C
    d. Option D

39. Which of the options listed in Table 2 would require the family to pay the highest amount of interest, total?
    a. Option A
    b. Option B
    c. Option C
    d. Option D

Table 3

	Cost	Franchise fee	Average gross monthly revenue	Average monthly expenses
Business A	**$500,000**	**5% of gross revenue**	**$20,000**	**$15,000**
Business B	**$440,000**	**4% of gross revenue**	**$16,000**	**$10,000**
Business C	**$320,000**	**None**	**$10,000**	**$5,000**
Business D	**$175,000**	**None**	**$8,000**	**$5,000**

40. Refer to Table 3. Sarah has up to $550,000 to invest, and is trying to decide which of four catering businesses she wants to purchase. Which of the options below correctly lists the businesses in order of average monthly profit from largest to smallest when the franchise fee is taken into consideration?
    a. A, B, C, D
    b. C, D, A, B
    c. B, C, A, D
    d. C, B, A, D

41. If Sarah wanted to get her initial investment back as quickly as possible, which of the following options would you advise her to choose, based upon the information in Table 3?
    a. Business A
    b. Business B
    c. Business C
    d. Business D

42. A consumer's credit score may be factor in all but which of the following transactions?
    a. Buying a car
    b. Buying a home
    c. Getting a personal loan
    d. Opening a bank account

43. Comprehensive car insurance typically covers:
    a. Damage the insured does to the property of others while driving the insured vehicle
    b. Medical expenses others incur as a result of a collision with the insured vehicle
    c. Damage done to the insured's vehicle by someone else
    d. All of the above

44. Which of the following is not typically cited as a potential cause of oil price increases?
    a. Price increases for consumer goods and services in the U.S.
    b. Increased global demand for oil
    c. Speculation in the oil market
    d. Insufficient refinery capacity

45. Nations whose economies rely primarily of the export of non-oil commodities like rubber or copper are:
    a. Typically located in Northern and Western Europe
    b. Often referred to as "developing countries" or "emerging markets"
    c. Known for their world class education systems
    d. Among usually among the wealthiest countries in the world

46. A company considering manufacturing a product in several different emerging markets will most likely consider which of the following factors in choosing between them?
    a. Likelihood of political instability
    b. Labor costs and regulations
    c. Cost of shipping goods from that country to the destination country
    d. All of the above

47. Adam Smith is best known for:
    a. Founding the doctrine of mercantilism
    b. Supporting the spread of communism
    c. Arguing for free market economics
    d. Arguing that the government should redistribute income

48. According to standard economic theories, countries that have a comparative advantage in the production of cotton should:
    a. Export another product, and import cotton
    b. Export cotton, and import other products
    c. Implement tariffs to protect their domestic cotton industry
    d. Work hard to reduce their comparative advantage and diversify their economy

49. An advantage of protectionism for countries that implement it is that it:
    a. Improves the country's global competitiveness
    b. Ensures that domestic jobs will be retained in the short term
    c. Encourages economic growth
    d. Prevents corruption

50. GDP measures a country's:
    a. Employment level
    b. Education level
    c. Total economic output
    d. Wage levels

51. A human resources manager is likely to be responsible for all but which of the following:
    a. Sales
    b. Payroll
    c. Hiring
    d. Training

52. The main function of a human resources department is to:
    a. Meet the company's recruiting goals
    b. Maximize employee productivity while minimizing pay
    c. Facilitate communication between the employer and the employees
    d. Prevent lawsuits

53. Which of the following questions would it be illegal to ask a job candidate at a pre-employment interview?
    a. Have you ever requested workers' compensation benefits?
    b. Do you have any disabilities that would interfere with your ability to perform this job?
    c. Both A and B
    d. Neither A nor B

54. Technological aids can be used to directly fulfill all but which of the following human resources functions:
    a. Soliciting resumes for open positions
    b. Assessing a new employee's job readiness
    c. Communicating information about employee benefits
    d. Resolving disputes between employees and management

55. A new manager with ABC Industries has noticed that many of his employees are chronically late to work. To remedy the problem, the manager decides to implement a bonus system that will financially reward employees who are on time to work for ten consecutive days. According to B.F. Skinner's Operant Conditioning theory, what type of behavior modification approach is the manager using?
    a. Extinction
    b. Punishment
    c. Negative reinforcement
    d. Positive reinforcement

Table 4

Management Approach	**Characteristic**
1. Classical Theory	A. Productivity can be improved through the application of mathematical models
2. Behavioral Theory	B. Understanding the worker's perspective is key to successful management
3. Management Science Approach	C. There is no single "correct" theory; instead, managers should apply the theory that is most sensible in a given situation
4. Contingency Approach	D. Productivity can be maximized by presenting the right combination of incentives, and correctly designing jobs

56. Refer to Table 4, and correctly match each Management Approach in the right column with the characteristic in the left column that best describes it.
    a. 1-D, 2-B, 3-A, 4-C
    b. 1-A, 2-C, 3-B, 4-D
    c. 1-A, 2-C, 3-D, 4-B
    d. 1-D, 2-A, 3-B, 4-C

57. A successful manager will be able to effectively delegate:
    a. Responsibility
    b. Accountability
    c. Authority
    d. Ability

58. According to Fayol's Administrative Theory of Management, which of the following is a correct list of the five essential functions of management?
    a. Controlling, composing, planning, organizing, implementing
    b. Containing, controlling, implementing, planning, organizing
    c. Composing, coordinating, controlling, planning, organizing
    d. Controlling, commanding, coordinating, planning, organizing

59. According to the National Environmental Policy Act of 1967, a business is required to prepare an environmental impact statement (EIS) when it:
    a. Hires a new worker
    b. Makes a charitable contribution
    c. Develops a new marketing initiative
    d. Builds a new factory

60. A manufacturing company implements anti-pollution measures as outlined by applicable legislation, but opts not to adopt any additional anti-pollution measures. This company has most likely adopted which of the following approaches to business-society relations?
    a. Social Responsiveness Approach
    b. Social Responsibility Approach
    c. Social Obligation Approach
    d. Cost-benefit Approach

61. Which of the following constitutes a binding contract?
    a. An agreement signed and dated by one party and one witness
    b. An agreement signed and dated by both parties
    c. An agreement signed by both parties and witnessed by a third party
    d. An agreement signed and dated by both parties and a witness

62. Corporation X, the largest oil refiner in the U.S., wants to purchase Corporation Y, the only other oil refiner in the U.S. This situation may be of concern to the government because:
    a. It may violate environmental laws
    b. It may constitute a violation of antitrust laws
    c. It could violate labor laws by reducing employees' choice of employers
    d. It could constitute a pyramid scheme

63. The Equal Employment Opportunity Commission (EEOC) is responsible for enforcing all but which of the following laws?
    a. Civil Rights Act of 1964
    b. Equal Pay Act
    c. Environmental Protection Act
    d. Americans with Disabilities Act

64. Anna is interested in purchasing a computer for her small landscaping business. She wants to be able to compose simple fliers and advertising materials, communicate with clients via email, and order supplies online. Which of the following lists best describes the hardware and software components that Anna's computer should have?
    a. Internet connection, Quickbooks, and at least 10 GB of memory
    b. Word processing software, Quickbooks, and an Internet connection
    c. Word processing software, an Internet connection, and 1-5 GB of memory
    d. Quickbooks, an Internet connection, and 1-5 GB of memory

65. Microsoft Excel would most likely be used for which of the following tasks?
    a. Developing a strategic plan
    b. Filing invoices
    c. Creating a sales presentation
    d. Analyzing numerical sales data

66. Which of the following steps might a company take in order to prevent unauthorized individuals from accessing confidential data?
    a. Requiring a username and password to access its computer system
    b. Constructing a firewall to protect its computer system
    c. Both A and B
    d. Neither A nor B

67. In order to facilitate communication between employees within a company, the company is considering providing all employees with unlimited access to a file that contains employee names, work phone numbers and addresses, work email addresses, birthdates, and social security numbers. What confidentiality issues would this new policy raise?
    a. None, the value of improved communication between employees would outweigh any confidentiality issues
    b. Many employees may object to their social security numbers and birthdays being shared with others; the company should publish the birthdays anyway, but withhold the social security numbers
    c. Many employees may object to their social security numbers and birthdays being shared with others; the company should withhold both of these
    d. Releasing of any of this information is a violation of employees' privacy

68. A business education teacher has allotted one class period to help students identify potential career options. Which of the following activities would be most appropriate given these circumstances?
    a. Having students complete an internship
    b. Having each student deliver a five-minute presentation describing their parents' jobs
    c. Administering a test that advises students about what careers might fit their interests and talents
    d. Asking students to write an essay describing their "dream job"

69. Which of the following business careers could a teacher safely recommend for a student who would not enjoy working with the public on a regular basis?
    a. Financial advisor
    b. Insurance salesperson
    c. Real estate agent
    d. None of the above

70. Choose the list below that best describes the most important contents of a resume:
    a. Salary requirements, relevant work experience, educational attainment, objective
    b. Contact information, grade point average, relevant work experience, objective
    c. References, objective, educational attainment, salary requirements
    d. Contact information, objective, educational attainment, relevant work experience

71. At a meeting with shareholders, an executive would be most likely to use which of the following visual aids to present a report on monthly stock gains and losses over a one-year period?
    a. Bar chart
    b. Pie chart
    c. Line graph
    d. Scatterplot

72. When manually proofreading a business document for a colleague, which of the following answers describes the correct way one would indicate that a section of text should be removed?
    a. An X should be drawn through the text
    b. A caret should be drawn at the beginning and end of the text
    c. A diagonal line should be drawn through the text from bottom left to top right
    d. A horizontal line should be drawn through the text with a loop at the right end of the line

73. When researching a presentation about a national shipping business, the most detailed and comprehensive source of information about the top management of the company and its competitors would most likely be:
    a. Microfilm records from local newspapers
    b. Hoovers.com
    c. LexisNexis.com
    d. The catalogue at your local library

74. Which of the following lists contains only types of computer software?
    a. Internet, Microsoft Office, Quicken
    b. Motherboard, Quicken, Excel
    c. Quicken, Peoplesoft, Microsoft Office
    d. Monitor, Mouse, Keyboard

75. Search engine optimization (SEO) is the process of:
    a. Designing a search engine to operate as efficiently as possible
    b. Designing a website to maximize its placement in search engine results for particular keywords, thus increasing traffic to the site
    c. Improving the visual aesthetic of a search engine
    d. Making a search engine more user-friendly

76. On the Internet, links are used in all but which of the following ways?
    a. They direct Internet users to other websites that have additional relevant information
    b. They are used for marketing purposes, to entice Internet users to navigate away from one website to view another one
    c. They allow Internet users to open additional windows that explain a webpage's content or provide technical assistance
    d. They allow computer users to open software programs on their PC

77. When designing a website for an online business, the web developer would include a site map in order to:
    a. Give website users directions to the business
    b. Provide website users with a list of links to all of the pages on the website
    c. Convince website users that it is safe to purchase products from the website
    d. Help website users decide which products to buy from the website

78. Better Business Bureau certification is useful for businesses that engage in e-commerce because it:
    a. Protects them from legal action by defrauded consumers
    b. Exempts them from paying state taxes
    c. Proves that they are certified by the government
    d. Reassures customers that the company is reliable

79. Businesses can increase the security of confidential customer information by:
    a. Destroying paper records of credit card information
    b. Conducting employee background checks
    c. Installing a firewall and virus protection software for computer systems
    d. All of the above

80. A high school student expresses interest in starting her own auto repair business after graduating from high school. She could best prepare for such a career by:
    a. Getting a college degree in finance and then completing an MBA program
    b. Taking small business finance, law, and accounting courses
    c. Getting an internship or part time job at an auto-repair shop
    d. B and C only

81. A business education teacher wants to evaluate her program in terms of how well graduates are prepared for the workforce. Which of the following strategies would be most likely to provide the best data to answer this question?
    a. Setting up an advisory committee of local employers to gather feedback on graduates' performance in the workplace
    b. Asking students to complete internships with local employers
    c. Conducting a survey of recent graduates to see if they were able to find jobs with local employers
    d. Asking the business professors at a local community college to provide feedback

82. Which of the following activities that are conducted by high school student leadership organizations would be the most effective tool for teaching business skills?
    a. Raising money by selling concessions at athletic events
    b. Performing community service by painting a local elementary school
    c. Holding an awards ceremony to honor scholarship winners
    d. Tutoring middle school students in math and reading

83. A business education teacher is asked to serve as an advisor to the local chapter of a student leadership organization. The teacher's primary responsibility as an advisor is most likely to:
    a. Ensure that students follow established procedures for conducting meetings
    b. Ensure the health and safety of student participants in the organization
    c. Design and implement activities for the group
    d. Collect and account for dues and fundraising proceeds

84. Which of the following activities provides the best example of collaboration between business education teachers and teachers of other subject areas?
    a. Students in a business education class are asked to write cover letters and resumes
    b. Students in a business education class read case studies about research and development for new products
    c. A business education teacher and a math teacher coordinate their lesson plans so that the concepts taught in math class are subsequently applied to real situations in the business class
    d. Students in a business class learn to balance checkbooks

85. Which of the following activities would most effectively and comprehensively assess students' mastery of learning objectives for a unit about small business?
    a. Asking students to create and market a new invention
    b. Asking students to design and implement a community service project
    c. Requiring students to complete an internship or externship
    d. Having students write and present a business plan

86. A business education teacher wants students to complete an activity that teaches them skills that are necessary for working in a culturally diverse environment. Which of the following activities would fulfill this goal?
    a. Collaborating with the social studies teacher to teach students about work customs in other cultures
    b. Asking students to read and discuss written accounts of minorities' experiences in the workplace
    c. Teaching students about laws and regulations that protect people from diverse ethnic and cultural backgrounds
    d. All of the above

Table 5

Name of Business	**Credit Rating**
Business A	BBB
Business B	BB
Business C	AA
Business D	AAA

87. Based on the information in Table 5, which of the following lists correctly orders the businesses from least to most risky for investors?
    a. Business B, Business A, Business C, Business D
    b. Business A, Business B, Business D, Business C
    c. Business D, Business C, Business A, Business B
    d. Business C, Business D, Business B, Business A

Table 6

Time card: Scott Smith			
Date	**Clock in**	**Clock out**	
11/01	11:00 AM	3:00 PM	4
11/02	8:00 AM	12:00 PM	4
11/03	8:00 AM	12:00 PM	4
11/05	11:00 AM	3:00 PM	4
11/07	8:00 AM	12:00 PM	4

88. If part time employee Scott Smith, whose time card is shown in Table 6, is paid $10.00 per hour on weekdays (Monday-Friday), and $11.00 per hour on weekends, and November 1st is a Monday, how much should he be paid for the week of November 1st through November 7th?
   a. $160.00
   b. $200.00
   c. $204.00
   d. $240.00

89. Only full time employees of Scott Smith's company, whose time card is shown in Table 6, have health insurance and 401k benefits deducted from their paychecks. Based on the number of hours Smith worked from November 1st through November 7th, which of the following is a correct list of his payroll deductions if he is a W-4 employee?
   a. 401k and health insurance
   b. Social security and Medicare
   c. Social security, Medicare, and income taxes
   d. None of the above

90. The company that Scott Smith works for provides full time employees with a 100% 401k match after one year on the job if they contribute 4% of their paycheck. If Scott becomes a full time employee after a year, makes $2,000 per paycheck, and contributes 4% to his 401k each pay period, how much would the company have to contribute to his 401k during each pay period?
   a. $160
   b. $80
   c. $40
   d. Cannot be determined

91. Accounts receivable are:
   a. Fixed assets
   b. Fixed liabilities
   c. Current assets
   d. Current liabilities

92. Owners' equity is comprised of:
   a. The personal net worth of the owners plus the amount of their initial investment in the business
   b. The amount of the owners' initial investment in the business
   c. The owners' unclaimed profits from the business' operation
   d. Both B and C

93. Which of the following are not protected by copyright law?
    a. Architectural drawings
    b. Scripts for plays
    c. Advertising slogans
    d. Books of poetry

94. A phrase that is associated with a particular product would be protected by which of the following?
    a. Trademark law
    b. Patent law
    c. Copyright law
    d. Both A and C

95. Which of the following is true of a corporation?
    a. It is always owned by shareholders
    b. Its shareholders are personally liable if it fails
    c. Its board of directors is personally liable if it fails
    d. It cannot sue another entity or be sued

96. Which of the following would be a violation of the Occupational Safety and Health Act (OSHA)?
    a. An employee becoming injured while commuting to work
    b. An employee becoming injured because an employer did not provide equipment in good working order
    c. An employer requiring employees to work with toxic chemicals
    d. An employer failing to accompany an OSHA compliance officer on an inspection

97. The following are each sentences from a job description. Select the sentence that clearly and correctly communicates its intended meaning.
    a. The employee, will have excellent oral communication skills.
    b. The employees oral communication skills will be excellent.
    c. The employee will communicate orally and in writing well.
    d. The employee will have excellent writing skills.

98. Which of the following is true of a Wide Area Network (WAN)?
    a. A WAN is equivalent to a LAN
    b. Businesses usually have their own WAN
    c. The Internet is an example of a WAN
    d. Businesses prefer WANs to LANs because their data transfer speed is higher

99. A business education teacher teaches two classes of 30 9th graders during a semester. At the end of the class, students are given identical tests of the course material. Students in Class 1, which was taught using a traditional lecture approach, scored an average of 73% on the test. Students in Class 2, which was taught using interactive exercises and computer-based simulations, scored an average of 82% on the test. What can be concluded from this experiment?

a. The students in Class 2 are more intelligent than those in Class 1
b. The teaching methods used for Class 2 are superior to those used for Class 1
c. Nothing can be concluded from these results because one semester is not a long enough period of time to accurately measure learning
d. Nothing can be concluded from these results because students' baseline performance on these tests was not measured before the experiment

100. Which of the following would violate federal child labor regulations?

a. Hiring your own child to work in your small business if the child is under 14
b. Employing someone under 14 as a newspaper carrier
c. Employing someone under 18 in a job deemed hazardous
d. Employing anyone under 18 as a babysitter

Answer Key

Number	Answer	Number	Answer	Number	Answer
1	D	**45**	B	**89**	C
2	C	**46**	D	**90**	B
3	D	**47**	C	**91**	C
4	C	**48**	B	**92**	D
5	B	**49**	B	**93**	C
6	C	**50**	C	**94**	A
7	D	**51**	A	**95**	A
8	D	**52**	C	**96**	B
9	A	**53**	C	**97**	D
10	B	**54**	D	**98**	C
11	A	**55**	D	**99**	D
12	B	**56**	A	**100**	C
13	A	**57**	C		
14	A	**58**	D		
15	D	**59**	D		
16	C	**60**	C		
17	D	**61**	D		
18	C	**62**	B		
19	C	**63**	C		
20	A	**64**	C		
21	B	**65**	D		
22	B	**66**	C		
23	A	**67**	C		
24	C	**68**	C		
25	C	**69**	D		
26	C	**70**	D		
27	C	**71**	C		
28	D	**72**	D		
29	A	**73**	B		
30	B	**74**	C		
31	B	**75**	B		
32	C	**76**	D		
33	D	**77**	B		
34	B	**78**	D		
35	A	**79**	D		
36	C	**80**	D		
37	A	**81**	A		
38	C	**82**	A		
39	B	**83**	B		
40	C	**84**	C		
41	D	**85**	D		
42	D	**86**	D		
43	D	**87**	C		
44	A	**88**	C		

Answer Explanations

1. D: A command economy (also known as a planned economy) is characterized by the government controlling nearly all aspects of the economy, including prices and production. This type of economy is traditionally associated with Communist economies where prices, wages and production quotas are set by the government. A, B, and C are all incorrect because they imply some form of private sector autonomy.

2. C: The Securities and Exchange Commission (SEC) is responsible for regulating securities, investigating insider trading, and processing applications for initial public offerings (IPOs) of stock. However, the Federal Reserve is responsible for setting interest rates.

3. D: In marketing, the demand for a product is determined both by customers' desire for that product, coupled with their ability to obtain it if they want it. For example, even if customers want a product, demand for it may be decreased if it is illegal or prohibitively expensive. Answer C, availability of a given product, refers to supply, not demand.

4. C: The Sarbanes-Oxley Act of 2002 was intended to fight corporate and accounting fraud in the wake of several huge scandals that brought down major U.S corporations. This bill reformed the rules and regulations governing corporations' financial disclosures, and increased financial reporting obligations.

5. B: The employee's net pay, or total take-home pay after deductions, is $1,615.64. This is calculated by subtracting the employee's taxes (totaling 14%, or $280.00) and insurance ($104.36) from the gross pay of $2,000.00.

6. C: A market in which product availability is greater than product demand is called a buyer's market, because when supply (product availability) exceeds demand, the prices paid by buyers decrease. This decrease in prices benefits the buyer of a product and decreases the seller's profits.

7. D: Supply and demand is not a part of Maslow's hierarchy of needs. This hierarchy is part of Maslow's theory that once people satisfy basic needs like food, water, and physical security, they begin to pursue needs higher up the hierarchy, like social acceptance, self-esteem, and self-actualization.

8. D: China is not part of NAFTA. NAFTA refers to the North American Free Trade Agreement, which is an agreement to encourage trade between the U.S., Canada, and Mexico.

9. A: A consumer's credit score is directly influenced by the individual's payment history on car and home loans, credit cards, etc. While marital status, employment history, and income level may indirectly influence the credit score by affecting the consumer's ability to pay bills on time, only payment history itself is a direct factor in credit score calculations.

10. B: The primary organization upon which the international community relies to deal with claims of unfair protectionism by one country against another is the World Trade Organization (WTO). NATO is a military alliance among many North American and European countries, OPEC is an organization of oil-producing countries that regulates supply and prices, and the Red Cross is an international humanitarian organization.

11. A: A 30-year fixed rate mortgage at 6% would provide the lowest monthly payment on the $200,000 mortgage loan, because it has both the longest term (30 years) and the lowest interest rate (6%). This means that the consumer would be paying less interest on a yearly basis, and the total would be divided over the maximum number of monthly payments.

12. B: The biggest factor that leads American companies to manufacture their products in developing countries is lower labor cost. Labor costs in developing countries (countries with a comparatively low GDP per capita) are lower than in the U.S. because unemployment is higher and labor regulations are less stringent.

13. A: The accounting equation for a sole proprietorship is correctly stated as Assets = Liabilities + Owners' equity. In the accounting equation for a corporation, owners' equity is replaced by shareholders' equity.

14. A: In order to present a business plan to a group of potential investors, a businessperson would most likely use Powerpoint, which allows an individual to present text and pictures in a slide format using a PC. Quickbooks is used for accounting, Peoplesoft is used by human resources professionals, and Excel is used for storing and analyzing numerical and categorical data.

15. D: In order to start an online business, an individual would need an Internet connection, email, and a web domain, but a fax machine would not necessarily be required, since documents can be scanned and sent via email.

16. C: Real estate is not subject to depreciation. While real estate often appreciates (increases) in value, assets like vehicles and computer equipment inevitably depreciate (decline in value) due to normal wear and tear.

17. D: When itemizing deductions on a federal tax return, a taxpayer may be able to deduct all of the things listed here except for food costs. Mortgage interest, losses from theft and charitable donations are all tax-deductible under certain circumstances.

18. C: When an individual enters into an agreement with a company to use the company's business model within a given territory, this is called a franchise agreement. In most cases, the individual pays the company a franchise fee, usually a percentage of gross revenue, in order to use the company's business model.

19. C: The par value of a bond is the value of the bond when it is issued. The par value is typically the amount that the bond issuer pays the buyer when the bond matures, as well.

20. A: Expanding opportunities for home ownership was Congress' primary purpose in setting up Freddie Mac. This organization was charged with increasing the availability of money for home loans by pooling mortgages together to create mortgage-backed securities.

21. B: India is the only country listed here that would be considered an emerging market. Emerging markets exist only in countries that are in the process of rapidly industrializing. Countries like Britain, Japan, and Canada have slower-growing, mature economies that have long passed the emergent stage. As in the case of India, emerging markets are often the destination for outsourced jobs.

22. B: If the exchange rate between the Euro (€) and the U.S. dollar ($) is $2.5 to € 1, it would take $3,950.00 to purchase a plane ticket that costs € 1580.00. This is calculated by multiplying the number of dollars to one Euro (2.5) by the cost of the plane ticket in Euros (1580).

23. A: If the U.S. Federal Reserve concludes that there is a significant risk of inflation, it will most likely raise interest rates. By raising interest rates, a central bank like the Federal Reserve can increase the cost of borrowing money, thus slowing economic growth and the price inflation that results from increased demand.

24. C: A combination of slow economic growth and high inflation is called stagflation. This can occur when slow economic growth (little or none of the wage and job increases that create demand) is coupled with price increases caused by external factors like rising energy costs.

25. C: If a shareholder owns 200 shares of stock XYZ at $58 each and there is a 2-1 stock split, the shareholder would then own 400 shares at $29 per share. Companies split stock in order to decrease the price and stimulate trading. In a two for one split, the number of shares is doubled, but the price is halved.

26. C: Stock dividends are usually taxable, they may be discontinued or reduced at any time, and they are offered voluntarily by companies to make their stock more attractive. However, the amount and frequency of dividend payments are determined by the company's board of directors, not by shareholders at large.

27. C: If a stock has a high P/E ratio, this means that the stock's price is high considering the value of its earnings per share (EPS). The P/E ratio is calculated by dividing the share price by the company's EPS. The closer the result is to zero, the cheaper the stock is in relation to the amount of money the company is earning.

28. D: An individual who is about to retire and wants to earn interest without risking his or her principal would most likely be advised to invest in U.S. Treasury bonds. Value stocks, index funds, and mutual funds are all tied to the stock market, which is far more volatile and risky than U.S. Treasury bonds. (Some other bond investments, like junk bonds, can be quite risky). Since this investor is more concerned with protecting the principal than with earning high returns, an investment in bonds would best match his or her objective.

29. A: A company that is included in the Dow Jones Industrial Average most likely would be a well-known corporation with a large market capitalization. The Dow lists only thirty companies, most of which are household names.

30. B: Investor B is exposed to the greatest amount of risk, because 85% of the money in Investor B's portfolio is invested in stocks. Stocks are historically riskier than bonds or cash, so Investor B is more vulnerable than the other investors to large market fluctuations. However, this also means that Investor B has the largest potential to earn higher returns.

31. The correct answer is B, 7%. If stocks return 8.8% during the year, and bonds return 5.2%, then Investor D's overall return would be the average of both halves of the portfolio, since 50% was in bonds and 50% was in stocks. The overall return is equal to the weighted average of the returns from all investments, in this case the average of 8.8% and 5.2%.

32. C: If one is planning to start a small business, one's first step should be to assess one's personal financial situation in order to determine how much start-up capital one has, and how long one can afford to support oneself before one's business begins to turn a profit. Conducting these types of calculations will help one determine how large a loan one needs to request, and whether one needs a partner. Banks would also require this information before they issued a loan.

33. D: Frank could improve his chances for a comfortable retirement by using the $10,000 bonus to pay down his high interest credit card debt. Since the high interest rate on the credit card debt means that Frank is paying more in interest than he would be earning in either his savings account or his retirement account, paying down this debt will increase his ability to save over the long term. Since the credit card interest rate is higher than the mortgage interest rate, the credit card should be paid off first.

34. B: If a country is a net exporter, this means that the value of the goods that it exports exceeds the value of the goods that it imports. Net exporters have positive trade balances, meaning that the value of the goods that they sell to other countries exceeds the value of the goods that they buy from other countries.

35. A: If a government implements a tariff on imported consumer electronics, it is most likely trying to protect its domestic consumer electronics industry from foreign competition. By increasing tariffs, the government will increase the domestic prices for foreign-made consumer electronics, thus making domestically-produced products more attractive to consumers and reducing the overall level of competition in the industry.

36. C: If the business owner has invested $100,000 into the business, and makes an average monthly profit of $3,000 ($8,000 average gross revenue minus the $5,000 monthly costs of running the business), it will take approximately 33.3 months for her to make back her initial $100,000 investment.

37. A: If the family is looking for the lowest overall cost, Option A would total only $11,880 ($330 multiplied by 36 months). Option B would cost $12,600 overall, option C would cost $15,000, and option D would cost $19,400, including the down payment and monthly payments.

38. C: If the family wanted to ensure that they pay the lowest amount of interest possible, Option C would be the best choice. The total cost of the car, $15,000, divided by the number of payments (60) equals the monthly payment exactly, meaning that the family pays no interest at all for this option. Interest can be calculated by subtracting the car's sticker price from the total amount actually paid over the life of the loan.

39. B: Option B would require the family to pay the highest amount of interest total. Option B pays a total of $12,600 ($160 multiplied by 60 months plus $3000 in down payment) for an $8,000 vehicle, so $4,600 of that payment is interest. The others have lower interest payments.

40. C: Business B has the highest average monthly profit, at $5,360. This is calculated by adding the franchise fee to the total monthly expenditures, and subtracting this total from the average gross monthly revenue. Business C makes an average monthly profit of $5,000, Business A makes around $4,000 per month, and Business D makes just $3,000 per month.

41. D: If Sarah wanted to get her initial investment back as quickly as possible, she would be best advised to choose Business D, which would allow her to recoup her initial investment of $175,000 in just over 58 months. One can estimate how long it will take to recoup the initial investment for a business by dividing the cost of buying the business by the average monthly profit.

42. D: A consumer's credit score may be considered when a consumer buys a car or home if the transaction involves a loan, and it will also be considered if an individual applies for a personal loan. However, one's credit score is not considered when opening a bank account, because the account holder is depositing money rather than borrowing it.

43. D: Comprehensive insurance typically covers damage that the insured does to others and their property while driving the car, as well as damage that is done to the insured and the insured's property, assuming the other party is not insured. Collision insurance only covers damage done by the insured to others and their property.

44. A: Many economists argue that price increases for consumer goods and services in the U.S. increase as a result of oil price increases, but they are not typically cited as a potential cause of them.

45. B: Nations whose economies rely primarily on the export of non-oil commodities like rubber or copper are often referred to as "developing countries" or "emerging markets." Because of the instability of commodity prices, and these countries' often disproportionate reliance on commodity exports, developing countries are typically poorer and less able to provide social services than are countries that rely more heavily on manufacturing and service industries.

46. D: All of the above. Political instability could put the company's investment at risk, and the labor and shipping costs associated with a given country can be a decisive factor in investment decisions.

47. C: Adam Smith is best known for writing *The Wealth of Nations*, a treatise on free market economics in which he describes an "invisible hand" which guides the marketplace through individuals protecting their own self-interest. He argued that economic competition through a free market would be the best way to increase economic efficiency, productivity, and ultimately human happiness.

48. B: Economic theory states that countries with a comparative advantage in producing a particular product should produce and export that product, and use the proceeds to import the other products that they need from other countries.

49. B: An advantage of protectionism for countries that implement it is that it helps ensure that domestic jobs will be retained in the short term. By implementing protectionist measures that decrease the competitiveness of otherwise cheaper foreign goods,

governments can protect the domestic industries that produce those goods and preserve the jobs of the people who work in them.

50. C: GDP (gross domestic product) measures a country's total economic output, including goods and services, over a given period of time. Usually, GDP is reported annually.

51. A: A human resources manager is likely to be responsible for hiring, training, and payroll, but not sales. Human resources managers are in charge of employer-employee relations, including any activity that involves recruiting and retaining valuable employees.

52. C: The main function of a human resources department is to facilitate communication between the employer and the employees. While human resources departments are primarily responsible to the company's upper management, they are intended to provide a "neutral" conduit through which personnel policies can be devised and implemented, and through which employees can express and resolve concerns.

53. C: It would be illegal to ask either of the questions listed in answers A and B at a job interview. The Americans with Disabilities Act prohibits employers from attempting to ascertain a prospective employee's disability status prior to hiring the job candidate. Questions like, "Have you ever requested workers' compensation benefits," or, "Do you have any disabilities that would interfere with your ability to perform this job," would both fall into this category of illegal interview questions.

54. D: Technological aids such as email and computer software programs can be used to directly fulfill human resources functions like soliciting resumes for open positions, assessing a new employee's job readiness, or communicating information about employee benefits. However, a complicated situation such as an employee-employer dispute requires listening and negotiation skills and judgment that cannot be replaced by a computer.

55. D: The manager is using positive reinforcement. According to Skinner's theory, undesirable behavior such as tardiness can be dealt with using positive reinforcement, negative reinforcement, punishment, or extinction (discontinuing an existing practice that encourages or rewards that behavior).

56. A: The Classical Theory of management argues that productivity can be maximized by presenting the right combination of incentives, and correctly designing jobs. The Behavioral Theory emphasizes that understanding the worker's perspective is key to successful management, and the Management Science approach asserts that productivity can be improved through the application of mathematical models. More recently, proponents of the Contingency Approach have argued that there is no single "correct" theory; instead, managers should apply the theory that is most sensible in a given situation.

57. C: A successful manager will be able to effectively delegate authority. As a leader, the manager always retains accountability for results and ultimate responsibility for employees' actions. However, the manager must be able to delegate decision-making authority to subordinate employees in order to fulfill his or her job function. Ability D can be improved through training, but it cannot be automatically delegated.

58. D: According to Fayol's Administrative Theory of Management, the five essential functions of management are controlling, commanding, coordinating, planning, and organizing. Henri Fayol, a French engineer, pioneered the Classical Theory of Management. He argued that any individual who performed these five functions could be considered a manager, regardless of his or her actual job title.

59. D: According to the National Environmental Policy Act of 1967, a business is required to prepare an environmental impact statement (EIS) when it builds a new factory, but not when it hires a new worker, makes a charitable contribution, or develops a new marketing initiative. Environmental impact statements assess the possible environmental concerns and damage that could result from a proposed action. Hiring new workers, making charitable contributions, and even developing marketing initiatives may be important decisions from a business perspective, but they are unlikely to have any major negative impact on the environment, and thus are exempted from the EIS requirement.

60. C: A manufacturing company that implements anti-pollution measures as outlined by applicable legislation, but that opts not to introduce any additional anti-pollution measures, has most likely adopted the Social Obligation Approach to business-society relations. This means that the business will follow all applicable laws, but will not make any supplemental attempts to improve the environment or contribute to social welfare. This model is based upon cost-benefit calculations, but such calculations are not an approach to business-society relations in and of themselves. The Social Responsibility and Social Responsiveness approaches denote moderate and high levels of social involvement, respectively.

61. D: A binding contract is an agreement signed and dated by both parties, and a witness.

62. B: This situation may constitute a violation of antitrust law. If the only two oil refiners in the U.S. merged, this would mean that there would be only one oil refiner in the U.S., thus creating a monopoly. Monopolies are generally illegal because they eliminate competition that ensures fair prices for consumers.

63. C: The Equal Employment Opportunity Commission (EEOC) is responsible for enforcing Civil Rights Act of 1964, the Equal Pay Act, and the Americans with Disabilities Act, but not the Environmental Protection Act. The EEOC is primarily responsible for enforcing civil rights, while the Environmental Protection Administration (EPA) is responsible for enforcing environmental protection statutes.

64. C: Anna would need word processing software, an Internet connection, and 1-5 GB of memory. Word processing software would allow Anna to compose simple fliers and advertising materials, and an Internet connection would allow Anna to communicate with clients via email and order supplies online. 1-5 GB of memory is what standard home and small business computers need, and Quickbooks is a type of accounting software that may be useful for Anna, but would not be necessary for the tasks listed in this question.

65. D: Microsoft Excel would most likely be used to analyze numerical sales data. This software program allows users to apply mathematical formulas to numerical and categorical data. While it does also produce charts and graphs that may ultimately be used in a sales presentation, such a presentation would probably be constructed using PowerPoint.

66. C: In order to prevent unauthorized individuals from accessing confidential data, a company might require a username and password to access its computer system, and also construct a firewall to protect the computer system. By requiring passwords, the company can prevent unauthorized users such as former employees from accessing its computer system, and firewalls are designed to prevent hackers from accessing the data.

67. C: Employees may object to their social security numbers and birthdays being shared with others, and disclosing either of these could result in employee complaints and possible legal action. While information like name and work contact information must be shared in order for the business to function properly, information like Social Security numbers and birthdays is not relevant to the business, and thus should not be shared without employees' consent.

68. C: If a business education teacher has allotted one class period to help students identify potential career options, the most appropriate activity given these circumstances would be to administer a test that advises students about what careers might fit their interests and talents. While an internship might be useful, this would not fit the allotted time period. The other two options, describing a parent's job and describing a "dream job," may also be useful. However, they are not personalized, and they do not provide students with new options that he or she may not have considered before.

69. D: Real estate agents, insurance salespeople, and financial advisors all have extensive interaction with the public and require excellent people skills. Such jobs would not be suitable for those with an aversion to working with the public.

70. D: The four most important parts of a resume are the applicant's contact information, objective, educational attainment, and relevant work experience. The contact information is crucial because it allows the employer to get in touch with the applicant, and the objective is important because it explains why the applicant is sending the resume, and what position the applicant hopes to obtain. Educational attainment and work experience are important credentials for any job, while salary requirements and employment references are typically provided in the cover letter or upon request.

71. C: The most effective way to convey information about monthly stock gains and losses over a one-year period would be to use a line graph, which would clearly indicate month-to-month changes in stock price over time. Bar and pie charts are most effective for conveying categorical information about things like market share and sector weighting, and scatter plots are usually used to show results that are comprised of many individual responses, like survey results.

72. D: When manually proofreading documents, the correct way to indicate that a section of text should be removed is to draw a horizontal line through the text with a loop at the right end. Carets are used to indicate that something should be inserted into the text, and diagonal lines are used to indicate that a letter should be lower case instead of capitalized. Xs are not standard proofreading marks.

73. B: When researching a presentation about a national shipping business, the most detailed and comprehensive source of information about the top management of the company and its competitors would most likely be Hoovers.com. LexisNexis.com is also useful for business research, but it is a searchable database of academic and news articles, rather than a database of information about specific companies and industries, like Hoovers. The local newspaper or library would be unlikely to have detailed information about competitors across the country, although it may have specific information about those located in the immediate vicinity.

74. C: Quicken, PeopleSoft, and Microsoft Office are all types of computer software. Quicken is used by individuals and small businesses for basic accounting functions, PeopleSoft is used primarily by human resources professionals, and Microsoft Office is the most widely-used word processing software on the market. The Internet is not a type of software, because it is not a program that can be installed and run on a single computer's operating system. The monitor, mouse, motherboard, and keyboard are all hardware, or equipment which is required to make software usable.

75. B: Search engine optimization (SEO) is the process of designing a website to maximize its placement in search engine results for particular keywords, thus increasing traffic to the site. Modifications are made to the website in order to make it highly relevant to certain search keywords, so that it will be among the first results Internet users see when they search for the designated keyword. This marketing tactic increases traffic to the website, and should increase sales on that website as well.

76. D: Links are used in all of the ways described here, except that they do not allow computer users to open software programs on their PC. In order to do that, one would click on an icon on one's own PC. Links, on the other hand, are inserted into a website's source code in such a way that clicking on them leads the Internet user to another website or webpage within the same site.

77. B: When designing a website for an online business, the web developer would include a site map in order to provide website users with a list of links to all of the pages on the website. Site maps, also called indexes, list each webpage that is part of the website.

78. D: Better Business Bureau certification is useful for businesses that engage in e-commerce because it reassures customers that the company is reliable and not trying to scam them. Better Business Bureau certification does not carry tax or legal protection, and the Better Business Bureau is not a governmental agency. Instead, it is a group of dues-paying members that are committed to setting and enforcing honest business practices.

79. D: Businesses can increase the security of confidential customer information by destroying paper records of credit card information, conducting employee background checks, and installing firewall and virus protection software to protect their computer systems. Firewalls and virus protection software prevent the theft of information stored on computers, and shredding paper records prevents theft as well. By conducting background checks prior to hiring employees, businesses can prevent theft by screening for individuals who have committed information or identity theft in the past.

80. D: A high school student who expresses interest in starting her own auto repair business after graduating from high school could best prepare for such a career by getting an internship or part time job at an auto-repair shop and by taking small business finance, law, and accounting courses. While experience and a basic understanding of how to run a small business would be crucial for success, a college degree and MBA would not be appropriate because they would not provide the student with the necessary industry experience she would need to be successful.

81. A: The best way for a business education teacher to evaluate her program in terms of how well graduates are prepared for the workforce would be to consult with local business leaders to find out where graduates have room for improvement. Asking students to complete internships would help prepare students for the workforce, but it would not provide the necessary feedback on students' preparedness. Surveying recent graduates would be useful, but it would provide less direct and detailed information about their performance in the workforce. Last, community college professors would be more familiar with students' performance in college courses than their performance in the workplace.

82. A: Of the activities listed here, the most effective tool for teaching business skills would be raising funds by selling concessions at athletic events. This would teach students how to attain permits and licenses, purchase and price inventory, develop a supply process, schedule employees, provide customer service, and account for sales, among many other functions that are necessary for running a small business. The other activities listed here would teach important skills, but fundraisers teach skills most directly relevant to business.

83. B: A business education teacher who is asked to serve as an advisor the local chapter of a student leadership organization is most likely to be responsible for ensuring the health and safety of student participants in the organization. In order to teach leadership and business skills, students are usually primarily responsible for holding meetings, planning activities, and accounting for funds. Advisors are present to guide students and protect students' health and safety.

84. C: A business education teacher and a math teacher coordinating their lesson plans so that the concepts taught in math class are subsequently applied to real situations in the business class is the best example of interdisciplinary collaboration. While the other examples do require students to use skills learned in other classes like math and language arts, only example B involves active coordination between teachers in two different subject areas.

85. D: The activity that would most effectively and comprehensively assess how well students have mastered learning objectives for a unit about small business would be writing and presenting a business plan. While marketing is an important aspect of running a small business, developing a business plan would more comprehensively and directly measure and reinforce students' knowledge about small businesses.

86. D: All of the activities described here would teach skills that are necessary for working in a culturally diverse workplace. Students need to know the legal rights and responsibilities of employees and employers vis-à-vis this issue. They should also understand the perspectives of people from culturally diverse backgrounds, as well the unique problems they face in the workplace.

87. C: Based upon the information in Table 2, the correct order for the list is Business D, Business C, Business A, Business B. The triple A rating indicates the least risk, followed by double A, triple B, and double B.

88. C: If Scott Smith is paid $10 per hour on weekdays and $11 per hour on weekends, he worked a total of 16 weekday hours for $160 and 4 weekend hours for $44, for a total of $204.00.

89. C: Smith, who is a part time employee, should have social security, Medicare, and income taxes deducted from his check, because he is a W-4 employee. Since he worked less than 40 hours from November 1st through November 7th, though, he is not a full time employee and does not have health insurance or 401k deductions.

90. B: If Scott contributes 4% of his $2,000 paycheck to his 401k, this would total $80 per pay period, and the company would have to match 100% of this contribution, which would be $80.

91. C: Accounts receivable are current assets, also known as short-term assets. This term refers to open accounts that are not yet due. For example, if a landscaping company mows Anna's lawn today and the company sends her a bill for the service that is due one month later, then Anna's account would be in "account receivable" status until the due date.

92. D: Owners' equity is comprised of the amount of their initial investment in the business plus any unclaimed profits from the business' operation. (Unclaimed profits are also called retained earnings).

93. C: According to the Copyright Act of 1976, creative works like plays, poems, and architectural plans are protected by copyright law so long as they are written down. Advertising slogans are not protected because they fall under the jurisdiction of trademark law.

94. A: A phrase that is associated with a particular product would be protected by trademark law. Copyright law protects creative work, while trademarks protect business-related slogans, symbols, etc., which distinguish one product from another.

95. A: A corporation is always owned by shareholders. This means that the corporation is a separate legal entity from its shareholders. As a consequence of this, shareholders' only personal financial risk is their investment. They, unlike the corporation itself, cannot be sued by debtors if the company fails.

96. B: If an employee becomes injured because an employer did not provide equipment in good working order, this would be an example of an OSHA violation by the employer. Employees are allowed to work in hazardous conditions, so long as the employer provides adequate safety protection. Employers have the right to accompany an OSHA compliance officer on an inspection, but they are not required to do so. Employees are not covered by the OSHA act during normal commutes to and from work.

97. D: "The employee will have excellent writing skills" states the desired qualification clearly and correctly. "The employee, will have excellent oral communication skills" is incorrect because the comma is unnecessary. In the second sentence, "employee's" is

possessive, and should have an apostrophe (employees'). In the third sentence, the word "well" is an adverb that would be best placed next to the verb which it modifies ("communicate well" would be correct).
98. C: The Internet is an example of a Wide Area Network (WAN). WANs are networks that cover an extremely large area. LANs (local area networks) cover smaller areas, like offices. LANs usually have faster data transfer speeds than WANs.

99. D: Nothing can be concluded from these results because students' baseline performance on these tests was not measured before the experiment. It is possible that one group of students already knew more about business, or were more academically advanced to start with. In order to account for this possibility, each group of students should have been tested prior to the beginning of the class. The effectiveness of the two teaching methods could then be compared based on the change in students' scores between the first and second test administrations.

100. C: It is illegal to employ someone under 18 in a job deemed hazardous. Such jobs include mining and manufacturing. Youths aged 16 and 17 can work in any job that is not hazardous, and youths under 14 can work in certain designated jobs like newspaper delivery and babysitting. In cases were state and federal laws conflict, the law that is more protective of minors takes precedence.

Secret Key #1 - Time is Your Greatest Enemy

Pace Yourself

Wear a watch. At the beginning of the test, check the time (or start a chronometer on your watch to count the minutes), and check the time after each passage or every few questions to make sure you are "on schedule."

If you are forced to speed up, do it efficiently. Usually one or more answer choices can be eliminated without too much difficulty. Above all, don't panic. Don't speed up and just begin guessing at random choices. By pacing yourself, and continually monitoring your progress against your watch, you will always know exactly how far ahead or behind you are with your available time. If you find that you are one minute behind on the test, don't skip one question without spending any time on it, just to catch back up. Take 15 fewer seconds on the next four questions, and after four questions you'll have caught back up. Once you catch back up, you can continue working each problem at your normal pace.

Furthermore, don't dwell on the problems that you were rushed on. If a problem was taking up too much time and you made a hurried guess, it must be difficult. The difficult questions are the ones you are most likely to miss anyway, so it isn't a big loss. It is better to end with more time than you need than to run out of time.

Lastly, sometimes it is beneficial to slow down if you are constantly getting ahead of time. You are always more likely to catch a careless mistake by working more slowly than quickly, and among very high-scoring test takers (those who are likely to have lots of time left over), careless errors affect the score more than mastery of material.

Secret Key #2 - Guessing is not Guesswork

You probably know that guessing is a good idea - unlike other standardized tests, there is no penalty for getting a wrong answer. Even if you have no idea about a question, you still have a 20-25% chance of getting it right.

Most test takers do not understand the impact that proper guessing can have on their score. Unless you score extremely high, guessing will significantly contribute to your final score.

Monkeys Take the Test

What most test takers don't realize is that to insure that 20-25% chance, you have to guess randomly. If you put 20 monkeys in a room to take this test, assuming they answered once per question and behaved themselves, on average they would get 20-25% of the questions correct. Put 20 test takers in the room, and the average will be much lower among guessed questions. Why?

1. The test writers intentionally writes deceptive answer choices that "look" right. A test taker has no idea about a question, so picks the "best looking" answer, which is often wrong. The monkey has no idea what looks good and what doesn't, so will

consistently be lucky about 20-25% of the time.

2. Test takers will eliminate answer choices from the guessing pool based on a hunch or intuition. Simple but correct answers often get excluded, leaving a 0% chance of being correct. The monkey has no clue, and often gets lucky with the best choice.

This is why the process of elimination endorsed by most test courses is flawed and detrimental to your performance- test takers don't guess, they make an ignorant stab in the dark that is usually worse than random.

$5 Challenge

Let me introduce one of the most valuable ideas of this course- the $5 challenge:

You only mark your "best guess" if you are willing to bet $5 on it.
You only eliminate choices from guessing if you are willing to bet $5 on it.

Why $5? Five dollars is an amount of money that is small yet not insignificant, and can really add up fast (20 questions could cost you $100). Likewise, each answer choice on one question of the test will have a small impact on your overall score, but it can really add up to a lot of points in the end.

The process of elimination IS valuable.

However, if you accidentally eliminate the right answer or go on a hunch for an incorrect answer, your chances drop dramatically: to 0%. By guessing among all the answer choices, you are GUARANTEED to have a shot at the right answer.

That's why the $5 test is so valuable- if you give up the advantage and safety of a pure guess, it had better be worth the risk.

What we still haven't covered is how to be sure that whatever guess you make is truly random. Here's the easiest way:

Always pick the first answer choice among those remaining.

Such a technique means that you have decided, **before you see a single test question**, exactly how you are going to guess- and since the order of choices tells you nothing about which one is correct, this guessing technique is perfectly random.

This section is not meant to scare you away from making educated guesses or eliminating choices- you just need to define when a choice is worth eliminating. The $5 test, along with a pre-defined random guessing strategy, is the best way to make sure you reap all of the benefits of guessing.

Secret Key #3 - Practice Smarter, Not Harder

Many test takers delay the test preparation process because they dread the awful amounts of practice time they think necessary to succeed on the test. We have refined an effective method that will take you only a fraction of the time.

There are a number of "obstacles" in your way to succeed. Among these are answering questions, finishing in time, and mastering test-taking strategies. All must be executed on the day of the test at peak performance, or your score will suffer. The test is a mental marathon that has a large impact on your future.

Just like a marathon runner, it is important to work your way up to the full challenge. So first you just worry about questions, and then time, and finally strategy:

Success Strategy

1. Find a good source for practice tests.
2. If you are willing to make a larger time investment, consider using more than one study guide- often the different approaches of multiple authors will help you "get" difficult concepts.
3. Take a practice test with no time constraints, with all study helps "open book." Take your time with questions and focus on applying strategies.
4. Take a practice test with time constraints, with all guides "open book."
5. Take a final practice test with no open material and time limits

If you have time to take more practice tests, just repeat step 5. By gradually exposing yourself to the full rigors of the test environment, you will condition your mind to the stress of test day and maximize your success.

Secret Key #4 - Prepare, Don't Procrastinate

Let me state an obvious fact: if you take the test three times, you will get three different scores. This is due to the way you feel on test day, the level of preparedness you have, and, despite the test writers' claims to the contrary, some tests WILL be easier for you than others.

Since your future depends so much on your score, you should maximize your chances of success. In order to maximize the likelihood of success, you've got to prepare in advance. This means taking practice tests and spending time learning the information and test taking strategies you will need to succeed.

Since you have to pay a registration fee each time you take the test, don't take it as a "practice" test. Feel free to take sample tests on your own, but when you go to take the official test, be prepared, be focused, and do your best the first time!

Secret Key #5 - Test Yourself

Everyone knows that time is money. There is no need to spend too much of your time or too little of your time preparing for the test. You should only spend as much of your precious time preparing as is necessary for you to pass it.

Once you have taken a practice test under real conditions of time constraints, then you will know if you are ready for the test or not.

If you have scored extremely high the first time that you take the practice test, then there is not much point in spending countless hours studying. You are already there.

Benchmark your abilities by retaking practice tests and seeing how much you have improved. Once you score high enough to guarantee success, then you are ready.

If you have scored well below where you need, then knuckle down and begin studying in earnest. Check your improvement regularly through the use of practice tests under real conditions. Above all, don't worry, panic, or give up. The key is perseverance!

Then, when you go to take the test, remain confident and remember how well you did on the practice tests. If you can score high enough on a practice test, then you can do the same on the real thing.

General Strategies

The most important thing you can do is to ignore your fears and jump into the test immediately- do not be overwhelmed by any strange-sounding terms. You have to jump into the test like jumping into a pool- all at once is the easiest way.

Make Predictions

As you read and understand the question, try to guess what the answer will be. Remember that several of the answer choices are wrong, and once you begin reading them, your mind will immediately become cluttered with answer choices designed to throw you off. Your mind is typically the most focused immediately after you have read the passage and question and digested its contents. If you can, try to predict what the correct answer will be. You may be surprised at what you can predict.

Quickly scan the choices and see if your prediction is in the listed answer choices. If it is, then you can be quite confident that you have the right answer. It still won't hurt to check the other answer choices, but most of the time, you've got it!

Answer the Question

It may seem obvious to only pick answer choices that answer the question, but the test writers can create some excellent answer choices that are wrong. Don't pick an answer just because it sounds right, or you believe it to be true. It MUST answer the question. Once you've made your selection, always go back and check it against the question and make sure that you didn't misread the question, and the answer choice does answer the question posed.

Benchmark

After you read the first answer choice, decide if you think it sounds correct or not. If it doesn't, move on to the next answer choice. If it does, tentatively check that answer choice.

This doesn't mean that you've definitely selected it as your answer choice, it just means that it's the best you've seen thus far. Go ahead and read the next choice. If the next choice is worse than the one you've already selected, keep going to the next answer choice. If the next choice is better than the choice you've already selected, check the new answer choice as your best guess.

The first answer choice that you select becomes your standard. Every other answer choice must be benchmarked against that standard. That choice is correct until proven otherwise by another answer choice beating it out. Once you've decided that no other answer choice seems as good, do one final check to ensure that your answer choice answers the question posed.

Valid Information

Don't discount any of the information provided in the question. Every piece of information may be necessary to determine the correct answer. None of the information in the question is there to throw you off (while the answer choices will certainly have information to throw you off). If two seemingly unrelated topics are discussed, don't ignore either. You can be confident there is a relationship, or it wouldn't be included in the question, and you are probably going to have to determine what is that relationship for the answer.

Avoid "Fact Traps"

Don't get distracted by a choice that is factually true. Your search is for the answer that answers the question. Stay focused and don't fall for an answer that is true but incorrect. Always go back to the question and make sure you're choosing an answer that actually answers the question and is not just a true statement. An answer can be factually correct, but it MUST answer the question asked. Additionally, two answers can both be seemingly correct, so be sure to read all of the answer choices, and make sure that you get the one that BEST answers the question.

Milk the Question

Some of the questions may throw you completely off. They might deal with a subject you have not been exposed to, or one that you haven't reviewed in years. While your lack of knowledge about the subject will be a hindrance, the question itself can give you many clues that will help you find the correct answer. Read the question carefully, and look for clues. Watch particularly for adjectives and nouns describing difficult terms or words that you don't recognize. Regardless of if you understand a word or not, replacing it with the synonyms used for it in the question may help you to understand what the questions are asking.

Look carefully for these descriptive synonyms (nouns) and adjectives and use them to help you understand the difficult terms. Rather than wracking your mind about specific detail information concerning a difficult term in the question, use the more general description or synonym provided to make it easier for you.

The Trap of Familiarity

Don't just choose a word because you recognize it. On difficult questions, you may not recognize a number of words in the answer choices. The test writers don't put "make-believe" words on the test; so don't think that just because you only recognize all the words in one answer choice means that answer choice must be correct. If you don't recognize words in all but one answer choices, then focus on the one that you do recognize. Is it correct? Try your best to determine if it is correct. If it does, that is great, but if it doesn't, eliminate it. Each word and answer choice you eliminate increases your chances of getting the question correct, even if you then have to guess among the unfamiliar choices.

Eliminate Answers

Eliminate choices as soon as you realize they are wrong. But be careful! Make sure you consider all of the possible answer choices. Just because one appears right, doesn't mean that the next one won't be even better! The test writers will usually put more than one good answer choice for every question, so read all of them. Don't worry if you are stuck between two that seem right. By getting down to just two remaining possible choices, your odds are now 50/50. Rather than wasting too much time, play the odds. You are guessing, but guessing wisely, because you've been able to knock out some of the answer choices that you know are wrong. If you are eliminating choices and realize that the last answer choice you are left with is also obviously wrong, don't panic. Start over and consider each choice again. There may easily be something that you missed the first time and will realize on the second pass.

Tough Questions

If you are stumped on a problem or it appears too hard or too difficult, don't waste time. Move on! Remember though, if you can quickly check for obviously incorrect answer choices, your chances of guessing correctly are greatly improved. Before you completely give up, at least try to knock out a couple of possible answers. Eliminate what you can and then guess at the remaining answer choices before moving on.

Brainstorm

If you get stuck on a difficult question, spend a few seconds quickly brainstorming. Run through the complete list of possible answer choices. Look at each choice and ask yourself, "Could this answer the question satisfactorily?" Go through each answer choice and consider it independently of the other. By systematically going through all possibilities, you may find something that you would otherwise overlook. Remember that when you get stuck, it's important to try to keep moving.

Read Carefully

Understand the problem. Read the question and answer choices carefully. Don't miss the question because you misread the terms. You have plenty of time to read each question thoroughly and make sure you understand what is being asked. Yet a happy medium must be attained, so don't waste too much time. You must read carefully, but efficiently.

Face Value

When in doubt, use common sense. Always accept the situation in the problem at face value. Don't read too much into it. These problems will not require you to make huge leaps of logic. The test writers aren't trying to throw you off with a cheap trick. If you have to go beyond creativity and make a leap of logic in order to have an answer choice answer the question, then you should look at the other answer choices. Don't overcomplicate the problem by creating theoretical relationships or explanations that will warp time or space. These are normal problems rooted in reality. It's just that the applicable relationship or explanation may not be readily apparent and you have to figure things out. Use your common sense to interpret anything that isn't clear.

Prefixes

If you're having trouble with a word in the question or answer choices, try dissecting it. Take advantage of every clue that the word might include. Prefixes and suffixes can be a huge help. Usually they allow you to determine a basic meaning. Pre- means before, post- means after, pro - is positive, de- is negative. From these prefixes and suffixes, you can get an idea of the general meaning of the word and try to put it into context. Beware though of any traps. Just because con is the opposite of pro, doesn't necessarily mean congress is the opposite of progress!

Hedge Phrases

Watch out for critical "hedge" phrases, such as likely, may, can, will often, sometimes, etc, often, almost, mostly, usually, generally, rarely, sometimes. Question writers insert these hedge phrases, to cover every possibility. Often an answer choice will be wrong simply because it leaves no room for exception.

Switchback Words

Stay alert for "switchbacks". These are the words and phrases frequently used to alert you to shifts in thought. The most common switchback word is "but". Others include although, however, nevertheless, on the other hand, even though, while, in spite of, despite, regardless of.

New Information

Correct answer choices will rarely have completely new information included. Answer choices typically are straightforward reflections of the material asked about and will directly relate to the question. If a new piece of information is included in an answer choice that doesn't even seem to relate to the topic being asked about, then that answer choice is likely incorrect. All of the information needed to answer the question is usually provided for you, and so you should not have to make guesses that are unsupported or choose answer choices that require unknown information that cannot be reasoned on its own.

Time Management

On technical questions, don't get lost on the technical terms. Don't spend too much time on any one question. If you don't know what a term means, then since you don't have a dictionary, odds are you aren't going to get much further. You should immediately recognize terms as whether or not you know them. If you don't, work with the other clues that you have, the other answer choices and terms provided, but don't waste too much time trying to figure out a difficult term.

Contextual Clues

Look for contextual clues. An answer can be right but not correct. The contextual clues will help you find the answer that is most right and is correct. Understand the context in which a phrase is stated. This will help you make important distinctions.

Don’t Panic

Panicking will not answer any questions for you. Therefore, it isn’t helpful. When you first see the question, if your mind goes blank, take a deep breath. Force yourself to mechanically go through the steps of solving the problem and using the strategies you've learned.

Pace Yourself

Don’t get clock fever. It’s easy to be overwhelmed when you’re looking at a page full of questions, your mind is full of random thoughts and feeling confused, and the clock is ticking down faster than you would like. Calm down and maintain the pace that you have set for yourself. As long as you are on track by monitoring your pace, you are guaranteed to have enough time for yourself. When you get to the last few minutes of the test, it may seem like you won’t have enough time left, but if you only have as many questions as you should have left at that point, then you’re right on track!

Answer Selection

The best way to pick an answer choice is to eliminate all of those that are wrong, until only one is left and confirm that is the correct answer. Sometimes though, an answer choice may immediately look right. Be careful! Take a second to make sure that the other choices are not equally obvious. Don’t make a hasty mistake. There are only two times that you should stop before checking other answers. First is when you are positive that the answer choice you have selected is correct. Second is when time is almost out and you have to make a quick guess!

Check Your Work

Since you will probably not know every term listed and the answer to every question, it is important that you get credit for the ones that you do know. Don’t miss any questions through careless mistakes. If at all possible, try to take a second to look back over your answer selection and make sure you’ve selected the correct answer choice and haven’t made a costly careless mistake (such as marking an answer choice that you didn’t mean to mark). This quick double check should more than pay for itself in caught mistakes for the time it costs.

Beware of Directly Quoted Answers

Sometimes an answer choice will repeat word for word a portion of the question or reference section. However, beware of such exact duplication – it may be a trap! More than likely, the correct choice will paraphrase or summarize a point, rather than being exactly the same wording.

Special Report: What Your Test Score Will Tell You About Your IQ

Did you know that most standardized tests correlate very strongly with IQ? In fact, your general intelligence is a better predictor of your success than any other factor, and most tests intentionally measure this trait to some degree to ensure that those selected by the test are truly qualified for the test's purposes.

Before we can delve into the relation between your test score and IQ, I will first have to explain what exactly is IQ. Here's the formula:

Your IQ = 100 + (Number of standard deviations below or above the average)*15

Now, let's define standard deviations by using an example. If we have 5 people with 5 different heights, then first we calculate the average. Let's say the average was 65 inches. The standard deviation is the "average distance" away from the average of each of the members. It is a direct measure of variability - if the 5 people included Jackie Chan and Shaquille O'Neal, obviously there's a lot more variability in that group than a group of 5 sisters who are all within 6 inches in height of each other. The standard deviation uses a number to characterize the average range of difference within a group.

A convenient feature of most groups is that they have a "normal" distribution- makes sense that most things would be normal, right? Without getting into a bunch of statistical mumbo-jumbo, you just need to know that if you know the average of the group and the standard deviation, you can successfully predict someone's percentile rank in the group.

Confused? Let me give you an example. If instead of 5 people's heights, we had 100 people, we could figure out their rank in height JUST by knowing the average, standard deviation, and their height. We wouldn't need to know each person's height and manually rank them, we could just predict their rank based on three numbers.

What this means is that you can take your PERCENTILE rank that is often given with your test and relate this to your RELATIVE IQ of people taking the test - that is, your IQ relative to the people taking the test. Obviously, there's no way to know your actual IQ because the people taking a standardized test are usually not very good samples of the general population- many of those with extremely low IQ's never achieve a level of success or competency necessary to complete a typical standardized test. In fact, professional psychologists who measure IQ actually have to use non-written tests that can fairly measure the IQ of those not able to complete a traditional test.

The bottom line is to not take your test score too seriously, but it is fun to compute your "relative IQ" among the people who took the test with you. I've done the calculations below. Just look up your percentile rank in the left and then you'll see your "relative IQ" for your test in the right hand column-

Percentile Rank	Your Relative IQ		Percentile Rank	Your Relative IQ
99	135		59	103
98	131		58	103
97	128		57	103
96	126		56	102
95	125		55	102
94	123		54	102
93	122		53	101
92	121		52	101
91	120		51	100
90	119		50	100
89	118		49	100
88	118		48	99
87	117		47	99
86	116		46	98
85	116		45	98
84	115		44	98
83	114		43	97
82	114		42	97
81	113		41	97
80	113		40	96
79	112		39	96
78	112		38	95
77	111		37	95
76	111		36	95
75	110		35	94
74	110		34	94
73	109		33	93
72	109		32	93
71	108		31	93
70	108		30	92
69	107		29	92
68	107		28	91
67	107		27	91
66	106		26	90
65	106		25	90
64	105		24	89
63	105		23	89
62	105		22	88
61	104		21	88
60	104		20	87

Special Report: Retaking the Test: What Are Your Chances at Improving Your Score?

After going through the experience of taking a major test, many test takers feel that once is enough. The test usually comes during a period of transition in the test taker's life, and taking the test is only one of a series of important events. With so many distractions and conflicting recommendations, it may be difficult for a test taker to rationally determine whether or not he should retake the test after viewing his scores.

The importance of the test usually only adds to the burden of the retake decision. However, don't be swayed by emotion. There a few simple questions that you can ask yourself to guide you as you try to determine whether a retake would improve your score:

1. What went wrong? Why wasn't your score what you expected?

Can you point to a single factor or problem that you feel caused the low score? Were you sick on test day? Was there an emotional upheaval in your life that caused a distraction? Were you late for the test or not able to use the full time allotment? If you can point to any of these specific, individual problems, then a retake should definitely be considered.

2. Is there enough time to improve?

Many problems that may show up in your score report may take a lot of time for improvement. A deficiency in a particular math skill may require weeks or months of tutoring and studying to improve. If you have enough time to improve an identified weakness, then a retake should definitely be considered.

3. How will additional scores be used? Will a score average, highest score, or most recent score be used?

Different test scores may be handled completely differently. If you've taken the test multiple times, sometimes your highest score is used, sometimes your average score is computed and used, and sometimes your most recent score is used. Make sure you understand what method will be used to evaluate your scores, and use that to help you determine whether a retake should be considered.

4. Are my practice test scores significantly higher than my actual test score?

If you have taken a lot of practice tests and are consistently scoring at a much higher level than your actual test score, then you should consider a retake. However, if you've taken five practice tests and only one of your scores was higher than your actual test score, or if your practice test scores were only slightly higher than your actual test score, then it is unlikely that you will significantly increase your score.

5. Do I need perfect scores or will I be able to live with this score? Will this score still allow me to follow my dreams?

What kind of score is acceptable to you? Is your current score "good enough?" Do you have to have a certain score in order to pursue the future of your dreams? If you won't be happy with your current score, and there's no way that you could live with it, then you should consider a retake. However, don't get your hopes up. If you are looking for significant improvement, that may or may not be possible. But if you won't be happy otherwise, it is at least worth the effort.
Remember that there are other considerations. To achieve your dream, it is likely that your grades may also be taken into account. A great test score is usually not the only thing necessary to succeed. Make sure that you aren't overemphasizing the importance of a high test score.

Furthermore, a retake does not always result in a higher score. Some test takers will score lower on a retake, rather than higher. One study shows that one-fourth of test takers will achieve a significant improvement in test score, while one-sixth of test takers will actually show a decrease. While this shows that most test takers will improve, the majority will only improve their scores a little and a retake may not be worth the test taker's effort.

Finally, if a test is taken only once and is considered in the added context of good grades on the part of a test taker, the person reviewing the grades and scores may be tempted to assume that the test taker just had a bad day while taking the test, and may discount the low test score in favor of the high grades. But if the test is retaken and the scores are approximately the same, then the validity of the low scores are only confirmed. Therefore, a retake could actually hurt a test taker by definitely bracketing a test taker's score ability to a limited range.

Special Report: What is Test Anxiety and How to Overcome It?

The very nature of tests caters to some level of anxiety, nervousness or tension, just as we feel for any important event that occurs in our lives. A little bit of anxiety or nervousness can be a good thing. It helps us with motivation, and makes achievement just that much sweeter. However, too much anxiety can be a problem; especially if it hinders our ability to function and perform.

"Test anxiety," is the term that refers to the emotional reactions that some test-takers experience when faced with a test or exam. Having a fear of testing and exams is based upon a rational fear, since the test-taker's performance can shape the course of an academic career. Nevertheless, experiencing excessive fear of examinations will only interfere with the test-takers ability to perform, and his/her chances to be successful.

There are a large variety of causes that can contribute to the development and sensation of test anxiety. These include, but are not limited to lack of performance and worrying about issues surrounding the test.

Lack of Preparation

Lack of preparation can be identified by the following behaviors or situations:

Not scheduling enough time to study, and therefore cramming the night before the test or exam
Managing time poorly, to create the sensation that there is not enough time to do everything
Failing to organize the text information in advance, so that the study material consists of the entire text and not simply the pertinent information
Poor overall studying habits

Worrying, on the other hand, can be related to both the test taker, or many other factors around him/her that will be affected by the results of the test. These include worrying about:

Previous performances on similar exams, or exams in general
How friends and other students are achieving
The negative consequences that will result from a poor grade or failure

There are three primary elements to test anxiety. Physical components, which involve the same typical bodily reactions as those to acute anxiety (to be discussed below). Emotional factors have to do with fear or panic. Mental or cognitive issues concerning attention spans and memory abilities.

Physical Signals

There are many different symptoms of test anxiety, and these are not limited to mental and emotional strain. Frequently there are a range of physical signals that will let a test taker know that he/she is suffering from test anxiety. These bodily changes can include the following:

Perspiring
Sweaty palms
Wet, trembling hands
Nausea
Dry mouth
A knot in the stomach
Headache
Faintness
Muscle tension
Aching shoulders, back and neck
Rapid heart beat
Feeling too hot/cold

To recognize the sensation of test anxiety, a test-taker should monitor him/herself for the following sensations:

The physical distress symptoms as listed above
Emotional sensitivity, expressing emotional feelings such as the need to cry or laugh too much, or a sensation of anger or helplessness
A decreased ability to think, causing the test-taker to blank out or have racing thoughts that are hard to organize or control.

Though most students will feel some level of anxiety when faced with a test or exam, the majority can cope with that anxiety and maintain it at a manageable level. However, those who cannot are faced with a very real and very serious condition, which can and should be controlled for the immeasurable benefit of this sufferer.

Naturally, these sensations lead to negative results for the testing experience. The most common effects of test anxiety have to do with nervousness and mental blocking.

Nervousness

Nervousness can appear in several different levels:

The test-taker's difficulty, or even inability to read and understand the questions on the test
The difficulty or inability to organize thoughts to a coherent form
The difficulty or inability to recall key words and concepts relating to the testing questions (especially essays)
The receipt of poor grades on a test, though the test material was well known by the test taker

Conversely, a person may also experience mental blocking, which involves:

Blanking out on test questions
Only remembering the correct answers to the questions when the test has already finished.

Fortunately for test anxiety sufferers, beating these feelings, to a large degree, has to do with proper preparation. When a test taker has a feeling of preparedness, then anxiety will be dramatically lessened.

The first step to resolving anxiety issues is to distinguish which of the two types of anxiety are being suffered. If the anxiety is a direct result of a lack of preparation, this should be considered a normal reaction, and the anxiety level (as opposed to the test results) shouldn't be anything to worry about. However, if, when adequately prepared, the test-taker still panics, blanks out, or seems to overreact, this is not a fully rational reaction. While this can be considered normal too, there are many ways to combat and overcome these effects.

Remember that anxiety cannot be entirely eliminated, however, there are ways to minimize it, to make the anxiety easier to manage. Preparation is one of the best ways to minimize test anxiety. Therefore the following techniques are wise in order to best fight off any anxiety that may want to build.

To begin with, try to avoid cramming before a test, whenever it is possible. By trying to memorize an entire term's worth of information in one day, you'll be shocking your system, and not giving yourself a very good chance to absorb the information. This is an easy path to anxiety, so for those who suffer from test anxiety, cramming should not even be considered an option.

Instead of cramming, work throughout the semester to combine all of the material which is presented throughout the semester, and work on it gradually as the course goes by, making sure to master the main concepts first, leaving minor details for a week or so before the test.

To study for the upcoming exam, be sure to pose questions that may be on the examination, to gauge the ability to answer them by integrating the ideas from your texts, notes and lectures, as well as any supplementary readings.

If it is truly impossible to cover all of the information that was covered in that particular term, concentrate on the most important portions, that can be covered very well. Learn these concepts as best as possible, so that when the test comes, a goal can be made to use these concepts as presentations of your knowledge.

In addition to study habits, changes in attitude are critical to beating a struggle with test anxiety. In fact, an improvement of the perspective over the entire test-taking experience can actually help a test taker to enjoy studying and therefore improve the overall experience. Be certain not to overemphasize the significance of the grade - know that the result of the test is neither a reflection of self worth, nor is it a measure of intelligence; one grade will not predict a person's future success.

To improve an overall testing outlook, the following steps should be tried:

Keeping in mind that the most reasonable expectation for taking a test is to expect to try to demonstrate as much of what you know as you possibly can.
Reminding ourselves that a test is only one test; this is not the only one, and there will be others.
The thought of thinking of oneself in an irrational, all-or-nothing term should be avoided at all costs.
A reward should be designated for after the test, so there's something to look forward to. Whether it be going to a movie, going out to eat, or simply visiting friends, schedule it in advance, and do it no matter what result is expected on the exam.

Test-takers should also keep in mind that the basics are some of the most important things, even beyond anti-anxiety techniques and studying. Never neglect the basic social, emotional and biological needs, in order to try to absorb information. In order to best achieve, these three factors must be held as just as important as the studying itself.

Study Steps

Remember the following important steps for studying:
Maintain healthy nutrition and exercise habits. Continue both your recreational activities and social pass times. These both contribute to your physical and emotional well being.
Be certain to get a good amount of sleep, especially the night before the test, because when you're overtired you are not able to perform to the best of your best ability.
Keep the studying pace to a moderate level by taking breaks when they are needed, and varying the work whenever possible, to keep the mind fresh instead of getting bored.
When enough studying has been done that all the material that can be learned has been learned, and the test taker is prepared for the test, stop studying and do something relaxing such as listening to music, watching a movie, or taking a warm bubble bath.

There are also many other techniques to minimize the uneasiness or apprehension that is experienced along with test anxiety before, during, or even after the examination. In fact, there are a great deal of things that can be done to stop anxiety from interfering with lifestyle and performance. Again, remember that anxiety will not be eliminated entirely, and it shouldn't be. Otherwise that "up" feeling for exams would not exist, and most of us depend on that sensation to perform better than usual. However, this anxiety has to be at a level that is manageable.

Of course, as we have just discussed, being prepared for the exam is half the battle right away. Attending all classes, finding out what knowledge will be expected on the exam, and knowing the exam schedules are easy steps to lowering anxiety. Keeping up with work will remove the need to cram, and efficient study habits will eliminate wasted time. Studying should be done in an ideal location for concentration, so that it is simple to become interested in the material and give it complete attention. A method such as SQ3R (Survey, Question, Read, Recite, Review) is a wonderful key to follow to make sure that the study habits are as effective as possible, especially in the case of learning from a textbook. Flashcards are great techniques for memorization. Learning to take good notes will mean that notes will be full of useful information, so that less sifting will need to be done to seek out what is pertinent for studying. Reviewing notes after class and then again on occasion will keep the information fresh in the mind. From notes that have been taken summary sheets and outlines can be made for simpler reviewing.

A study group can also be a very motivational and helpful place to study, as there will be a sharing of ideas, all of the minds can work together, to make sure that everyone understands, and the studying will be made more interesting because it will be a social occasion.

Basically, though, as long as the test-taker remains organized and self confident, with efficient study habits, less time will need to be spent studying, and higher grades will be achieved.

To become self confident, there are many useful steps. The first of these is "self talk." It has been shown through extensive research, that self-talk for students who suffer from test anxiety, should be well monitored, in order to make sure that it contributes to self confidence as opposed to sinking the student. Frequently the self talk of test-anxious students is negative or self-defeating, thinking that everyone else is smarter and faster, that they always mess up, and that if they don't do well, they'll fail the entire course. It is important to decreasing anxiety that awareness is made of self talk. Try writing any negative self thoughts and then disputing them with a positive statement instead. Begin self-encouragement as though it was a friend speaking. Repeat positive statements to help reprogram the mind to believing in successes instead of failures.

Helpful Techniques

Other extremely helpful techniques include:

Self-visualization of doing well and reaching goals
While aiming for an "A" level of understanding, don't try to "overprotect" by setting your expectations lower. This will only convince the mind to stop studying in order to meet the lower expectations.
Don't make comparisons with the results or habits of other students. These are individual factors, and different things work for different people, causing different results.
Strive to become an expert in learning what works well, and what can be done in order to improve. Consider collecting this data in a journal.
Create rewards for after studying instead of doing things before studying that will only turn into avoidance behaviors.
Make a practice of relaxing - by using methods such as progressive relaxation, self-hypnosis, guided imagery, etc - in order to make relaxation an automatic sensation.
Work on creating a state of relaxed concentration so that concentrating will take on the focus of the mind, so that none will be wasted on worrying.
Take good care of the physical self by eating well and getting enough sleep.
Plan in time for exercise and stick to this plan.

Beyond these techniques, there are other methods to be used before, during and after the test that will help the test-taker perform well in addition to overcoming anxiety.

Before the exam comes the academic preparation. This involves establishing a study schedule and beginning at least one week before the actual date of the test. By doing this, the anxiety of not having enough time to study for the test will be automatically eliminated. Moreover, this will make the studying a much more effective experience, ensuring that the learning will be an easier process. This relieves much undue pressure on the test-taker.

Summary sheets, note cards, and flash cards with the main concepts and examples of these main concepts should be prepared in advance of the actual studying time. A topic should never be eliminated from this process. By omitting a topic because it isn't expected to be on the test is only setting up the test-taker for anxiety should it actually appear on the exam. Utilize the course syllabus for laying out the topics that should be studied. Carefully go over the notes that were made in class, paying special attention to any of the issues that the professor took special care to emphasize while lecturing in class. In the textbooks, use the chapter review, or if possible, the chapter tests, to begin your review.

It may even be possible to ask the instructor what information will be covered on the exam, or what the format of the exam will be (for example, multiple choice, essay, free form, true-false). Additionally, see if it is possible to find out how many questions will be on the test. If a review sheet or sample test has been offered by the professor, make good use of it, above anything else, for the preparation for the test. Another great resource for getting to know the examination is reviewing tests from previous semesters. Use these tests to review, and aim to achieve a 100% score on each of the possible topics. With a few exceptions, the goal that you set for yourself is the highest one that you will reach.

Take all of the questions that were assigned as homework, and rework them to any other possible course material. The more problems reworked, the more skill and confidence will form as a result. When forming the solution to a problem, write out each of the steps. Don't simply do head work. By doing as many steps on paper as possible, much clarification and therefore confidence will be formed. Do this with as many homework problems as possible, before checking the answers. By checking the answer after each problem, a reinforcement will exist, that will not be on the exam. Study situations should be as exam-like as possible, to prime the test-taker's system for the experience. By waiting to check the answers at the end, a psychological advantage will be formed, to decrease the stress factor.

Another fantastic reason for not cramming is the avoidance of confusion in concepts, especially when it comes to mathematics. 8-10 hours of study will become one hundred percent more effective if it is spread out over a week or at least several days, instead of doing it all in one sitting. Recognize that the human brain requires time in order to assimilate new material, so frequent breaks and a span of study time over several days will be much more beneficial.

Additionally, don't study right up until the point of the exam. Studying should stop a minimum of one hour before the exam begins. This allows the brain to rest and put things in their proper order. This will also provide the time to become as relaxed as possible when going into the examination room. The test-taker will also have time to eat well and eat sensibly. Know that the brain needs food as much as the rest of the body. With enough food and enough sleep, as well as a relaxed attitude, the body and the mind are primed for success.

Avoid any anxious classmates who are talking about the exam. These students only spread anxiety, and are not worth sharing the anxious sentimentalities.

Before the test also involves creating a positive attitude, so mental preparation should also be a point of concentration. There are many keys to creating a positive attitude. Should fears become rushing in, make a visualization of taking the exam, doing well, and seeing an A written on the paper. Write out a list of affirmations that will bring a feeling of confidence, such as "I am doing well in my English class," "I studied well and know my material," "I enjoy this class." Even if the affirmations aren't believed at first, it sends a positive message to the subconscious which will result in an alteration of the overall belief system, which is the system that creates reality.

If a sensation of panic begins, work with the fear and imagine the very worst! Work through the entire scenario of not passing the test, failing the entire course, and dropping out of school, followed by not getting a job, and pushing a shopping cart through the dark alley where you'll live. This will place things into perspective! Then, practice deep breathing and create a visualization of the opposite situation - achieving an "A" on the exam, passing the entire course, receiving the degree at a graduation ceremony.

On the day of the test, there are many things to be done to ensure the best results, as well as the most calm outlook. The following stages are suggested in order to maximize test-taking potential:

Begin the examination day with a moderate breakfast, and avoid any coffee or beverages with caffeine if the test taker is prone to jitters. Even people who are used to managing caffeine can feel jittery or light-headed when it is taken on a test day.
Attempt to do something that is relaxing before the examination begins. As last minute cramming clouds the mastering of overall concepts, it is better to use this time to create a calming outlook.
Be certain to arrive at the test location well in advance, in order to provide time to select a location that is away from doors, windows and other distractions, as well as giving enough time to relax before the test begins.
Keep away from anxiety generating classmates who will upset the sensation of stability and relaxation that is being attempted before the exam.
Should the waiting period before the exam begins cause anxiety, create a self-distraction by reading a light magazine or something else that is relaxing and simple.

During the exam itself, read the entire exam from beginning to end, and find out how much time should be allotted to each individual problem. Once writing the exam, should more time be taken for a problem, it should be abandoned, in order to begin another problem. If there is time at the end, the unfinished problem can always be returned to and completed.

Read the instructions very carefully - twice - so that unpleasant surprises won't follow during or after the exam has ended.

When writing the exam, pretend that the situation is actually simply the completion of homework within a library, or at home. This will assist in forming a relaxed atmosphere, and will allow the brain extra focus for the complex thinking function.

Begin the exam with all of the questions with which the most confidence is felt. This will build the confidence level regarding the entire exam and will begin a quality momentum. This will also create encouragement for trying the problems where uncertainty resides.

Going with the "gut instinct" is always the way to go when solving a problem. Second guessing should be avoided at all costs. Have confidence in the ability to do well.

For essay questions, create an outline in advance that will keep the mind organized and make certain that all of the points are remembered. For multiple choice, read every answer, even if the correct one has been spotted - a better one may exist.

Continue at a pace that is reasonable and not rushed, in order to be able to work carefully. Provide enough time to go over the answers at the end, to check for small errors that can be corrected.

Should a feeling of panic begin, breathe deeply, and think of the feeling of the body releasing sand through its pores. Visualize a calm, peaceful place, and include all of the sights, sounds and sensations of this image. Continue the deep breathing, and take a few minutes to continue this with closed eyes. When all is well again, return to the test.

If a "blanking" occurs for a certain question, skip it and move on to the next question. There will be time to return to the other question later. Get everything done that can be done, first, to guarantee all the grades that can be compiled, and to build all of the confidence possible. Then return to the weaker questions to build the marks from there.

Remember, one's own reality can be created, so as long as the belief is there, success will follow. And remember: anxiety can happen later, right now, there's an exam to be written!

After the examination is complete, whether there is a feeling for a good grade or a bad grade, don't dwell on the exam, and be certain to follow through on the reward that was promised...and enjoy it! Don't dwell on any mistakes that have been made, as there is nothing that can be done at this point anyway.

Additionally, don't begin to study for the next test right away. Do something relaxing for a while, and let the mind relax and prepare itself to begin absorbing information again. From the results of the exam - both the grade and the entire experience, be certain to learn from what has gone on. Perfect studying habits and work some more on confidence in order to make the next examination experience even better than the last one.

Learn to avoid places where openings occurred for laziness, procrastination and day dreaming.

Use the time between this exam and the next one to better learn to relax, even learning to relax on cue, so that any anxiety can be controlled during the next exam. Learn how to relax the body. Slouch in your chair if that helps. Tighten and then relax all of the different muscle groups, one group at a time, beginning with the feet and then working all the way up to the neck and face. This will ultimately relax the muscles more than they were to begin with. Learn how to breathe deeply and comfortably, and focus on this breathing going in and out as a relaxing thought. With every exhale, repeat the word "relax."

As common as test anxiety is, it is very possible to overcome it. Make yourself one of the test-takers who overcome this frustrating hindrance.

Special Report: Additional Bonus Material

Due to our efforts to try to keep this book to a manageable length, we've created a link that will give you access to all of your additional bonus material.

Please visit http://www.mometrix.com/bonus948/osatbusinessed to access the information.